John Roy Musick

A Century Too Soon

A Story of Bacon's Rebellion

John Roy Musick

A Century Too Soon
A Story of Bacon's Rebellion

ISBN/EAN: 9783743399464

Manufactured in Europe, USA, Canada, Australia, Japa

Cover: Foto ©ninafisch / pixelio.de

Manufactured and distributed by brebook publishing software (www.brebook.com)

John Roy Musick

A Century Too Soon

"HERE! SHOOT ME! 'FORE GOD, A FAIR MARK!"

COLUMBIAN HISTORICAL NOVELS. VOLUME VI.

A CENTURY TOO SOON

A STORY OF BACON'S REBELLION

BY

JOHN R. MUSICK

Author of "Columbia," "Estevan," "St. Augustine," "Pocahontas,"
"The Pilgrims," Etc., Etc.

Illustrations by

FREELAND A. CARTER

New York
FUNK & WAGNALLS COMPANY
LONDON AND TORONTO

COPYRIGHT, 1893, BY THE
FUNK & WAGNALLS COMPANY

[*Registered at Stationers' Hall, London, Eng.*]

Printed in the United States.

To
MY WIFE,

WHO SHARES MY JOYS AND SORROWS, TOILS AND CARES,

THIS BOOK

IS AFFECTIONATELY DEDICATED

BY

THE AUTHOR

PREFACE.

HISTORIANS have bestowed little attention to that important period in our great commonwealth, just after the restoration in England. Though one hundred years before liberty was actually obtained, the sleeping goddess seemed to have opened her eyes on that occasion and yawned, though she closed them the next moment for a sleep of a century longer. Events produce such strange and lasting impressions on individuals as well as on nations, that the historian may not be much out of the way, who fancies that he sees in the reign of Cromwell the outgrowth of republicanism, which culminated in the establishment of a free and independent English-speaking people on the American continent. The two principal classes of English colonists were the cavaliers and the Puritans, though there were also Quakers, Catholics, and settlers of other creeds. Generally the cavaliers were the "king's men," or royalists, and the Puritans republicans. The different characteristics of these two sects were quite marked. The Puritans were sober and industrious, quiet, fanatically religious and strict, while the cavaliers were polite, gallant, brave, good livers and quite fond of display. They were nearly all of the Church of England, with rather loose morals, fond of fox-hunting and gay society. During the time of the Commonwealth of England, the Puritans were in power, and the king's people, cavaliers, or royalists were reinstated on the restoration of monarchy in 1660.

Sir William Berkeley, a bigoted churchman, a lover of royalty, and one who despised republicanism and personal liberty so heartily that he could "thank God that there were neither printing-presses nor public schools in Virginia," was appointed by Charles II. governor of Virginia. Berkeley, whose early career was bright with promise, seems in his old age to have become filled with hatred and avarice. He was too stubborn to listen to the counsel even of friends. Being engaged in a profitable traffic with the Indians, he preferred to let them slaughter the people on the frontier, rather than to allow his business to be interfered with. Berkeley's tyranny was carried to such an extreme, that rebellion was the natural consequence. Rebellion always follows some injury or misplaced confidence in the powers of the government. This rebellion came a "century too soon," being just one hundred years before the great revolution, which set at liberty all the colonies of North America.

In this story we take up John Stevens and his son Robert, the son and grandson of Philip Stevens, whose story was told in "Pocahontas." The object has been to give a complete history of the period and to depict home life, manners and customs of the time in the form of a pleasing story. It remains for the reader to say if the effort has been a success.

JOHN R. MUSICK.

KIRKSVILLE, MO., August 1st, 1892.

TABLE OF CONTENTS.

CHAPTER I.
	PAGE
THE DUCKING STOOL,	1

CHAPTER II.
SEEKING BETTER FORTUNE,	20

CHAPTER III.
THE COLONIES OF THE NEW WORLD,	39

CHAPTER IV.
THE STORM AND SHIPWRECK,	59

CHAPTER V.
JOHN STEVENS' CHARGE,	77

CHAPTER VI.
THE ISLAND OF DESOLATION,	92

CHAPTER VII.
IN WIDOW'S WEEDS,	107

CHAPTER VIII.
THE STEPFATHER,	126

CONTENTS.

CHAPTER IX.
THE MOVING WORLD, ... 144

CHAPTER X.
THE FUGITIVE AND HIS CHILD, ... 162

CHAPTER XI.
TYRANNY AND FLIGHT, ... 181

CHAPTER XII.
THE DAUGHTER OF A REGICIDE, ... 197

CHAPTER XIII.
LEFT ALONE, ... 213

CHAPTER XIV.
THE TREASURE SHIP, ... 231

CHAPTER XV.
THE ANGEL OF DELIVERANCE, ... 244

CHAPTER XVI.
KING PHILIP'S WAR, ... 261

CHAPTER XVII.
NEARING THE VERGE, ... 280

CHAPTER XVIII.
THE SWORD OF DEFENCE, ... 296

CHAPTER XIX.
THE MYSTERIOUS STRANGER, ... 314

CHAPTER XX.

BACON A REBEL, ... 331

CHAPTER XXI.

BURNING OF JAMESTOWN, ... 350

CHAPTER XXII.

VENGEANCE WITH A VENGEANCE, ... 366

CHAPTER XXIII.

CONCLUSION, ... 382

HISTORICAL INDEX, ... 393

CHRONOLOGY, ... 401

LIST OF ILLUSTRATIONS.

	PAGE
"Here! Shoot me! 'Fore God, a fair mark!" (See page 337), ... *Frontispiece*	
Ducking stool, ...	1
"I'll scratch your eyes out!"	17
Once more he bent over the sleeping children, . .	37
Kieft from the ramparts watched the burning wigwams, ...	43
Stuyvesant, ...	48
The squaw, with a yell of fear, wheeled to fly for her life, ...	49
Blanche could not utter a word of consolation, . .	101
Oliver Cromwell, ...	113
"Peter the Headstrong," unable to control his passion, tore the letter into pieces, ...	115
Tomb of Stuyvesant, ...	116
The door was thrown open, and the boy Robert entered to take a part in the scene, . .	133
His temper flamed out in words, ...	154
His tired child was at his side uncomplainingly, .	171
"Are you ready?"	199
Sir Henry Vane, ...	202
"Our journey is not one half over!"	221
"You are not lost, if you follow me!" . . .	260
He fell upon his face in the mud and water with his gun under him, ...	279
He flung him down the front steps where he lay in a heap on the ground, ...	299
Ruins of Jamestown, ...	363
The ball struck four or five feet to Robert's left, and in front of him, splashing up a jet of water, .	372
Map of the period, ...	248

xiii

A CENTURY TOO SOON.

CHAPTER I.

THE DUCKING-STOOL.

Blow, wind, and crack your cheeks! rage! blow!
You cataracts and hurricanes, spout
Till you have drenched our steeples, drowned the cocks!
You sulphurous and thought-executing fires,
Vaunt couriers to oak-cleaving thunderbolts,
Singe my white head! And thou, all-shaking thunder,
Strike flat the thick rotundity o' the world."
—SHAKESPEARE.

A CROWD of bearded men, some in the sad-colored clothes and steeple-crowned hats of Puritans, others in loose top-boots, scarlet coats, lace and periwigs of the cavaliers of the Cromwellian period, intermixed with women, some wearing hoods and others bareheaded, was assembled on the banks of a deep pond within sight of Jamestown, Va. A curious machine, one which at the present day would puzzle the beholder to guess its use, had been constructed near the edge of the water. It was a simple contrivance and rude in structure; but the freshly hewn timbers were proof of its virgin newness. This machine was a long pole fastened upon an upright post, almost at the water's edge, so that it could revolve or dip at the will of the manipulators. On the heavy end of the pole was a seat or chair fastened, with a rest for the feet, and straps and buckles so arranged that when one was buckled down escape was impossible. On the opposite end of the pole a rope was tied, the end hanging down to the ground. This contrivance, to-day unknown, was once quite familiar to English civilization, and was called the "ducking-stool." The founders of the American colonies, whatever may have been their original designs for the promotion of universal happiness, found it necessary very soon to allot a portion of the virgin soil to the humiliation, punishment and degradation of their fellow creatures.

Thus we find, in addition to the prison, the whipping-post and the pillory, the ducking-stool. From the vast throng assembled about the pond on that mild June day in 1653, one might suppose that the entire colony had turned out to witness some great event. Nearly four years before the opening of our story, Cromwell had established the "Commonwealth" in England; but it was not until 1653 that the Parliament party, or "Roundheads," as they were contemptuously termed, conquered the colony of Virginia. Many of the royalists were still elected to the House of Burgesses, and the cavaliers in boots and lace, with riding-whips in hand, predominated in the throng we have just described. The continual neighing of horses in the woods told of the arrival of fresh troops of planters and fox-hunting cavaliers.

The merry cavalier was easily distinguished from the sedate Puritan. The latter gazed solemnly on the instrument of torture as a thing essential to the performance of a duty, while the cavaliers seemed to have come more for the enjoyment of some rare sport, than to witness an execution of the law. Occasionally a snake-eyed aborigine mingled with the throng, gazing in wonder on the scene, or a negro, granted a half-holiday, stood grinning with barbarous delight on what was more sport than punishment in his eyes.

There is something hideous about the ducking-stool in the present age of reason and enlightenment, more especially as it was designed to punish the weaker sex and usually those advanced in years. Before the ugly machine and between it and the road which ran past the pond to the village was a grass-plot, much overgrown with burdock, pigweed, plantain and such unsightly vegetation, which seemed to find something congenial in the soil that bore an instrument for the torture of the gentler sex; but on one side of the post and leaning against it was a wild rosebush covered with fragrant flowers.

It was still an early hour, for the morning dew sparkled in the deeper recesses of the grand old forest, and the moisture of dawn yet lingered on the air. Strange as it may seem, that instrument was regarded with careless indifference, even by the gentler sex of this period.

Meagre and cold was the sympathy which a transgressor might expect from the assembly at the pond. The women mingled freely with the crowd and appeared to take a peculiar interest in the punishment about to be inflicted. The age had not so much refinement, that any sense of impropriety kept the wearers of petticoats and farthingales from elbowing their way through the densest throngs to witness the executions. Those wives and maidens of English birth and breeding were morally and materially of coarser fibre than their fair descendants, who would swoon at the thought of torture and punishment. They were not all hard-featured amazons in that throng, for, mingled with the stout, broad-shouldered dames, were maids naturally shy, timid and beautiful. The ruddy cheeks and ruby lips indicated health, and the brawny arms of many women bore evidence of physical toil.

The cavaliers were jesting and laughing, while the Puritans were silent, or conversing in low, measured tones on the purpose of the assembly.

There was enough of gloom and solemnity in the one party to prove that the execution was not to be a farce, and enough merriment in the other to convince a beholder that the punishment was not capital. A young cavalier, all silk and lace, with heavy riding-boots, galloped up to the scene and, dismounting, handed the rein to a negro slave, who had run himself out of breath to keep up with his master, and hastened down to the water.

"Good morrow, Roger!" said the new-comer to a young man of about twenty-five years of age, like himself a gentleman of ease.

"Good morrow, Hugh," Roger answered.

"What gala scene have they prepared for our amusement?" asked Hugh, his dark gray eyes twinkling with merriment. "I trow it is one that you and I need never fear."

"The magistrates have adjudged Ann Linkon to be ducked."

"Marry! what hath she done?"

"Divers offences, all petty, but aggravating in themselves. She is not only a common scold, but a babbling woman, who often hath slandered and scandalized her neighbors, for which her poor husband is often brought into chargeable and vexatious suits and cast in great damages."

Hugh gave utterance to a genuine cavalier-like laugh, and, striking his boot-top with his riding-whip, returned:

"Marry! but she will make a merry sight soaring through the air like a fisher-bird to be plunged beneath the water."

"It will be a goodly sight, Hugh, and one I knew you would wish to see; therefore I sent for you."

"You have my thanks; but where is the culprit?"

"They have not arrived with her yet. Did you come from Greenspring Manor this morn?"

"Yes."

"How is Sir William Berkeley?"

"He is well, and still lives in the hope of seeing the king restored to his throne."

"Hath he invited our wandering prince to Virginia?"

"Sh—! speak not so loud," said Hugh in an undertone. "There are some of those Puritans, the cursed Roundheads, near, and it would mean death to Sir William if it were known that he but breathed such thoughts."

The two young men walked a little apart from

the others and sat down upon the green, mossy banks, where they might converse uninterrupted and still be near enough to witness the ducking when the officers arrived with the victim.

"Keep a still tongue in your head, Roger," said Hugh when they were seated. "Greenspring Manor is beset with spies, and the Roundheads long for some pretext to hang Sir William for his devotion to our king; but Sir William says that the commonwealth will end with Cromwell and the son of our murdered king will be restored."

"The rule of the Roundheads is mild."

"Mild, bah!" interrupted Hugh in contempt. "They are men without force, groundlings, the common trash from the earth with whom the best do not mingle."

"But they permit the people to send royalists to the House of Burgesses."

"That they do; yet there they must mingle with leetmen and indented slaves whose terms have expired," and Hugh heaved a sigh and dug his boot heel into the ground, adding, "It was not a merry day for old England when they struck off the king's head."

While the young royalists were discussing politics and awaiting the arrival of the guard with Ann Linkon, the women were not all silent.

"Good wives," said a hard-featured dame of fifty,

"I will tell you a piece of my mind. It would be greatly for the public behoof, if we women being of mature age and church members in good repute like Ann Linkon might speak our minds of such baggage as Dorothe Stevens without being adjudged and sent to the ducking-stool as she is to be done. Wherefore is Dorothe Stevens so great that one must not say ill of her that they be plunged in the pond? Did she but have her deserts, would she be at home and Ann Linkon on the stool? Marry! I trow not!"

"Prythee, good dame Woodley, be more chary of your tongue, lest you be brought to judgment," interposed a more cautious sister.

Dame Woodley scowled and ground her teeth in silence for a short interval, and then resumed:

"I speak only to you five who know the wife of John Stevens truly. Despite all her airs and efforts to assume to herself a superiority, we know full well she hath her faults."

"Verily, she hath," interposed a female who had her hood drawn low over her face to protect it from the morning sun.

"And I have heard that she does lead poor John Stevens a miserable life. What with her extravagance, her temper, and the way she does hate his old mother whom he loves, his life must be a burden," continued dame Woodley.

"Little the pity for him, though," interposed the woman whose weak eyes were half-hidden by her hood.

"Why say ye so, Sarah Drummond?"

"The more fool he to maintain such a creature."

"Marry! think you, Sarah, that a wife is like a shoe to be cast off at will? John Stevens hath two children, whom he loves as ardently as ever parent loved."

"I have known Dorothe Stevens to be kind and gentle," interposed a woman who had not spoken before.

"Yet she is haughty, and she would have all the world believe her of superior flesh and blood to ourselves. Doth not the Scriptures say that 'Pride goeth before destruction and a haughty spirit before a fall'? Yea, verily, I wish she would break her neck when she doth fall."

At this moment, one of the petty officers came to the group of gossipers and cried:

"Go to! hold your peace, you prating dames! The prisoner comes."

A confused murmur swelled to a general hubbub as two men appeared over the hill leading between them a woman about fifty-five years of age. She was a strong, thin-visaged woman, whose cheek had been bronzed by sun and weather. She was bareheaded, and her hair was gathered in a knot at the back. Her gown, of a thick woollen stuff, fit closely to her person, as if it had been made on purpose for the punishment she had been adjudged to receive. She was talking in a loud voice and gesticulating angrily with her head, for her arms were confined.

"I will give ye a piece of my mind," she declared to her guards.

"Hold your peace, Ann!" cried the eldest of the guards.

"Hold my peace! Verily, I will not hold my peace about such a hussy as Dorothe Stevens. That I, a Christian and Puritan, should be ducked for slandering one so foul as she! I choke at the thought."

"Marry! I wish you were silent."

"Silent, Joshua Chard, silent, indeed! Think ye that the fear of all the water in James River will awe me to silence?"

"No, by the mass, it will not," answered his companion.

"Lawrence Evans, unholy papist, do not touch me!"

"I am not a papist."

"Come, Ann Linkon, let us have this execution done with," put in Joshua, dragging the woman along.

The scene was now ridiculous enough to excite

the laughter of even the gravest Puritans. The pond and ducking-stool were in sight, and Ann Linkon, with a persistence and strength that was marvellous, began to pull back, and when she had set her heels firmly in the ground it required the united strength of both guards to move her.

"I won't go! I won't be ducked! I won't! I won't!" she screamed at the top of her voice.

"Nay, Ann, bright flower of loveliness, you shall have a soft seat."

"Shame on you, Joshua, to drag an old woman like me by the arm."

"Marry! I am not dragging you, dame Linkon. Your heels do stick like a ploughshare in the ground."

The woman continued in her sharp, shrill voice to upbraid him:

"Ungrateful wretch, is it thus you serve one who fed you in your infancy, when your mother had deserted you? Unhand me, indented slave, and go back to your master, wretch—wretch—wretch!" she hissed, as she went sliding on her heels, her toes horizontal and her knees rigid. Her feet ploughed up the earth and stones, and the crowd hooted and jeered.

"Come on, Dame Linkon, and take your bath," cried some idle urchins, waiting at the water in anticipation of rare sport.

The victim continued to scream in her shrill voice:

"It's for that hussy! She bore false witness against me at the court and had me condemned. I will be avenged for this!"

"Marry! we will be more damp than you," said Joshua, wiping the perspiration from his forehead with the cuff of his coat.

"Joshua, is this payment for what I have done for you? When you were sick with fever I sat by your bedside and cared for you; when no one else would cook your food, it was I who did it, and is it thus you requite me?"

"Peace, good dame, I have my duty to perform."

"Duty; but such a duty!"

She still braced her heels against he ground, and it required all the strength of her guards to push and pull her along.

"Verily, I say such a duty," answered Joshua, on whose grave features there came a smile. "Dame Linkon, if you would limber your joints we could make more speed."

"I am in no hurry," she answered.

"I believe you; yet if you had not detained us, this affair would have been over."

The urchins and older persons began to cry:

"Hold back, Dame Linkon; make them earn their fees."

"I will scratch your eyes out!" she hissed, as she was forced down to the bank and made to sit in the chair. Joshua wound a strap about her waist and stooped to buckle it, when, with her freed hand, she seized his hair, causing him to yell with pain.

"Prythee, hold her hands, lest she make good her threat!" he cried to his companion.

The appearance of the victim and her guards brought everybody to their feet, and a silence fell over the group. The matrons ceased to gossip; the royalists left off talking politics, and all gathered about to witness the scene. Joshua's companion held the woman's arms, and he stooped to bind her feet to the chair, when one flew out like a bolt from a catapult, planting the toe in the pit of poor Joshua's stomach, causing him to roll over on the ground and howl with pain. The sheriff by this time came on the scene and summoned sufficient help to bind her to the chair.

"See to it that every strap and cord is secure, for if she should fall she would drown," said the sheriff, and the men drew the leather straps tight, while Ann Linkon continued to rail and abuse all about her.

"'Tis for the hussy that I am to suffer this," she cried. "Dorothe Stevens bore me false witness. I never slandered her. There—there is Hugh Price. Verily I spoke truly, as he knows."

Hugh Price, the young royalist who had been talking politics with his friend Roger, blushed.

At this moment, there appeared on the scene a young man twenty-eight years of age, whose light blue eyes and frank, open face spoke honesty and humanity. His knit brows and distressed features showed that he was not in accord with the proceedings. He led the sheriff aside and spoke hurriedly with him in an undertone, which no one could hear. It was quite evident that he was making some request which the sheriff would not grant, for he shook his head in a very emphatic manner, and those nearest heard the official answer:

"No, no, the judgment of the court, the judgment of the court."

Dame Woodley, turning to a matron near, whispered: "Sarah Drummond, there is John Stevens, the husband of the woman who had Ann Linkon adjudged. How dare he come here?"

"For shame!" whispered Sarah Drummond.

"Yea, verily."

"I wonder he could witness the wrong she hath done."

At this a young wife with a babe in her arms interposed:

"They do say that John Stevens had naught to do with the matter and did protest against having one so old as Ann Linkon ducked."

"John Stevens is a godly man," remarked still another. "He would not wrong any one."

"If he were my dearest foe," whispered goodwife Woodley, "he would have my sympathy for living with Dorothe Stevens."

"Whist, Dame Woodley; speak not your mind so freely," whispered Sarah Drummond, "for there be those in hearing on whose ears your words had best not fall."

All the while, Ann Linkon had been struggling with her executioners; but now, helpless and exhausted, she was bound in the chair. The sheriff, who was a humane man as well as a stern official, remonstrated with her.

"Ann Linkon, do not so exert and heat yourself, or else when you be plunged into the water you will take your death."

"Death! Take my death! That is what you want, wretch!" she screamed in her shrill voice.

"Peace, dame; be still!"

"I will not be silent. She is a hussy. John Stevens, I defy your wife," she added as her eyes lighted on Stevens who was near. "I told no falsehood on her. Go to your friend Hugh Price, and if he will speak the truth, he will say I spoke no falsehood."

Again Stevens was seen talking with the sheriff; but he shook his head with the inexorable:

"The judgment of the court—the judgment of the court."

Stevens turned away with a look of disappointment on his face. The sight of him seemed to increase the anger of Ann Linkon, and she railed and struggled until, exhausted, she panted for breath. The sheriff fanned her with his hat until she had partially cooled; but as soon as she regained her breath, she began again:

"It's a merry sight to you all to watch an old woman. Verily, I wish Satan would rend you limb from limb, all of ye."

"Go to! hold your peace, Ann!" said the sheriff.

"I will not," she screamed, the froth appearing upon her lips.

"Then you shall be plunged hot."

"I care not."

"It may be your death."

"That's what ye want."

"We don't."

"Ye lie, ye wretch!"

"Ann, I will duck you the full sentence if you don't hold your peace."

"You are a wretch!" she screamed.

The sheriff at this moment motioned the crowd to stand back and gave the signal to his two assistants, who went to the other end of the pole and seized the rope dangling there.

"I'LL SCRATCH YOUR EYES OUT!"

"You are a white-livered wretch!" the scold again yelled. At this moment she went soaring off into the air. A piercing shriek came from her lips as she found herself swinging out over the pond. "I'll scratch your eyes out!"

"Let her down," commanded the sheriff, and the men holding the rope allowed it to slip through their hands, and the woman in the chair darted down toward the water.

"I said it, as I say it yet; she's a hussy! she's a hussy!" shrieked the woman, whose vocabulary was insufficient for her rage. The chair rapidly descended until it struck the water with a splash, pushing the waves on either side and letting the scold down, down into the cold liquid. She gave utterance to a yell when she found the water coming up over her breast, almost taking her breath.

She was drawn all dripping from the pond and elevated high in the air so everybody could see her. A wild yell went up from the crowd, and an impudent urchin cried:

"Ann Linkon, how like you your bath?"

"I'll scratch your eyes out!" she shrieked, then again began to denounce her prosecutor as she once more descended, repeating, "She's a hussy!"

Down, down she went into the water, until it came to her chin, causing her to utter another shriek. Again she was lifted high in the air. The sheriff, who was superintending the enforcement of the sentence, turned to his assistants and said:

"You do not dip her under; let the stool go lower."

As Ann Linkon descended for the last time, she seemed to gather up all her energies and, in a voice overflowing with hate, shrieked:

"It's true! She is a hussy!"

Plunging down, down, down, until ducking-stool and occupant were completely buried beneath the water, sank the victim, and on the air came a gurgling sound: "She's a hussy!" The sheriff's assistants gave the rope a sudden pull, and in an instant the choking, strangling creature soared up in the air, gasping for breath with the water running in streams from her garments. She made several efforts to speak, but in vain. Her mouth, nostrils, eyes and ears were full of water, and she could only gasp. Poor Ann Linkon was humiliated and crushed. A ducking was a light punishment, yet the disgrace which attached to it was sufficient to break the spirit of one possessing any pride. The sheriff turned to his assistants and said:

"Put her on shore."

The people gave way, and the stool swung round on the pivot and was lowered to the sands. The sport was over, and the cavaliers began to jest and laugh over the scene, which, to them, had been one of amusement. Hugh and Roger once more retired to talk of politics, and the Dame Woodley, turning to Sarah Drummond, asked if she thought public morals had been improved by such a disgraceful scene. But few expressions of sympathy were offered to the coughing, shivering, dripping woman, who sat silently in the chair upon the sands. She was meek enough now when the guards came to unbuckle the straps and free her. Even after she was released, she sat in the chair, strangling, coughing and shivering.

John Stevens made his way through the crowd and, going up to the woman, who seemed almost lifeless, began:

"Dame Linkon, I am most truly sorry that this has been done—"

At sound of his voice, the half-inanimate form seemed suddenly inspired with life and vigor, and, bounding to her feet with a shriek of rage, she dealt him a blow with her open hand on the side of his head, which made him see more stars than can usually be discerned on the clearest night. He staggered and, but for the sheriff, would have fallen.

CHAPTER II.

SEEKING BETTER FORTUNE.

On peace and rest my mind was bent,
And fool I was I married;
But never honest man's intent
As cursedly miscarried.
—BURNS.

IN Virginia's colonial days, no man was better known than John Smith Stevens. His father was one of the original founders of Jamestown and, it was said, had felled the first tree to build the city. John Smith was his first born, and was named in honor of Captain John Smith, a personal friend.

John Smith Stevens was born about the year 1625, the same year that Governor Wyat defeated the Indians. He was four years of age when John Harvey became colonial governor in 1629, and a year later, 1630, Sir George Calvert came to Jamestown on his way to colonize Maryland under the charter of Lord Baltimore. He was old enough to remember the stormy days in the assembly, when, on the "28th of April, 1635, Sir John Harvey thrust out of his government, and Captain John

West acts as Governer till the king's pleasure is known." He never knew exactly why Sir John Harvey was thrust out; but he heard some one say he was interfering with the liberties of the people.

He knew that the king replaced him, however. Then the people said that all Virginia was divided into eight *Shires:* James City, Henrico, Charles City, Elizabeth City, Warwick River, Warrosquoyake, Charles River, and Accawmacke, and that a lieutenant was appointed over each to protect them against the Indians. John Stevens remembered when William Claybourne, the famous rebel of colonial Virginia, tried to urge the people, against the will of the king, to drive the colonists out of Maryland, which they claimed as a part of their domain.

Claybourne established a colony at Kent Island, from whence a burgess was sent. Leonard Calvert was governor of Maryland, and a misunderstanding arose between him and Claybourne on Kent Island. Claybourne must go, for the island was part of Maryland, although the right of his lordship's patent was yet undetermined in England. Claybourne resisted. He declared that he was on Virginia territory by the king's patent, and was the owner of Kent Island, and that he meant to stay there. He would also sail to and fro in his trading ship, the *Longtail*, to traffic with the Indians. If he were attacked he would defend himself. He soon had an opportunity to make good his boasts. Leonard Calvert seized the *Longtail*, and Claybourne sent a swift pinnace with fourteen fighting men to recapture her. This was in the year 1634, when John Stevens was nine years of age; but the affair was the talk of the time, and consequently was indelibly stamped on his young mind. Two Maryland pinnaces went to meet Claybourne, and a desperate fight occurred on the Potomac River. A volley of musket-balls was poured into Claybourne's pinnace, and three of his men fell dead. Calvert captured the pinnace; but Claybourne escaped. He was driven from Kent Island and escaped to Virginia; but Sir John Harvey refused to surrender him, and John Stevens saw the rebel when he embarked for England, where he made a strong fight before the throne for Kent Island. Although he seemed for a while about to triumph, the lords commissioners of plantations finally decided against his claims, thus dispelling the rosy dreams of Claybourne.

In 1642, there came to Virginia as governor of the colony Sir William Berkeley, then almost forty years of age, when John Stevens was only seventeen. Berkeley was a man of charming manners, proverbially polite, and he delighted the Virginians, who had a weakness for courtliness. He belonged to an ancient English family, and believed in monarchy as a devotee believes in his saint, "and he brought to the little capital at Jamestown all the graces, amenities, and well-bred ways which at that time were characteristic of the cavaliers. He was a cavalier of the cavaliers, taking the word to signify an adherent of monarchy and the established church," and thoroughly hated anything resembling republicanism. For his king and church, this smiling gentleman, with his easy and friendly air, was going to fight like a tiger or a ruffian. Under his glove of velvet was a hand of iron, which would fall inexorably alike on the New England Puritans and the followers of Bacon. With the courage of his convictions, he was ready to deal out banishment for the dissenters; shot and the halter for rebels. He lived on his estate of about a thousand acres at Greenspring, not far from Jamestown. "Here he had plate, servants, carriages, seventy horses, fifteen hundred apple trees, besides apricots, peaches, pears, quinces and mellicottons. When, in the stormy times, the poor cavaliers flocked to Virginia to find a place of refuge, he entertained them after a royal fashion in this Greenspring Manor house. As to the Virginians, they were always welcome, so that they did not belong to the independents, haters of the church and king."

From the very first, John Stevens did not like Governor Berkeley and in a short time learned that he was a tyrant. Berkeley issued his proclamation against the Puritan pastors, prohibiting their teaching or preaching publicly or privately.

John Smith Stevens participated in the Indian war in 1644, and saw Opechancanough, at this time almost a hundred years of age, captured and brought to Jamestown, where he requested his captors to hold open his eyes, that he might see and upbraid Sir William Berkeley for making a public exhibition of him. A short hour afterward the aged chieftain was treacherously wounded by his guard.

In the year 1648, John Stevens married Dorothe Collier, the daughter of a clergyman of the church of England. This naturally united him to the cavalier or church party, while his mother, brother and sister were Puritans. Sometimes John thought he had the best wife living, at others he was almost persuaded that she was intolerable. She was a beautiful brunette, with great dark eyes which smiled when the sky was fair, but in which appeared the lustre of a tigress when enraged. Love in its full strength and beauty seldom dwells in the heart of both husband and wife through all the vicissitudes of life. It was so in John's case. When the honeymoon waned and practical existence began, the wife became ambitious for a more showy manner of life and more pleasures than the husband could afford. He was prosperous; but his wife's extravagance, in which he indulged her at first, kept him poor. Poverty became a burden and marriage a mockery. He who had been insanely in love, and who was unable to live out of her presence, proved an indifferent husband before the honeymoon was over. Why? John had thought his wife an angel, and marriage had shattered his idol. His ideal woman had fallen so far below his expectations that disappointment drove him to indifference. His wife thought herself his superior, and John, to her, was more a convenience than a husband.

Gradually Dorothe grew indifferent toward her husband's mother and young sister, who idolized him, and though they bore her no thought of ill, she came to despise them. John's mother saw that her son's wife was ruining him by her extravagance, yet she dared not interpose as it would make the rupture complete. Dorothe was a haughty cavalier and despised all Puritans and, most of all, her husband's mother; but the cavaliers were in trouble. King Charles was tried, condemned and beheaded in 1649, and a protectorate (Oliver Cromwell) ruled over England a few months after the execution of the king. John Stevens' wife gave birth to a son who was named Robert for his wife's father.

Though England was a commonwealth, Virginia remained loyal to the wandering prince, who slept in oaks and had more adventures than any other man of his day. Berkeley, it is said, even invited him to come and rule over Virginia, assuring him of his support; but Parliament took notice of the saucy colony and, in 1650, ordered a fleet to conquer it. The fleet did not reach Jamestown until 1652, when, after a little fluster, Sir William Berkeley retired to Greenspring, and the government was turned over to the roundheads, who chose Richard Bennet, Esquire, to be governor of the colony for one year. On the day of Bennet's inauguration, John Steven's second child, a daughter, whom he named Rebecca, was born. These two links of love made his wife more dear to him. At times she was pleasant; but usually she studied to thwart his will. She was humbled with the cavaliers and hated the Puritans. Ann Linkon, an old woman given to gossiping, incurred the displeasure of Dorothe Stevens, because she gossiped about her extravagance. She had her arrested, condemned and ducked as we have seen. There was no open rupture between Dorothe and her husband's relatives. She still greeted them with half-smiles; but those half-smiles were cold and uncongenial, and there seemed to be a settled purpose on her part as well as theirs to dislike each other. To no one did Dorothe express this dislike save to her husband, and to him she never lost an opportunity for doing so.

In 1654, Claybourne, who was in possession of Kent Island, was threatened by the Catholics from Maryland, and John Stevens, with his friend Hugh Price and half a dozen more, went to aid in the defence of the island. They camped at the mouth of the Severn, in the vicinity of the present city of Annapolis, where they were joined by Claybourne and a body of three hundred men.

On the 25th of March, 1654, Stone sailed with a force down the river, landed and attacked Claybourne. At early dawn the sleeping Puritans were awakened by the boom of cannon and volleys of muskets. They arose, formed their lines of battle and poured a tremendous fire upon the enemy. The Marylanders landed and tried to storm their fort; but after an hour retreated, leaving twenty killed and twice as many wounded on the field. Claybourne had conquered and, for a brief space of time, was to hold sway over the Severn and Kent Island.

John Stevens returned to his home to find that his wife's extravagance had impoverished his estates and almost brought him to beggary. He had remonstrated with her without avail. She wrecked her husband's fortune for a few weeks of vain show.

"Were you more prudent, Dorothe," said John, "we could soon live at ease. I have fine estates and earn money sufficient to make us comfortable for life and leave a competency for our children."

"Peace, man! Do you disdain to labor for your wife and children? Do not other men support their families, and why not you, pray?"

"But other men have helpmates in their wives."

This was the spark which ignited the hidden fires. Her black eyes blazed, and her breast heaved. She upbraided him until he withdrew and, mounting his horse, rode away. At night he returned to find his wife silent and morose, and for nine days they scarcely spoke. This life was trying to John.

After a few days she grew more amiable and expressed sympathy with her husband in his financial straits.

"I am going to economize," she declared. "I will take no heed what I shall eat, nor what I shall drink, nor wherewithal I shall be clothed."

Again for the thousandth time he took heart. After all, Dorothe might become a helpmate. She was so beautiful and so cheerful in her pleasanter moods that he thought her a treasure. When he took his baby on his knee and felt her soft, warm cheek against his own, he realized that life might be endurable even in adversity.

One evening, as they talked over his financial troubles, he said:

"Our family has a fortune in Florida."

At the name of fortune, Mrs. Stevens' head became erect, and she was all attention like a warhorse at the blast of a trumpet.

"If you have a fortune there, why don't you go and get it?" she asked.

"We would, I trow, did we know we could have it for the going," he made answer.

"And wherefore can you not?"

"St. Augustine is under the Spanish rule, and we know not that they will permit an Englishman even to inherit property there. My grandfather was a Spaniard and died possessed of valuable property."

"Can you not get it? Can you not get it?" she asked.

"I do not know."

"Try."

"We have thought to try it."

His brother was sent to Florida, but failed, though assured by the lawyers that they might in time recover it.

There is no business so unprofitable as waiting

for dead men's money. Fortune flies at pursuit and smiles on the indifferent.

The prospects of John Stevens were certainly at a low ebb, and he found his affairs daily growing worse. Large consignments of tobacco sent to England remained unpaid for, and he stood in danger of losing all. He thought of making a voyage to London for the purpose of looking after his accounts. John Stevens had never been away from his family, save in the short campaign on the Severn, and he dreaded to leave home. He loved his children and, despite her faults, he loved his wife. As he held his baby in his arms and listened to her gentle crowing and heard the merry prattle of his boy at play, he asked himself if he should ever see those children again, were he to go away.

John had three friends in whom he reposed great confidence. They were Drummond, Lawerence, and Cheeseman. One evening he met them at the home of Drummond and, relating his condition, asked:

"Knowing all as you do, what do you advise?"

"By all means, go to London," answered Drummond.

"Ought I to leave my wife and children?"

"Wherefore not?"

"If I perish on the voyage, they will be wholly unprovided for."

"Your father was a sailor."

"But his son is not."

"Yet methinks the son should inherit some of the father's courage."

John Stevens' cheek reddened at the delicate insinuation against his courage, and he responded:

"Have I not, on more than one hard-fought field, established my claim to courage?"

"True, yet why shrink from this voyage?"

"A soothsayer once predicted that dire calamities would overcome me, were I ever to venture upon the sea."

At this Cheeseman and Drummond laughed and even the thoughtful Mr. Lawerence smiled. Though soothsayers in those days were not generally gainsaid, those four men at Drummond's house lived in advance of their age.

"Go on your voyage and save the sum in jeopardy," was Drummond's advice.

"If your going will make sure the sum, hesitate not a single moment," interposed Cheeseman.

"How much is involved?" asked the thoughtful Mr. Lawerence.

"Eight hundred pounds."

"Quite a sum."

"Verily, it is. The amount would at this day

relieve all my embarrassments; yet, if I go, I leave nothing behind, for my property is gone, and my family is unprovided for."

"Secure the eight hundred pounds and provide for them."

With this advice in mind, he went home, and that same evening Hugh Price, the young royalist, who lived with Sir William Berkeley at Greenspring, called to see him, and once more the voyage to London was discussed.

"By all means, go," Hugh advised. "It is your duty to go."

Mrs. Stevens was consulted and thought she should go also; she saw no reason in his taking a pleasure voyage and leaving his wife at home; but this was out of the question, for the baby was too young to endure the voyage; besides, the cost of taking her would more than double the expense. Then Mrs. Stevens, who thought only of a pleasant time, wanted to know why she could not be sent in his stead. He explained that it was a matter of business which a woman could not perform; but Mrs. Stevens became unreasonable, declaring:

"You wish to go to London and pass your time in gay society."

"I do not," he answered.

"Verily, you do. You tire already of your wife; you would seek another."

"Dorothe, I would wed no other woman living," answered John, with a sigh.

"They all say that; yet no sooner is the wife laid in the grave than they are anxious to find one younger and more fair."

"Women do the same," John ventured to urge in defence of his sex.

"Not so often as the men."

Then Mrs. Stevens began a harangue on the evils of second marriages and wound up by declaring they were compacts of the devil. John Stevens returned to the original question of his going to London.

"My friends all declare that it is my duty to go," he said.

"Your friends! who are your friends?"

"Drummond."

"An ignorant Scotchman."

Drummond was far from being ignorant, yet he stood not in favor with Mrs. Stevens.

"Mr. Lawerence advises it."

"He is a canting hypocrite."

"Mr. Edward Cheeseman also thinks it advisable."

"Verily, he is a scheming man, who will swindle you out of the eight hundred pounds when you have secured it."

"Hugh Price agrees with them."

"Does he?" asked Mrs. Stevens.

"He does."

"I don't believe it."

Hugh Price was, in her estimation, the perfection of manhood. He was of the same church, a thorough royalist and a close friend of Sir William Berkeley the deposed governor.

"Dorothe, I said he recommended it. Pray do not doubt it."

The matter was settled next day when Hugh Price himself said to Mrs. Stevens that it was best for her husband to go. She secretly resolved that during her husband's absence she would enjoy herself.

"John," she said, "if you are going away to London to enjoy yourself, you must leave with me two or three hundred pounds."

John Stevens interrupted her with a sarcastic laugh.

"Dorothe, had I two or three hundred pounds, I would not go."

"Verily, how do you expect me to pass the dreary interval of your absence, if I have no luxuries."

"Luxuries in our poor country are uncommon, and what few we have are expensive. Think not of luxuries, but rather of necessities. Husband the little money I shall be able to leave you and be prepared against adversity. I may never return."

"Wherefore not?" cried Mrs. Stevens. "Do you contemplate an elopement? You were seen holding converse with Susan Colgate."

Mrs. Stevens had, among other weaknesses, enough of the "green-eyed monster" to make herself miserable. Susan Colgate was a pretty maiden at Jamestown, whose charms John Stevens had praised in his wife's presence. He smiled at her interruption and, after assuring her that he had no intention of eloping, said:

"The ship may sink; then you and these two little children will be unprovided for. I beseech you, husband the little I leave."

"Have no fears, I shall care for them in some way; but I am not going to forego anything in anticipation of disaster. Surely you will come back. My great grief at the absence of my husband will rend my heart so sorely that I must needs have some pleasure to drive away the sorrow and perpetuate the bloom on these cheeks and the brightness in these eyes for you."

Silly John Stevens yielded to his wife and consented to set apart for luxuries some of the small amount he was to leave. Mrs. Stevens was born to squander. Ann Linkon had said of her:

"She could cast from the window more than

the good husband could throw in at the door."
But Ann was adjudged of slander, and ducked for
the charge.

John paid his mother a visit before departing.
That sweet, gentle mother greeted her unhappy
son with tears. It was seldom Dorothe permitted
him to visit her. His mother knew it and always
assumed a cheerfulness she was far from feeling.
Ofttimes poor John had a hard struggle between
duty to his mother and fidelity to wife. It was a
struggle in which no earthly friend could aid him.

The day to sail came. At an early hour the
vessel was to weigh anchor, and just as the approaching day began to paint the eastern horizon
an orange hue, John rose and prepared to depart.
All the town was quiet. His children were sleeping, and he bent over them and pressed a kiss upon
the cheek of each, murmuring a faint:

"God bless you!"

"Shall I awake them?" his wife asked.

"No, no; the parting will be much easier if
they sleep.

"Dear, I do so regret your going!" sobbed Mrs.
Stevens, genuine tears gathering in her eyes.

"Heaven grant, Dorothe, it may not be for long."

"I will go with you to the boat," she said, hurriedly dressing herself.

John's small effects had been carried aboard the

evening before, so he had only to go on board himself. As Mrs. Stevens buckled her shoes, she repeated:

"I do so regret your going. I shall be so anxious about you and so lonesome."

John heard her, but made no answer. He was standing with folded arms gazing on his sleeping

ONCE MORE HE BENT OVER THE SLEEPING CHILDREN.

children. Moisture gathered in his eyes, and he murmured a silent but fervent prayer to God to bless and spare them. There came a knock at the door. It was a sailor come to tell him the boat was waiting to carry him on board the ship, that the tide and wind were fair and they only awaited his arrival to sail.

Once more he tenderly bent over the sleeping children and pressed a kiss on the face of each. A tear fell on the chubby cheek of little Rebecca, causing her to smile.

"Farewell, little darling!" and the father quitted his home and, accompanied by his wife, hurried to the beach. Here was a short pause, a last embrace, a fond adieu, and the husband left the weeping wife on the strand, while he was rowed to the great ship which had already begun to hoist anchor.

CHAPTER III.

THE COLONIES OF THE NEW WORLD.

> We love
> The king who loves the law, respects his bounds,
> And reigns content within them; him we serve
> Freely and with delight, who leaves us free:
> But recollecting still that he is a man,
> We trust him not too far.
> —COWPER.

The Dutch, who still held possession of Manhattan Island and the territory now known as New York, were not enjoying the peace and tranquillity promised the just. Because some swine had been stolen from the plantation of De Vries on Staten Island, the Dutch governor sent an armed force to chastise the innocent Raritans in New Jersey, believing that a show of power would disarm the vengeance of the savages. The event was so grossly unjust that it not only aroused the Raritans, but all neighboring tribes, and they prepared for war. The hitherto peaceful Raritans killed the whites whenever they found them alone in the forest. Fifteen years before some of Minuet's men murdered an Indian belonging to a tribe seated beyond the Harlem River. His nephew, then a boy, who saw the outrage and made a vow of vengeance, had now grown to be a lusty man. He executed his vow by murdering a wheelwright while he was examining his tool-chest for a tool, cleaving his skull with an axe. Governor Kieft demanded the murderer; but his chief would not give him up, saying he had sought vengeance according to the customs of his race.

The governor, who cared little for the "customs of the race," determined to chastise that tribe as he had the Raritans, and called upon the people to shoulder their muskets for the fray; but they, seeing the danger to which the rashness of the governor was leading them, refused. They had been witnesses of his rapacity and greed, and they now charged him with seeking war that he might "make a wrong reckoning with the colony," and reproached him with selfish cowardice.

"It is all well for you," they said, "who have not slept out of a fort a single night since you came, to endanger our lives and homes in undefended places."

The autocrat was transformed by the bold attitude of the people. Reason dawned upon his dull brain, and he invited all the heads of families in New Amsterdam to meet him in convention to consult upon public affairs. The result of this invitation was the selection of twelve men to act as representatives for the people, which formed the first popular assembly and first representative congress for political purposes in the New Netherlands. Thus were planted the seeds of a representative democracy, in the year 1641, almost on the very spot where, a century and a half later, our great republic, founded upon similar principles, was inaugurated, when Washington took the oath of office as the first president of the United States.

These twelve representatives of the people chose De Vries as president of their number. To that body the governor submitted the question whether the murderer of the wheelwright ought to be demanded of his chief, and whether, in case of the chief's refusal, the Dutch ought to make war upon his tribe and burn the village wherein he dwelt. The twelve counselled peace and proceeded to consider the propriety of establishing a government similar to that of the fatherland. To this the governor cunningly agreed to make popular concessions if the twelve would authorize him to make war on the offending tribe at the proper time, to which they foolishly assented. Then the surly governor dissolved them, saying he had no further use for them, and forbade any popular assemblage thereafter.

Next spring (1642) Kieft sent an expedition against the offending tribe, but a treaty disappointed his thirst for military glory. The river Indians were tributary to the Mohawks, and in midwinter, 1643, a large party of the Iroquois came down to collect by force of arms tribute which had not been paid. The natives along the lower Hudson, to the number of about five hundred, fled before the invaders, taking refuge with the Hackensacks at Hoboken and craving the protection of the Dutch. At the same time many of the offending Westchester tribe and others fled to Manhattan and took refuge with the Hollanders. De Vries thought this a good opportunity to establish a permanent peace with the savages; but Kieft, who still seemed to thirst for blood, made it an occasion for treachery and death.

One dark, cold night, late in February, 1643, when the snow fell fast, and the wind blew loud and shrill, and there was not a star to be seen in the sky, eighty men were sent by Kieft to attack the fugitives at Hoboken and those at "Colaer's Hook," who were slumbering in fancied security. Forty of those at the Hook were massacred, while the Hollanders, who had stealthily crossed the river through floating ice, were making the snows at Hoboken crimson with blood of confiding Indians and lighting up the heavens with the blaze of their wigwams. They spared neither age nor sex. "Warrior and squaw, sachem and child, mother and babe," says Brodhead, "were alike massacred. Daybreak scarcely ended the furious

KIEFT, FROM THE RAMPARTS, WATCHED THE BURNING WIGWAMS.

slaughter. Mangled victims, seeking safety in the thickets, were driven into the river, and parents, rushing to save their children, whom the soldiery had thrown into the stream, were driven into the waters and drowned before the eyes of their unrelenting murderers."

It has been estimated that fully one hundred perished in this ruthless butchery. Historians state that Kieft, from the ramparts at Fort Amsterdam, watched the burning wigwams. This treachery and wholesale murder roused the fiery hatred of the savages and kindled a war so fierce that Kieft was frightened by the fury of the tempest which his wickedness and folly had raised, and he humbly asked the people to choose a few men again to act as his counsellors. The colonists, who had lost all confidence in the governor, chose eight citizens to relieve them from the fearful net of difficulties in which they were involved. Almost the first these eight advisers did was to ask the states-general at home to recall Governor Kieft, which was promptly done, and while on his way to Europe with his ill-gotten gains, his vessel went down, and the governor perished.

Peter Stuyvesant, the brave soldier who had lost a leg in the West Indies, was sent as governor to New Amsterdam, and he arrived in May, 1647. The stern, stubborn old soldier was received with great demonstrations of joy by the Hollanders. Despite all his stubbornness, Stuyvesant was a man of keen sagacity. He was despotic, yet honest and wise. He set about some much needed reforms, refusing to sell liquors and arms to the Indians. He soon taught the Indians to respect and fear him; but at the same time they learned to admire his honesty and courage.

By prudent and adroit management, Stuyvesant swept away many annoyances in the shape of territorial claims. When the Plymouth Company assigned their American domain to twelve persons, they conveyed to Lord Stirling, the proprietor of Nova Scotia, a part of New England and an island adjacent to Long Island. Stirling tried to take possession of Long Island, but failed. At his death, in 1647, his widow sent a Scotchman to assert the claim and act as governor. He proclaimed himself as such, but was promptly arrested by Stuyvesant and put on board a ship bound for Holland. The vessel touched at an English port, where the "governor" escaped, and no further trouble with the family of Lord Stirling ensued.

Stuyvesant went to Hartford and settled by treaty all disputes with the New Englanders which had annoyed his predecessors. Then he turned his attention to the suppression of the expanding power and influence of the Swedes on the Delaware. The accession of a new queen to the throne of Sweden made it necessary to make a satisfactory adjustment of the long-pending dispute about the territory. Stuyvesant was instructed to act firmly but discreetly. Accompanied by his suite of officers, he went to Fort Nassau on the New Jersey side of the Delaware, whence he sent Printz, the governor of New Sweden, an abstract of the title of the Dutch to the domain and called a council of the Indian chiefs in the neighborhood. These chiefs declared the Swedes to be usurpers and by solemn treaty gave all the land to the Dutch. Then Stuyvesant crossed over and, near the site of New Castle in Delaware, built a fort, which he called Fort Cassimer. Governor Printz protested in vain. The two magistrates held friendly personal intercourse, and they mutually promised to "keep neighborly friendship and correspondence together." This strange friendly conquest was in the year 1651. The following year an important concession was made to the inhabitants of New Amsterdam. A constant war was waged between Stuyvesant and the representatives of the people called the "Nine." The governor tried to repress the spirit of popular freedom; the Nine fostered it. They wanted a municipal government for their growing capital and, fearing the governor, made a direct application to the states-general for the privilege. It was granted, and the people of New Amsterdam were allowed a government like the free cities of Holland, the officers to be appointed by the governor. Under this arrangement, New Amsterdam (afterward New York) was, early in 1653, organized as a city. Stuyvesant was very much annoyed by this "imprudent entrusting of power with the people."

Stuyvesant was a royalist, and for years he struggled with the increasing spirit of republicanism, which was constantly growing among his people; but he was not troubled by his domestic affairs alone; his foreign relations were once more disturbed. Governor Printz returned to Sweden, and in his place the warlike magistrate John Risingh came to the Delaware with some soldiers under the bold Swen Schute, and appeared before Fort Cassimer demanding its surrender.

The Dutch residents fled to the fort demanding protection; but Bikker the commander said:

"I have no powder. What can I do?"

After an hour's parley, Bikker went out, leaving the gate of the fort wide open, and shook hands with Schute and his men, welcoming them as friends. The Swedes fired two shots over the fort in token of its capture and then, blotting out the Dutch garrison, named it Fort Trinity, as the surrender was on Trinity Sunday, 1654.

Stuyvesant was enraged and perplexed by this surrender. At that time he was expecting an attack from the English, and the doughty governor prepared to wipe out the stain on Belgic prowess caused "by that infamous surrender." On the first Sunday in September, 1655, with seven vessels carrying more than six hundred soldiers, he sailed from New Amsterdam for the Delaware. He landed his force on the beach between Fort Cassimer and Fort Christina near Wilmington, and

STUYVESANT.

an ensign with a drum was sent to the fort to demand the surrender. The warlike Schute complied next day, and in the presence of Stuyvesant and his suite he drank the health of the governor in a glass of Rhenish wine. So ended the bloodless conquest.

On his return to Manhattan, Stuyvesant found the wildest confusion reigning because of a sudden uprising of the Indians. A former civil officer named Van Dyck had a very fine peach orchard which caused him no little annoyance on account of the constant pilfering of the Indians. Van Dyck, had grown exasperated and had vowed to kill the next Indian whom he should discover stealing his fruit. One day while the stout Dutchman was at his midday meal, his son ran in to tell him that he had seen an Indian squaw enter the orchard. Van Dyck sprang from the table vowing vengeance, and from the rack made of deer's horns

he took down his fusee and rushed into the orchard, taking care to conceal himself until he was within easy range. The squaw saw him and, with a yell of fear, wheeled to fly for her life; but Van Dyck was a true shot and, bringing his gun to his shoulder, killed her as she ran.

THE SQUAW, WITH A YELL OF FEAR, WHEELED TO FLY FOR HER LIFE.

The fury of the tribe was kindled, and the long peace of ten years was suddenly broken. One morning before daybreak almost two thousand river Indians in sixty large war-canoes landed, distributed themselves through the town and, under pretence of looking for northern Indians, broke into several dwellings in search of Van Dyck. A council of the inhabitants was immediately held at the fort, and the sachems of the invaders were summoned before them. The Indian leaders agreed to leave the city and pass over to Nutten (now Governor's Island), before sunset; but they broke their promise. That afternoon Van Dyck was discovered, and they opened fire on him. He fled down the street, but was finally shot and killed, and the lives of others were threatened. The people flew to arms and drove the savages to their canoes. The Indians crossed the Hudson and ravaged New Jersey and Staten Island. Within three days a hundred inhabitants were killed, one hundred and fifty made captives, and the estates of three hundred utterly desolated by the dusky foe. In the height of the excitement, Stuyvesant returned and soon brought order out of chaos, yet distant settlements were still broken up, the inhabitants in fear flying to Manhattan for safety. To prevent a like calamity in the future, the governor issued a proclamation ordering all who lived in secluded places in the country to gather themselves into villages "after the fashion of our New England neighbors." After some desultory fighting on the frontier, Dutch and Indian hostilities in a great measure ceased, and for about ten years, beyond the threatenings of the English on the one hand and the Indians on the other, New Netherland enjoyed a season of peace and prosperity.

The New England colonies, with the exception of Rhode Island and a part of the Mason and Gorges claim, had, in 1644, formed a confederacy. The New England Confederacy—the harbinger of the United States of America—was simply a league of independent provinces, as were the thirteen states under the "Articles of Confederation," each jealously guarding its own privileges and rights against any encroachments of the general government. That central body was in reality no government at all. It was composed of a board of commissioners consisting of two church members from each colony, who were to meet annually, or oftener if required. Their duty was to consider circumstances and recommend measures for the general good. They had no executive or independent legislative powers, their recommendations becoming laws only after they had been acted upon and approved by the colonies. The doctrine of state supremacy was controlling. Though it was not a government, or at least only a government in embryo, yet the student can see from these separate colonies, jealous of their rights, the outcoming of the United States.

Of that famous league, Massachusetts assumed control because of her greater population and her superiority as a "perfect republic." It remained in force more than forty years, during which period the government of England was changed three times. When trouble arose between King Charles I. and Parliament, the New Englanders, being Puritans, were in sympathy with the roundheads. In 1649 King Charles lost his throne and life, and England for a brief time became a commonwealth. Unlike the Virginians, the New Englanders sympathized with the English republicans, and found in Oliver Cromwell, the ruler of England next to the beheaded Charles I., a sincere friend and protector. The growth of the colony of Massachusetts was particularly healthy. A profitable commerce between the colony and the West Indies, now that the obnoxious navigation laws were a dead letter, was created. That trade brought bullion, or uncoined gold and silver, into the colony, which led, in 1652, to the exercise of an act of sovereignty on the part of the authorities of Massachusetts by the establishment of a mint. It was authorized by the general assembly, in 1651, and the following year "silver coins of the denomination of threepence, sixpence and twelvepence, or shilling, were struck. This was the first coinage within the territory of the United States."

There lived in Boston at this time a family named Stevens. The head of the family was a white-haired old man named Mathew, whose dark eyes and complexion indicated southern blood. He was a foster-son of the Pilgrim Father, Mr. Robinson, and had come to New England in the *Mayflower* when she made her first memorable voyage to Plymouth, thirty-two years before.

Mathew Stevens had removed with his family from New Plymouth to Boston the year before the king of England lost his head. This man was a brother to the father of John Stevens of Virginia, and though he had Spanish blood in his veins, he was a Puritan. The Puritan of Massachusetts was, at this time, the straitest of his sect, an unflinching egotist, who regarded himself as eminently his "brother's keeper," whose constant business it was to save his fellow-men from sin and error, sitting in judgment upon their belief and actions with the authority of a divinely appointed high priest. His laws, found on the statute books of the colony, or divulged in the records of court proceedings, exhibit the salient points in his stern and inflexible character, as a self-constituted censor and a conservator of the moral and spiritual destiny of his fellow-mortals. A fine was imposed on every woman wearing her hair cut short like a man's; all gaming for amusement or gain was forbidden, and cards and dice were not permitted in the colony. A father was fined if his daughter did not spin as much flax or wool as the selectmen required of her. No Jesuit or Roman Catholic priest was permitted to make his residence within the colony. All persons were forbidden to run or even walk, "except to and from church" on Sunday, and a burglar, because he committed his crime on that sacred day, was to have one of his ears cut off. John Wedgewood was placed in the stocks for being in the company of drunkards. Thomas Petit, for "suspicion of slander, idleness and stubbornness," was severely whipped. Captain Lowell, a dashing ladies' man, more of a cavalier and modern society fop than a sober Puritan, was admonished to "take heed of his light carriage." The records show that Josias Plaistowe, for stealing four baskets of corn from the Indians, was ordered to return to them eight baskets, to be fined five pounds, and thereafter to "be called by the name of Josias, and not Mr. Plaistowe, as formerly." The grand jurors were directed to admonish those who wore apparel too costly for their income, and, if they did not heed the warning, to fine them, and in the year 1646 there was enacted a law in Massachusetts which imposed a penalty of flogging for kissing a woman on the street, even in the way of honest salute. This law remained in force for a hundred years, though it was practically ignored.

In this school of rigid Puritanism lived the northern family of Stevens, of the same Spanish branch as the Virginia family. The head of the family, having been trained by such devout men as John Robinson and William Brewster, of course grew up in the law and customs of the Puritans. Puritanism to-day has a semblance of fanaticism; but in the age of pioneers, when civilization was in its infancy, the frontierman naturally went to some extreme. Extreme Puritanism is better than the reign of lawlessness which characterized many frontier settlements in later years. It is sometimes difficult to distinguish between fanaticism and the keenest sagacity, and the folly of one age may become the wisdom of a succeeding century. Fanatic as the Puritan may be called, he was the sage of New England and gave to that land an impetus in the arts, literature, and science, which has enabled that country to eclipse any other part of the New World.

While New England was steadily progressing, despite changes in the home government, Maryland was without any historical event worth mentioning, save the trouble with Claybourne.

That portion of the United States known as New

Jersey and Delaware consisted at this time of only a few trading settlements hardly worthy of being called colonies. Except for the Swedish and Dutch troubles and the Indian wars mentioned, these countries were in the last decade wholly without historical interest. After all, territory is but the body of a nation. The people who inhabit its hills and valleys are its soul, its spirit and its life.

All south of Virginia was a wilderness occupied by tribes of Indians until the Spanish settlements were reached. That portion now known as Carolinia and Georgia was claimed by Spain. In 1630, a patent for all this territory was issued to Sir Robert Heath, and there is room to believe that, in 1639, permanent plantations were planned and contemplated by his assign William Howley, who appeared in Virginia as "Governor of Carolinia." The Virginia legislature granted that it might be colonized by one hundred persons from Virginia, "freemen, being single and disengaged of debt." The attempts were unsuccessful, for the patent was declared void, because the purpose for which it was granted had never been fulfilled. Besides, more stubborn rivals were found to have already planted themselves on the Cape Fear River. Hardly had New England received within her bosom a few scanty colonies, before her citizens began roaming the continent and traversing the seas in quest of untried fortune. A little bark, navigated by New England men, had hovered off the coast of Carolinia. They had carefully watched the dangers of its navigation, had found their way into the Cape Fear River, had purchased of the Indian chiefs a title to the soil, and had boldly planted a little colony of herdsmen far to the south of any English settlement on the continent. Already they had partners in London, and hardly was the grant of Carolinia made known before their agents pleaded their discovery, occupancy and purchase, as affording a valid title to the soil, while they claimed the privilege of self-government as a natural right. A compromise was offered, and the proprietaries, in their "proposal to all that would plant in Carolinia," promised emigrants from New England a governor and council to be elected from among a number whom the emigrants themselves should nominate; a representative assembly, independent legislation, subject only to the negative of the proprietaries, land at a rent of half a penny per acre and such freedom from customs as the charter would warrant.

Notwithstanding all these offers, but few availed themselves of them, and the lands were for most part abandoned to wild beasts and natives. From Nansemond, Virginia, a party of explorers was formed to traverse the forests and rivers that flow into the Albemarle Sound. The company which started in July, 1653, was led by Roger Green, whose services were rewarded by a grant of a thousand acres, while ten thousand acres were offered to any colony of one hundred persons who would plant on the banks of the Roanoke, or the south side of the Chowan and its tributary streams. These conditional grants seem not to have taken effect, yet the enterprise of Virginia did not flag, and Thomas Dew, once the speaker of the assembly, formed a plan for exploring the navigable rivers still further to the south, between Cape Hatteras and Cape Fear. How far this spirit of discovery led to immediate emigration, it is not possible to determine. The country of Nansemond had long abounded in nonconformists, and the settlements on Albemarle Sound were the result of spontaneous overflowings from Virginia. A few vagrant families were planted within the limits of Carolinia; but it is quite certain that no colony existed until after the restoration.

CHAPTER IV.

THE STORM AND SHIPWRECK.

> The wind
> Increased at night, until it blew a gale;
> And though 'twas not much to naval mind,
> Some landsmen would have looked a little pale,
> For sailors are, in fact, a different kind:
> At sunset they began to take in sail.
> —BYRON.

NEARLY two centuries and a half have made wonderful changes in ocean travel. The floating palaces of to-day which plough the deep on schedule time, regardless of storms, contrary winds and adverse tides, were unknown when John Stevens embarked for England in 1654.

The vessel in which he sailed was one of the best of the time. It was large, well manned and officered, and few had any fears of risking a voyage in the stanch craft *Silverwing;* but John Stevens could no more allay his fears than control the storm.

His wife, who stood weeping on the strand, became a speck in the distance and then disappeared from his view. The heart of the husband overflowed with bitterness, and he turned from the taffrail where he had been standing and walked forward to conceal his emotion.

All about him were gay groups of people, laughing and jesting. They were mostly men and women who had come from England and were happy now that they were going home. John's wife seemed to have lost her many faults, and the image that faded from his gaze was a creature of perfection. Only the beautiful face, the great dark eyes and the sunny smiles were remembered.

John went to his stateroom and, falling into his berth, wept. He may be called weak, but he was not. John had braved too many dangers and undergone too many hardships to be termed weak. His mind was filled with his wife and children. The face of his sleeping baby, whose warm, tender arms had been so often entwined about his neck, lingered in his mind. When the dinner hour came he was not hungry, so he remained in his cabin.

The vessel had gained the open sea by nightfall and was bowling along at a three-knot rate under full spread of canvas and fair wind. He went to supper, though little inclined to eat, and during the night was awakened with a load heavier than grindstones on his stomach.

"Surely I will die," he groaned, as each heaving

billow seemed to torture his poor stomach. He rose at dawn and found himself unable to stand. The sea was rough, and the ship was tossing and reeling like a drunken man. John found himself unable to lie down or sit up. He spent the day in rolling alternately in his berth or on the floor, groaning, "Surely I will die."

The purser came and laughed at his distress, assuring him that he would survive. Next day he felt better and crawled out upon the deck. The sea still ran high, though the sky was clear, and the sun shone on the wildly agitated sea.

He saw a wretch as miserable as himself crouching under a hencoop and holding both hands upon his tortured stomach. John Stevens paused for a moment at the rail, gasping with seasickness.

"Say, neighbor, are you having a hard time?" asked the seasick but cheerful individual under the hencoop.

"My head hurts," John gasped.

"Verily, I ache all over," returned the new acquaintance under the hencoop.

At this moment the cabin door was thrown suddenly and unceremoniously open, and a man past middle age darted forward as if he had been shot out of a cannon and went sprawling upon the deck, howling as he did so:

"Good morrow, stranger!"

John was not astonished at the sudden appearance of the man, but was rather alarmed at the violence of his fall. He ran to him and assisted him to rise.

"Are you injured?" he asked.

"Nay, nay; the fall was not violent."

The man under the hencoop, who had been a disinterested spectator, took occasion to remark:

"Marry! my friend, I wish it were I who had taken such a tumble; surely it would have crushed the stones in my stomach."

"I am not sick," the new-comer answered, rising to his feet. "I was thrown by the sudden lurch of the ship; but it will soon be over."

"I trust so," groaned the seasick man by the hencoop.

"But the sea runs high," the old man said, "let us go in."

John Stevens, who had partially recovered from his seasickness, went into the cabin with the stranger. He had formed no acquaintances since coming on board the vessel and was strangely impressed with this old gentleman. Men cannot always brood on the past and retain their senses. John Stevens was not a coward, yet the helpless condition of his wife and children made him dread danger. When they were seated he said:

"You do not belong at Jamestown."

"No. I am from London and know no one at Jamestown."

"You came in the last ship?"

"We did."

"You did not come alone?"

"No; my daughter Blanche came with me. She is all the child I have."

John Stevens remembered to have seen a very pretty girl on the streets of Jamestown, and for having praised her beauty, his wife had grown insanely jealous and given way to one of her outbursts of anger. The gentleman from London was Mr. Samuel Holmes, who had been a too warm friend of Charles I. to suit the Protectorate, and after Cromwellism had become a certainty, he considered it better to fly the country. As Virginia had been friendly to cavaliers, he had brought his daughter to Jamestown and spent six months there; but, being assured by friends that he could return with safety, he had decided to go home.

From that time John Stevens and Mr. Holmes became friends. In a day or two more the passengers had nearly all recovered from their seasickness, and the voyage promised to be a favorable one. John Stevens met Blanche Holmes, a pretty blue-eyed English girl, with light brown hair and ruddy cheeks. She was not over eighteen years of age, and was one of those trusting, confiding creatures, who win friends at first sight. By the strange, fortuitous circumstances which fate seems to indiscriminately weave about people, the maid and John Stevens were thrown much into each other's society.

She had many questions to ask about the New World. He, having passed all his life there and having explored the coast to Massachusetts and fought many battles with the Indians, was able to entertain her, and she never seemed to tire of listening to his adventures. It never occurred to John that there could be any impropriety in talking to this child, nor was there any, though modern society might condemn him. He never mentioned his family to either Blanche or her father.

That wife and children left at Jamestown were subjects too sacred for general conversation. When alone in his stateroom he knelt and breathed a prayer for them, and often in his dreams he heard his laughing boy at play, or felt the warm, soft hand of his baby on his cheek, or heard her sweet voice calling him. Often he awoke and sobbed like a child on discovering that the ship was hourly bearing him further and further from home.

Mr. Holmes was a cheerful companion at first, but gradually he grew melancholy, and at times inapproachable. One day John met him at the gangway, and he took the young man's arm and, leading him aft, said:

"I want to talk with you."

They sat upon some coils of rope, and Mr. Holmes resumed: "We are going to have bad weather. I am something of a sailor, and, in addition to my own experience, the captain says we will have a storm ere many hours."

There was something in the voice and manner of the man which chilled Stevens; but he retained his self-possession and answered:

"Of course you feel no serious apprehension? The ship is strong and able to weather any storm."

"I believe it is; yet in a storm at sea we have no assurance of safety. Our captain is incompetent and the vessel has, through a miscalculation, gone a long distance out of her true course. Now what I wish to say is this: should anything happen to me on this voyage, I want you to care for my daughter. You have seen and talked with her every day since first we met, and you know how good she is. I am her only relative on earth, and Cromwell has set a price on my head. Should I perish, she will be without a protector."

John Stevens was astonished at the strange request, but consented to accept the charge, provided he should be spared and Mr. Holmes should perish.

Mr. Holmes was not mistaken in his surmises

about the weather. The day of this interview was the nineteenth of September, and before night the sky was obscured by great fleecy clouds, and in the evening the rain fell in torrents. The firmament darkened apace; sudden night came on, and the horrors of extreme darkness were rendered still more horrible by the peals of thunder which made the sphere tremble, and the frequent flashes of lightning, which served only to show the horror of the situation, and then leave them in darkness still more intense. The wind grew more violent, and a heavy sea, raised by its force, united to add to the dangers of the situation.

"It is coming," Mr. Holmes whispered to John, whom he met in the gangway.

"We are going to have a terrible storm," John answered.

"Yes; remember your promise."

"I will not forget it, Mr. Holmes; but why do you refer to it? Surely you are as likely as I to outlive the tempest."

"No, no," Mr. Holmes answered, shaking his white head despairingly, "I have an impression that my time has surely come."

John Stevens was startled by the remark, for he too was living in the shadow of some expected calamity. He next met the passenger whom he had seen under the lee of the hencoop, and his despair and grimaces were enough to make even the discouraged John smile.

"Oh, I shall be drowned. I shall be drowned!" the poor fellow was groaning. "Pray for me, some of you who can. I cannot, for it would do no good; but some of you can surely pray. By the mass! I see the very whale that swallowed Jonah ready to gulp me down."

He was clinging to some ropes as if he expected momentarily to be swept away.

John Stevens went to bed, which was the most sensible thing he could do. By daylight on the morning of the twentieth, the gale had increased to a furious tempest, and the sea, keeping pace with it, ran mountains high. All that day the passengers were kept close below hatches, for the sea beat over the ship.

About seven o'clock on the morning of the twenty-first, John Stevens was alarmed by an unusual noise upon deck, and running up, perceived that every sail in the vessel, except the foresail, had been totally carried away. The sight was horrible, and the whole vessel presented a spectacle of despair, which the stoutest heart could not withstand. Fear had produced not only all the helplessness of despondency, but all the mischievous freaks of insanity. In one place stood the captain, raving, stamping and tearing his hair in handfuls from his head. Here some of the crew were upon their knees, clasping their hands and praying, with all the extravagance of horror depicted in their faces. Others were flogging their images with might and main, calling upon them to allay the storm. One of the passengers from England had got hold of a bottle of rum and, with an air of distraction and deep despair imprinted on his face, was stalking about in his shirt, crying:

"Come, drink to oblivion, death we must meet; let us make the dissolution easy." Perceiving that it was his intent to serve it out to the few undismayed members of the ship's crew, John rushed on him, seized the liquor and hurled it over into the raging sea.

Having accomplished this, Stevens next applied himself to the captain, endeavoring to bring him back to his senses, and a realization of the duty which he owed as commander to the passengers and crew. He appealed to his dignity as a man, exhorted him to encourage the sailors by his example, and strove to raise his spirits by saying that the storm did not appear so terrible as some he had before experienced. While he was thus employed, they shipped a sea on the starboard side, which all thought would send them to the bottom. For a moment the vessel seemed to sink beneath its weight, shivered and remained motionless. It was a moment of critical suspense, and, fancying that they were gradually descending into the great bosom of the ocean, John Stevens gave himself up for lost and summoned all his fortitude to bear the approaching death as became a brave man.

At this crisis, the water, which rushed with incredible force through all parts of the vessel, floated out. Mr. Holmes was almost drowned, and, had not John seized one arm which he swung wildly above his head, he probably would have been washed overboard. The vessel did not go down immediately as they thought it would, and Mr. Holmes, partially recovered, joined Stevens.

"The storm is terrible," said the old man. "The ship is going down, and I will go with it."

"Nay, nay; keep up a stout heart," urged John.

"Verily, how can I, when danger overwhelms even the captain?"

"If we must die, let us die like men, struggling for our lives," said John.

"Remember your pledge to me. Care for her, for I will go. The ship may be saved, but my end I feel is near."

John promised to obey his request, and then, being one whom hope never entirely deserted, he turned upon the captain of the ship and once more urged him to make some manly exertion to save himself and the crew.

"Throw the guns overboard as well as much of the weighty cargo," he cried, "and set the pumps a-going.

Mr. Holmes, having sufficiently recovered to realize the wisdom of the course pursued by Stevens, joined him in his entreaties, and they got the captain and some of his crew to make one more effort. The water, however, gained on the pumps, and it seemed as if they would not long be able to keep the vessel afloat.

At ten o'clock, the wind had increased to a hurricane; the sky was so entirely obscured with black clouds, and the rain poured in such torrents, that objects could not be discerned from the wheel to the ship's head. Soon the pumps were choked and could be no longer worked. Then dismay seized on all, and nothing but unutterable despair, anguish and horror, wrought up to frenzy, were to be seen. Not a single person was capable of an effort to be useful; all seemed more desirous to terminate their calamities in an embrace of death, than willing, by a painful exertion, to avoid it.

John Stevens, though despairing, yet determined to make a manly struggle for life, and he was staggering through the main cabin, when some one clutched his arm. He turned about and through the gloom saw Blanche's pale face.

"Are we going down?" she asked.

"God grant that it be not so!" he answered.

"But such fearful noises, such hideous sights."

"Be brave, young maid," he urged. "Where is your father?"

"His shoulder is injured, and his left arm is almost useless."

At this moment Mr. Holmes came along, holding his injured arm with his right hand.

"Aye, my friend, the worst is coming," he said, fixing his despairing eyes on the white face of his daughter. "I am pleased to find you together, for now I can say what I would to both of you. Blanche, he hath promised to care for you; he is a man of honor, rely on him."

A sudden lurch of the vessel sent all three in a heap at one side of the cabin, and, as soon as John could regain his feet and ascertain that the old gentleman and his daughter had sustained no injury, he went on deck. At about eleven o'clock, they could plainly distinguish a dreadful roaring noise resembling that of waves rolling against the rocks; but the darkness of the day and the accompanying rain made it impossible to see for any distance, and John realized that, if they were near rocks, they might be dashed to pieces on them before they were perceived. At twelve o'clock, however, the weather cleared a little, when they discovered breakers and reefs outside, so that it was evident they had passed in quite close to them, and were now fairly hemmed in between the rocks and the land.

At this very critical moment, the captain adopted the dangerous expedient of dropping anchor, to bring the ship up with her head to the sea. Any seaman of common sense and not frightened out of his wits must have known that no ship could ride at anchor in that storm. John Stevens, though no sailor, saw the folly of such a course and expostulated with the captain, but to no purpose. Scarcely had the anchor taken firm hold when an enormous sea, rolling over the ship, overwhelmed her and filled her with water, and every one on board concluded that she was sinking. On the instant a sailor, with presence of mind worthy of an English mariner, took an axe, ran forward and cut the cable.

The freed vessel again floated and made an effort to right herself, but she was almost completely waterlogged and heeled to larboard so much that the gunwale lay under water. They then endeavored to steer as fast as they could for land, which they knew could not be at any great distance, though through the hazy weather they were unable to see it. The foresail was loosened, and, by great efforts in bailing, she righted a little, her gunwale was raised above water, and they scudded as well as they could before the wind, which blew hard on shore, and at about two o'clock one of the sailors said he espied land ahead.

"We will never reach it," said Mr. Holmes, who was at the side of John Stevens.

"Do not despair," said John.

"But we can't reach the shore, look at those waves."

A tremendous sea rolling after them broke over the stern of the ship, tore everything before it, stove in the steerage, carried away the rudder, shivered the wheel to pieces and tore up the very ringbolts of the deck, carrying the men who stood on the deck forward and sweeping them overboard. Among them was the unfortunate captain of the *Silverwing*. John was standing at the time near the wheel, and fortunately had hold of the taffrail, which enabled him to resist in part the weight of the wave. He was, however, swept off his feet, and dashed against the main-mast. So violent was the jerk from the taffrail, that it seemed as if it would have dislocated his arms. However, it broke the force of the stroke, and, in all probability, saved him from being dashed to death against the mast.

John floundered about in the water at the foot of the mast, until at length he got upon his feet and seized a rope, which he held while considering what he should do to extricate himself. At this instant he perceived Mr. Holmes and his daughter on the capstan. How they had got there was a marvel to him which he had no time to investigate. Mr. Holmes beckoned with his lame hand to John, while he clung to his daughter with his right. A vivid flash of lightning lighted up the scene, and John saw that Blanche was very pale, but calm. Never had he seen a more beautiful picture than this pretty maiden with her face turned in resignation to the storm. He forgot his own danger, forgot wife and children at home in his unselfish eagerness to snatch the unfortunate girl from the impending danger.

It was no easy matter for John Stevens to break away from his hold on the main-mast and make his way to the capstan. At every roll of the ship and every surge of the waves, unfortunate passengers or sailors were washed overboard and plunged into the boiling, seething waves which thundered about them. Stevens made a bold push, however, and reached the capstan. Here he could survey the wreck, and he saw that the water was nearly breast-high on the quarter-deck of the vessel.

"It will soon be over," said Mr. Holmes in a voice so despairing that it rang in the ears of John Stevens to his dying day. "Crew and passengers are nearly all gone, and my turn will come soon."

Even as he spoke, the purser, two men and four

women were washed overboard, their drowning screams mingling with the hollow roars of the ocean.

"Take her! take her!" cried Mr. Holmes frantically. "I resign her to you. I am going; I can hold out no longer."

A wave more terrible than any that had preceded it at this moment seemed to bury the ship, which was driving straight toward the unknown shore. Instinctively John wound one arm about the girl and held to the capstan with the other. It seemed an age, and he was almost on the point of relaxing his hold on the capstan, when they once more rose above the water, and he got a breath of air. He still clung to Blanche in despair, though she lay so limp in his arms that he thought her dead.

It was now dark, for night had fallen upon the awful scene. A flash of lightning illuminated the wreck, Mr. Holmes was gone, and Stevens could not see another soul on the vessel. The wild roar of surf fell on his ears, and a moment later he felt the bottom of the ship grating on the sands. It seemed to glide further and further on the beach, as if the ship were being lifted and driven inland. The tide was at the full, and the wind was blowing a hurricane on shore, so that the wreck was driven far up on the beach, and at low tide it was high and dry.

John Stevens remained by the capstan, as it was highest point, holding Blanche in his arms long after the ship had settled in the sands. The waves leaped and raved angrily below; but not a human voice was heard. He asked himself if Blanche were dead or living. At last he felt her move and, placing his hand on her heart, was rejoiced to know that it still beat.

"Father—father!" she faintly murmured.

"He is gone," John answered.

"Is this you?" she asked.

"Yes."

"Cling to me."

"I will. We will survive or perish together."

Then she became silent, and the night grew blacker, while the storm howled; but the waves receded with the ebbing tide, and the broken hulk remained fast fixed in the sands. The poor girl shivered all through that night and clung to her preserver. She did not weep at the loss of her father, for the horror of their situation dried the fountains of grief. All night long the warring elements raged about the remaining castaways, who clung with the tenacity of despair to the wreck.

CHAPTER V.

JOHN STEVENS' CHARGE.

> The fair wind blew, the white foam flew,
>   The furrow followed free;
> We were the first that ever burst
>   Into that silent sea.
>
> Down dropped the breeze, the sails dropped down,
>   'Twas sad as sad could be;
> And we did speak only to break
>   The silence of the sea.
>   —COLERIDGE.

SINCE the art of navigation became known, there have been castaways in romance and reality without number. De Foe's celebrated Robinson Crusoe stands first, but not alone among the shipwrecked mariners of truth and fiction. How many countless thousands have suffered shipwreck and disaster at sea, whose wild narratives have never been recorded, will never be known.

John Stevens was not a reader of romance and poetry, which at his age were in their infancy in Virginia. The hardy pioneers of the New World were kept too busy fighting Indians and building plantations and cities to read romance or history. Consequently he had no similar adventures to compare with his own. John had enough of the sturdy Puritan in his nature to deeply feel the duty incumbent on him, and enough of the cavalier to be a gentleman, unselfish and kind.

Throughout the long night he held the half inanimate form of Blanche in his arms. The storm abated and the tide running out left the vessel imbedded in the sands. John watched for the coming morn as a condemned criminal looks for a pardon. He knew no east nor west in the darkness; but anon the sea and sky in a certain place became brighter and brighter. The clouds rolled away, and he saw the bright morning star fade, as the sable cloak of night was rent to admit the new born day.

Blanche sat up and gazed over the scene as the flashing rays of sunlight gleamed over the sea and shore.

"Are we all?" she asked.

"Yes."

"Was no one saved?"

"None but ourselves."

"And the ship?"

"Is a hopeless wreck on the sands," he answered.

As they rose to gaze upon their surroundings, John Stevens thought with regret that if the crew and passengers had remained below hatches, they would have been saved; but he and Blanche were all who remained, and he turned his gaze to the wild shores hoping to discover some sign of civilization. There was not a hamlet, house or wigwam to indicate that Christian or savage inhabited the land.

Blanche marked the troubled look on his face and asked:

"Do you know where we are?"

"No."

The shore was wild and rocky, and on their right it was covered with a dense growth of tropical trees. Farther inland rose two towering mountains. The beach directly before them was low and receding. A long, level plain, covered with a dense growth of coarse sea-grass, was between them and the hills, which were covered with palms, maguey and other tropical trees.

John feared that they had been wrecked on the coast of some of the Spanish possessions and would be made captives and perhaps slaves by the half-civilized colonists.

They could not live long on the wreck, and he began to look about the deck for some means of going ashore. The pinnace which had been stowed away between decks was an almost complete wreck. It would have been useless had it remained whole, for John and his companion could not have launched it. There was a small boat hanging by the davits, which had sustained no other injury than two holes in its side. He was a fair carpenter, and getting some tools from the carpenter's chest, he mended the boat. After no little trouble, he lowered the boat and, assisting Blanche into it, pulled to the shore half a mile away.

It was a shore on which no human foot had ever trod. The great black stones which lay piled in heaps along the coast to the northeast until they were almost mountain-high forbade the safe approach of a vessel. The entire coast was armed with bristling reefs to guard it against the approach of wandering ships. It was almost miraculous that they had been driven in between the reefs at the only visible opening. A hundred paces in either direction their vessel would have been forced upon the rocks

"Is this country inhabited?" asked Blanche, when they had landed, and made fast their boat to a great stone.

"I fear not," he answered; "or, if inhabited, it is probably by savages."

"Should that be true, ours will be a sad fate."

"I will not desert you," he answered.

They sat down on the dry white sand to rest and gazed at the wreck, with its head high in the air and its stern low in the water.

"We made a mistake in not bringing some arms to defend ourselves against savages or wild beasts," said John.

"Can we not go back for them?"

"Would you be afraid to remain on the beach while I went?" he asked.

She said she would not, though he noticed her cast nervous glances toward the thickets and forests inland. As he pushed out once more into the shallow waters lying between the beach and wreck, she came down so close to the water's edge that the waves almost touched her toes.

"You won't be long gone?" she called in a low, sweet voice, trembling with dread.

"No."

He reached the wreck and went on board by means of broken shrouds lashed to the gunwale. The sun shone as brightly and the sky was as peaceful as if no storm had ever swept over it. The deck was almost dry, and, the hatches having been fastened, John was agreeably surprised to find but little damage done by the water. He went down to the companion-way and found less water in the hold than he expected. He brought out two muskets, a pair of pistols, a keg of powder, and bullets enough for his arms. The guns and the pistols were all flint-locks, for at this time matchlock and wheel-lock had about gone out of use.

A dagger and a sword were also added to the armament, which John lowered into his boat. Then he remembered that Blanche had had no food, and he bethought himself of some provisions. He went again into the hold and, thanks to the care of the cook in stowing away the provisions, found most of them dry and snug in the fore-part of the vessel. He got out a small chest of sea biscuits, a Holland cheese, and some dried fish, which he carried to his boat. He paused a moment to gaze at Blanche, who sat on a stone watching him. The almost tropical sun beating down upon her defenceless head suggested the need of some sort of shelter, and he procured some canvas and threw in an axe and pair of hatchets to cut poles and arrange a tent or shelter for her.

Having at last loaded his boat he set out for shore. The tide was fast setting in and bore him rapidly onward. Landing he unloaded his boat, and asked:

"Have you seen any one?"

"No."

"I have brought some food."

"It will be useless without water. I am very thirsty," she said.

"We will go farther inland, where we must find fresh water," he said hopefully.

John saw that Blanche had no covering for her

head, and the sun's rays made her faint. He gave her his hat and for himself fashioned a cap of palm leaves. They went inland until they came to some tall trees, which afforded a grateful shade. Here he induced Blanche to rest, while he went further in search of fresh water. She was tired, and had a dread of being left alone in this strange land; but Blanche was reasonable and waited beneath the tall palms gazing on the coast, the sea and the wreck lying on the sands.

"It might have been worse," she thought. "While all our friends and companions have perished, we are saved. God surely will not desert us. Having preserved us thus far for some purpose, he will not suffer us to perish until that purpose is accomplished. I alone might have been spared to perish miserably in a strange land."

Meanwhile, John Stevens was roaming among the rocks and hills for fresh water. Great blackened stones parched and dry as the sands of Sahara met his view on every side, and no sight of water was found until he came to a dark shallow pool so warm that he could not drink it.

"Heaven help us ere we perish," he groaned, wandering among the rocks and trees. "If we don't find water soon she will die."

He threw himself on the ground in despair, and as he lay there, he thought he heard a trickling sound. He started up, fearing that his ears deceived him; but no, they did not. Beyond a moss-covered stone of great size was a clear, sparkling rivulet of bright, crystal water, falling into a stone basin of considerable depth. He stooped and found it sweet and cool. Oh, so refreshing! Slaking his thirst, he next thought of his suffering companion under the trees beyond the hill, and for the first time he reflected that he had failed to provide himself with any vessel to carry water. There was no bucket or cup nearer than the ship, and she might perish before he could bring anything from there. He set his gun against a rock and, plucking some broad palm leaves, made a cup which would hold about a pint.

All this required time, and he was constantly tortured with the recollection that his charge was suffering with thirst. With the improvised cup full of water, he hastened to the almost fainting girl and said gladly:

"I have found pure, sweet water in abundance. Drink of this, and we will go at once to the spring."

She eagerly seized the leaf cup and drank, then found herself strong enough to cross the hill to the precious fountain.

John left one of the guns with her, the other was at the spring; but the sword and pistols he kept at his belt.

Taking the provisions and musket they set out for the spring. Here they bathed their hot faces and refreshed themselves.

"Now let us have food," said John.

The sea-biscuit and dried fish were wholesome, and they ate with a relish. John Stevens wanted to climb a lofty hill about two miles away, from which he hoped to have a good view of the surrounding country.

"Can we from there determine what land we are on?" she asked.

"I hope so."

"If there be cities, will we see them?"

"We shall," he answered.

"Have you no hopes nor fears?"

"I have both."

"What are your hopes?"

"My hopes are that this is one of the Bermuda Islands."

"And your fears?"

"That this is one of the West India Islands, or a part of the Florida coast, under control of the Spaniards."

"Did you hear the captain say where we were before the ship struck?"

"No; he was a most incompetent master, and knew not where we were."

"Whether we are in the land of enemies or

friends, it will be better to know the truth," reasoned Blanche.

"Are you strong enough for the walk?"

She thought she was, and they started on their journey of exploration. One of the guns was left with the provisions at the spring; but John carried the other.

The distance to the hill proved greater than they had supposed, and before they reached the base, the sun, sinking low in the heavens, admonished them that night would overtake them before the summit could possibly be gained.

John called a halt and asked:

"Shall we go on, or return to the beach?"

Blanche gazed on the frowning hills and bluffs before them and thought it best to return. Those gloomy mountain wilds were terrible after dark, and she thought they would find it more congenial nearer the wreck.

They returned to the beach. The inflowing tide had lifted their boat and borne it further up on the sands.

"Will it not be carried off?" Blanche asked.

"No, I have it anchored with a heavy stone, so it cannot be carried out."

John cut four poles and drove them into the ground and spread the canvas over it, forming a shelter for Blanche. He had brought a blanket from the wreck, which, with some of the coarse grass he cut with his sword, formed a bed for his charge. A box which he had brought from the ship afforded her a seat.

They had not found a human being, nor had they seen a single animal. A few sea-birds flying high in the air were the only living creatures which had greeted their vision since landing.

"Will you be afraid to remain here while I go for the provisions and musket left at the spring?" asked John.

"No, we have nothing to fear."

"I believe this part of the coast to be entirely uninhabited."

She made no answer, and he went for the gun and provisions. The walk was longer than he thought, for he was tired with the day's toil and was compelled to walk slowly. When about half-way to the spot he heard a rustling in the tall grass and paused to discover the cause. Cocking his gun, he tried to pierce the jungle, not fully decided whether the noise were made by man or beast.

A moment later he heard something running away. It was beyond question a wild animal, frightened at his approach. He did not get a glimpse of it and was unable to tell what it was like.

"If a beast," he thought, "it is the only one I have met with since landing on the coast."

From the rustling it made, it was no doubt small and little to be feared. He listened for a moment, and then hurried on to the spring.

"Blanche will be lonesome," he thought. "Her father placed her in my charge, and I will protect her if I can."

Climbing the moss-grown stone, he descended into a dark ravine to the spring. The sun was set by this time, and the sombre shades of twilight began to spread over the scene. His eager eyes pierced the gathering gloom and discovered that the food left had been attacked by animals and the biscuit devoured.

He searched the ground, and saw footprints.

"Some animals have been here," he thought. "They evidently did not like dried fish, for, though they have trampled over them, they have devoured none; but the sea-biscuits are all gone."

It was impossible to determine what sort of animals they were, but he was quite sure they were not dangerous.

He took up the gun and returned to the tent, where he related to Blanche the loss of their biscuits.

"Then there are animals on the land," she said.

"Yes; but they are not dangerous," he returned. "These animals may prove useful to us for food."

"I hope so."

After several moments, she asked:

"How long must we stay?"

"I know not. Had I not better take the boat and go to the wreck for more food?"

"No, not to-night," she answered with a shudder. "I prefer to go without food than to be left an hour alone in the approaching night."

He had a sea-biscuit in his pocket, which he gave her and made his own supper of dried fish. With flint, steel and some powder, he kindled a fire near the tent and sat down before it with a gun across his knees and another at his side, his back against a tree. Thus he prepared to pass the night, urging his companion to go to sleep in the tent.

Patient, confiding Blanche went and laid down to sleep. She had borne up well, not uttering a single complaint throughout all their trying ordeals.

As John sat there keeping guard over his charge, his mind went back across the wild waste of waters to the home he had left. He seemed to feel the soft baby hands of little Rebecca on his face, or hear the prattling of his boy at play. His wife's great, dark eyes looked at him from out the gloom, and he sighed as he thought how improbable it was that he would ever see them again. Wrecked on an unknown shore, with dangers and difficulties to surmount, what hope had he of the future?

"Heaven watch over and guard my helpless ones at home, as I guard the charge entrusted to me," he prayed.

His fire was not so much to keep off the cold as wild animals. The distant roar of the ocean beating on the shore broke the silence. The low and melancholy sound fell on the ear of the unfortunate man, and, raising his eyes to the stars, he thought:

"The same stars shine for them, and the same God keeps watch over all. May his guardian angels watch over the loved ones at home until the father and husband returns."

John's heart was heavy. His fire had burned low, and he had forgotten to replenish it. Suddenly upon the air there came a half growl and half howl, and, looking up, he saw a pair of fiery eyes flashing upon him. An animal was approaching the tent. John cocked his gun, aimed at the two blazing eyes and fired.

In a moment the eyes disappeared, and Blanche, alarmed at the report of the gun, sprang from the tent and wildly asked:

"What was it? Are we attacked?"

"Peace! It was only an animal, which I should judge to be a fox," assured John.

The report of the gun awakened a thousand

slumbering sea-fowls, which arose screaming on the air in every direction. John listened to hear some animal, but not a growl and not a cry came on the air. After a few moments all was quiet once more, and he begged his charge to retire to sleep, while he took up his post as guard.

CHAPTER VI.

THE ISLAND OF DESOLATION.

> I am monarch of all I survey,
>   My right there is none to dispute:
> From the centre all round to the sea
>   I am lord of the fowl and the brute.
> O Solitude! where are the charms
>   That sages have seen in thy face?
> Better dwell in the midst of alarms
>   Than reign in this horrible place.
>   —COWPER.

NEXT morning Stevens went to find the animal, at whose eyes he had fired during the night; but it was gone without leaving even a trace of blood behind it. The boat had sustained some damages during the night from the surf dashing it against the rocks; but he managed to reach the wreck with it, where he quickly mended the seam started in its side.

He brought away a cask of fresh water, a chest of sea-biscuit, some Holland cheese, wine, salt pork and more dried fish. After they had dined, they set out to the nearest mountain, from the peak of which they hoped to get a survey of the surrounding country. He tried to induce Blanche to remain, but she insisted on accompanying him.

Nothing is more deceitful than distance, and they were compelled to pause and rest before they had reached the bluffs and foot-hills at the base of the mountain. While resting there, they heard a scampering of feet, accompanied by the loud snort of frightened animals flying from the plateau above them. They were gone before John and his companion were able to get a sight of them.

"What are they?" she asked.

"I know not, yet they seem to have a greater dread of us than we have of them."

Resuming their journey they had not proceeded half a mile, when John espied one of them looking down upon him and his companion from an airy cliff. Its bristling horns, long beard, and keen eyes were visible, though the ferns and grass concealed its body.

"It is a goat," he said. "The animals which we discovered were goats, and we have nothing to fear from them."

A little further on, he discovered a fox in the bushes. The animal was unacquainted with man and was very tame. It stood until they were within a few paces of it, and then it trotted off a short distance and halted to look at them. John's first impulse was to shoot it; but, on a second thought, he decided to reserve his fire for some larger and more useful game. At last the summit of the nearest hill was gained, and from it they had a survey of the country and discovered that they were on an island. Stevens' heart sank within him at the discovery, for now no human help was within their reach. The fear of Spaniards and savages gave place to the greater dread of passing their lives on a desolate island.

The island was about sixteen miles long by ten wide. It had four lofty mountains in the centre, one of which was so high as to be above the clouds and covered at the peak with snow. These lofty elevations supplied the island with an abundance of pure, fresh water. In the fertile valleys below grew bread-fruit and oranges in profusion and many wild berries and vegetables excellent for food. They spent four days in exploring the island, hoping to find some sort of inhabitants, but were disappointed. Goats, foxes and a species of gray squirrel were the principal animals on the island. None were very dangerous; but the foxes proved to be mischievous thieves, and stole all of their provisions they could come at. Stevens began an early war against them, and shot them wherever they could be found.

Far to the north were two more islands evidently not so large as the one on which they were cast.

Dangerous reefs lay between them and all about the three islands, making navigation difficult if not impossible.

Blanche bore the journey well and did not give way to despair even when they discovered that they were on an uninhabited island. For her sake Stevens kept up a show of courage, though he found despair rising within his breast.

"We must get the provisions and tools from off the wreck," he said, "and make our stay here as comfortable as possible."

"How long will that stay be?" she asked.

"God in heaven alone can tell."

"Surely some passing ship will see us."

He hoped so; but that reef-girt shore seemed to forbid the approach of a vessel. Nevertheless he set up long poles with flags on them at different points of the island, so that a passing ship might see them for miles out to sea.

Then he began the work of unloading the wreck. There was an inlet or mouth of a creek not far from the place where they first landed, and, constructing a raft on the wreck and loading it with arms, provisions, ammunition and tools, they took advantage of the tide to float it in to shore. This was repeated daily for weeks. Clothing, sails, provisions of all kinds, half a hundred guns and as many pistols and cutlasses, with other weapons, tools, books, writing material, and, in fact, everything that could possibly be of service was brought off from the wreck. They were favored with mild weather, and John, soon learning to take advantage of the tides, had no difficulty in landing the goods.

The shore was strewn with boxes, barrels, arms, bales and piles of goods, with tools, provisions, rafts and broken bits of lumber, for he decided to bring away as much of the wreck as he could, for the boards would be very useful in the construction of houses. Weeks were spent in this arduous toil, and their efforts were fully rewarded.

The foxes proved their only annoyance, and Stevens shot them until they became more shy. He killed nineteen in a single night. It became necessary to make a strong wooden cage, or box to keep their food in; but the salt junk was scented by the foxes, and they gathered about it in great numbers and made the night hideous with their howls.

At last he hit upon a plan which nearly exterminated the foxes and rid them of the nuisance. Among other articles brought from the ship was poison. He shot a goat and, while it was warm and bleeding, cut it open, poisoned the meat and left it where the foxes could get at it.

Early in the night the fighting, snapping and snarling began, and the next morning the woods were filled with dead foxes, so it was years before the howl of another was heard.

Fully realizing the importance of making haste in removing the wreck to the shore, he worked with more than human efforts until he had gotten off almost everything of value. Blanche aided him all she could, and when their tents were up, her womanly instincts as housekeeper gave a homelike appearance to them.

Having brought off all that was valuable, he built a house close under a bluff, where a projecting shelf of rock covered a small grotto, which he enlarged with pick and shovel. Before the rainy season set in, he had a comfortable house. They had a store of provisions enough to last for two years, and, in addition, John brought away Indian corn, barley, and wheat which he planted and, to his delight, discovered that it grew well. Being a farmer, it was only natural that he should give his thoughts to agriculture.

John was industrious, thoughtful and, having been brought up in the colony, was calculated to make the wilderness bloom as Virginia had done. His axe awoke the echoes of the forest, and he busied himself building houses, planting fields, and providing for their comforts. All the while the flags were kept flying from the hills, in hopes of attracting some passing ship.

Two years glided by, and not a sail had been seen on the ocean. The wreck had disappeared; but John and Blanche were provided with comfortable homes. They had tamed the goats, exterminated the foxes, and their fields waved with corn, wheat and barley. To grind their corn, John, who was something of a genius, invented a mill from two stones. The wild fruits and berries of the island improved under cultivation and yielded a greater abundance. Their floors were covered with rush mats, and the furniture brought from the wreck gave to the rooms a comfortable and homelike air.

It was evening, and the sitting-room was lighted by candles made of goat's tallow. John Stevens was reading aloud from a Bible and Blanche sat listening with rapt attention.

"Read more," she said when he had finished the page. "What a blessing to know that even in the uttermost parts of the earth God is with us."

"Verily, it is a comfort."

"Should we die here, He will be with us."

"God is everywhere. He will not desert us," John said.

"But I hope we will yet be rescued."

"I trust so."

He closed his book and placed it on the table at his side and buried his face in his hands. She watched his strong emotion with eyes which were moist with sympathy, and, rising, came to his side and placed her hand on his shoulder.

"You are stronger than I," she said, "why should you grieve more at our calamity? Surely God is with us."

The tears were trickling through his fingers and his frame was convulsed with emotion. She noted his grief and, to encourage him, added:

"God is everywhere; he is here; he will guard and watch over us, and, if it be his pleasure that we escape from this island, he will send some ship to our deliverance."

"My burden is greater than I can bear."

"Remember He said, 'Take my yoke upon you, for my yoke is easy and my burden is light.' Trust all to Jesus, and He will give you strength."

"You are all alone in the world, Blanche."

"Yes."

"You have not a relative living."

"No, my father was lost."

"I wish I had none. It is not for myself that I grieve, but the helpless ones at home."

"Helpless——"

"My wife and children."

Blanche, shocked and amazed, gazed at him in silence. The blood forsook her face, her breast heaved, and her breath came in painful gasps. He had never before in all the two years they had been alone upon the island mentioned his wife and children.

"I left them to better my fortune," he continued. "They were so helpless and I so poor; but I did what I thought best. Last night I saw them in my dreams, her great bright eyes all red with weeping, and my baby's warm little hands were again about my neck imploring me to come home in accents so pathetic and sweet, they melted my heart. My blue-eyed Robert was no longer gay, but melancholy. O God, give me the wings of a dove that I may go and see them again!"

His head fell on the table and his whole frame shook with emotion, while Blanche, with her own sad beautiful eyes swimming in tears, could not utter a word of consolation. When he had partially recovered she asked:

"Why did you not tell me this before, you might have had my sympathy all along."

"I did not care to burden you with my griefs."

"Trust in God."

"I do; but this dark uncertainty; my helpless children."

"They have their mother."

"She is unpractical, knows nothing of life and is as helpless as the children. The little money left her has been spent long before this, and they are—Heaven only knows what ills they may endure. So long as I was with them, I shielded them from the rude blasts of the world; but now they are without a protector."

Overcome with the sad picture he had created in his mind, he buried his face again in his hands. Once more Blanche sought to soothe his cares by

BLANCHE COULD NOT UTTER A WORD OF CONSOLATION.

assuring him that He who watched the sparrow's fall would in some way care for his loved ones at home.

The years rolled on, and day by day he climbed the top of the nearest hill and gazed off to the sea, hoping to discern a sail, but in vain.

He had brought the captain's glasses from the ship, and with this often gazed at the two islands toward the north with longing eyes. Did they connect with the main land where people dwelt, and from which they might find means of transportation to the home which he sometimes feared he might never again behold?

"Would it be too dangerous to undertake a voyage to those islands?" Blanche asked one day when they were gazing for the thousandth time at them.

"If we had a suitable boat we might attempt it."

"How is our own boat?"

"Too frail. The boards are almost rotten."

"Then why not make one?"

The idea was a good one, for it promised him employment. He felled a large tree and proceeded to make a dug-out such as the Indians of Virginia used.

Blanche helped him and was so cheerful, kind and considerate, that often, as he gazed on her beautiful face, he sighed:

"Had Dorothe possessed her spirit, this misery would have been averted." He felt a twinge of conscience at rebuking his wife, even in thought. No doubt she had paid dearly for her folly.

The boat at last was completed, and he rigged a sail for it, and together they set out for the distant islands. They glided over the water, catching a glimpse of a man-eating shark, which made them shudder with dread.

With fair wind and tide they reached the nearest island that day. It was nearly as large as their own, and the shore was fully as dangerous. The next was smaller, and both were wooded, with low hills, but poorly watered. They found goats and foxes abounding on each, but no indication that a human being had ever been there. All about on every side was the vast ocean, stretching as far as the eye could reach, with the eternal wash of waves on the rocks.

Spreading their tent on the shore, they passed the night on the island nearest their own, and were greatly annoyed by foxes and mosquitoes, so that with early dawn they were glad to return home.

One never knows how to appreciate home until they have been away, and John seemed to take a new interest in his house, fields and the tame goats of his island.

Yet in the night, when slumber had sealed his eyelids, he saw in that far-away home his wife's pale face, and felt his baby's soft arms once more about his neck, and in his agony he cried out:

"God send some ship to deliver me!"

Day by day as the years rolled on, John Stevens saw more and more to admire in the companion with whom his lot was cast. When he was sick or tired she watched over him with all the tender care of a sister or mother. When he was saddest she whispered words of hope and cheer in his ear. In fact Blanche was an ideal woman, a comforter and a helper.

"How could I live here without you, Blanche?" he said one day.

"Heaven tempers the wind to the shorn lamb," she answered. "Nothing is so bad that it could not be worse." Blanche was a pure Christian girl. No influence on earth could swerve her from a course marked out for her by her intellect and approved by her conscience. She was a devout Christian, and when her companion, in the bitterness of his soul, was rebellious, her sweet Christian influence led him back to God.

In the stillness of life, talent is formed; but in the storm and stress of adverse circumstances character is fashioned. Had Blanche returned to London she might have become a society lady; but here she was a consoler, binding up the broken heart. She would sit for hours by John's side talking with him about his wife and children in far-off Virginia, and she never went to sleep without praying Heaven by some means to take the father and husband back to his loved ones.

"I went to the cliff this morning," she said,

"thinking I might see a sail, but I was disappointed."

"Why did you think to see a sail, Blanche?" he asked.

"I dreamed last night that a ship came for you and took you home. Oh, how glad I was, when I saw you happy again with your dear wife and the baby on your knee, its little warm hands on your face!"

After a long silence, he asked:

"Blanche, how long have we been here?"

"Ten years," she answered.

Blanche not only had kept a complete journal since the day of their shipwreck, but had written a faithful description of the island, giving its resources and describing the coast. To John it seemed but yesterday since he kissed the tender cheek of his babe, bade his wife a farewell and sailed away.

Ten years had made their impress on him. His hair was growing gray, and his beard was quite frosty. It was not age that whitened his hair so much as it was his ten years of suffering. Ten years had developed Blanche from a beautiful girl to a glorious woman of twenty-eight, more beautiful at twenty-eight than eighteen.

"Blanche, would ten years change a baby?" John asked.

"Yes."

"Then my baby is a baby no longer," sighed the father.

"No; she is a pretty little girl now."

"And has no recollection of her father?"

"How could she?"

"But my little boy?"

"He was five when you left home?"

"No, not quite; four and some months."

"Then he would remember you."

"He is a good-sized boy."

"Almost fifteen," she answered.

"Heaven grant I may yet see them!"

"Amen!" replied Blanche. "God has not forgotten you; our prayers will be heard."

John made no answer. He arose, took his gun and went out among the hills.

"When he talks of them," Blanche thought, "he always goes to the hills. God grant he does not die of despair, for then I would be all alone on this island of desolation."

Tears gathered in her eyes and, falling on her knees, she breathed a fervent prayer.

CHAPTER VII.

IN WIDOW'S WEEDS.

Go; you may call it madness, folly;
You may not chase my gloom away.
There's such a charm in melancholy,
I would not, if I could, be gay.
—ROGERS.

DOROTHE STEVENS was not a woman to take misfortune much to heart. She watched the ship in which her husband sailed until it vanished from sight, shed a few tears, heaved a few sighs and went home to see if the negro slave had prepared breakfast. She smiled next day, and before the week was past she was quite gay. She said she was not going to repine and languish in sorrow.

Her conduct shocked the staid Puritans, and her fine apparel was ungodly in their eyes.

Weeks rolled on, and no news came from the good ship *Silverwing;* but they might not hear from her for months, and Mrs. Stevens did not borrow trouble. She did not dream that the ship could possibly be lost, or that her husband's voyage could be other than prosperous, so she plunged into a course of extravagance and pleasure that would have ruined a wealthier man than poor John Stevens.

"I must do something," she declared, "to relieve my mind from thoughts of my poor, dear, absent husband, for whom I grieve continually."

Once John's mother and sister came to see her; but she was entertaining some ladies from Greensprings and wholly neglected her visitors. The grandmother held the baby on her knee, kissed the face, while her tears fell on it; then silently the two unwelcome visitors departed for their home, while Mrs. Stevens was so busily engaged with the ladies from Greensprings that she did not even bid them adieu.

Dark days were in store for Dorothe Stevens. She heeded not the constant reduction of her money until it was gone. Then she reasoned that her husband would soon return with a goodly supply, and she began to use her credit, which had always been good; but she found that the merchants who once had smiled on her frowned when she came to ask for credit.

"Have you heard from your husband, Dorothe Stevens?" one asked, when she applied to him for credit.

"No."

"He has been a long time gone."

"Yes; but he will return."

"The *Silverwing* has not yet reached London."

"How know you that?" she asked, a momentary shadow coming over her face.

"The *Ocean Star* hath just arrived, but brought no report from the *Silverwing*."

"It left before the *Silverwing* arrived. The ship was delayed a little. It has reached there safely by this time, I am quite sure," and Mrs. Stevens' face grew bright as she made some purchases for which she had not the money to pay. The merchant sold to her reluctantly, and she, without dreaming that calamity could possibly befall her, went on enjoying herself. Ex-Governor Berkeley had invited her to spend a few days at Greenspring, where she met her husband's friend Hugh Price, with other gay cavaliers and ladies.

Dorothe was a thorough royalist, and she heard, while at the governor's, that Cromwell was in poor health, and there was a strong feeling that the exiled Prince Charles would be recalled to the throne. Berkeley had invited him to Virginia. Many of England's nobles, flying from Cromwell's persecutions, had taken refuge with ex-Governor Berkeley, and no other greater pleasure could Dorothe wish than to be associated with them.

When she returned to her home, it looked poor and mean in comparison with the governor's excellent manor house; but troubles thickened. Bills came pouring in upon her, which she was unable to meet, for she had not a farthing, and her creditors became clamorous.

"Why don't John come back with the money?" she asked, angry tears starting from her eyes. "I cannot meet these bills, and he knows I must live."

"You have been grossly extravagant, Mrs. Stevens," one heartless creditor returned. He was a merchant who had smiled on her most sweetly in her prosperous days, and had always welcomed her to his shop. "Had you economized with the money your husband left, you would not be in such sore straits."

Mrs. Stevens was shocked and indignant. She wept and asked for time. Ann Linkon, who had never forgiven Dorothe Stevens for the ducking she had caused her, now boldly declared that she had all along told the truth and, shaking her gray head, repeated:

"She is a hussy. She hath driven John to sea and perchance to death. She is a hussy."

No one attempted to prevent Ann's tongue from wagging, and to the unfortunate Dorothe it was quite evident that she was no longer the favorite of Jamestown.

"When John comes back, all will change," she thought; but, alas, the months crept slowly by, and John came not. There came a rumor which time confirmed that the *Silverwing* was lost. Dorothe, who was of a hopeful nature, would not believe it at first, though the news had a very disastrous effect to her credit. She was refused at every shop and store in Jamestown. In her distress she sold such articles as she could dispense with; but Jamestown was only a frontier hamlet, it had no such conveniences as pawnbrokers and second-hand clothiers, and what few articles she could dispose of were sold mainly to freed or indented servants at ruinous prices.

Dorothe's fashionable friends deserted her. The ladies and cavaliers at Greenspring became suddenly cold and she remained at home. Her slaves were taken away, so, finally, was the home, and, with her little children, she took up her abode in a miserable log cabin, where she became an object of charity. A year and a half had rolled away; but she had not wholly given up her husband for dead. The vessel might have blown out of its course, it might have been captured by pirates, or Spaniards, and her husband might yet escape.

She had been so cool toward his relatives, that they had not seen her for a year. She was proud and would have suffered death rather than appeal to them for aid; but her children—his children, were suffering, and, as she had to give up even the log cabin to rapacious creditors, at last she appealed to his mother and sister, whom she had despised.

"You are welcome. Come and share our home," was the response.

Almost heartbroken, yet proud, Dorothe with her children set out for the distant plantation in the county in which lived the relatives of her husband.

Political changes were coming, which were to have a marked effect on Dorothe, who gave up her husband for dead and donned the widow's weeds. Those changes were the restoration.

In 1658, Cromwell died and named his son Richard as his successor. From the death of Cromwell until the accession of Charles II., the government of England was in a state of chaos and was highly revolutionary without being in a state of actual anarchy. There was in reality no head to the government. Even the Puritans saw that the inevitable must come, and, in 1660, Charles II. was restored to the throne of England without any serious jar to the country or colonies. It was late in May, 1660, when the wandering prince, mounted on a gayly caparisoned steed, entered London between his brothers, the Dukes of York and Gloucester, and took up his abode in the palace of Whitehall, while flags waved, bells rang, cannons roared, trumpets brayed, shouts rent the air and fountains poured out costly libations of wine as tokens of public joy. After a twenty years' struggle between royalists and republicans, the monarchy was restored, and the English people again became subjects of the head of the Scottish house of Stuarts.

The accession of Charles II. soon caused a change in the affairs of America. The new king assigned to his brother James, Duke of York, the whole territory of New Netherland, with Long Island and a part of Connecticut. Charles had no more right to that domain than to the central province of Spain; but the brutal argument that "might makes right" justified the royal brothers, in their own estimation, in sending ships, men and cannon, the "last argument of kings," to take possession of and hold the territory. Four men-of-war, bearing four hundred and fifty soldiers, commanded by Colonel Richard Nicolls, a court favorite, arrived before New Amsterdam in the latter part of August, 1664. Governor Stuyvesant had been warned of their approach and tried to strengthen the fort; but money,

OLIVER CROMWELL.

men and will were wanting. The governor's violent temper, with English influence, had alienated the people, and they were indifferent. Some of them regarded the invaders as welcome friends. Stuyvesant began to make concessions to the popular wishes. It was too late; and New Amsterdam became an easy prey to the English freebooters.

Early in this year, revolutionary movements had taken place among the English on Long Island, which the governor could not suppress, and the province was rent by internal discord for several months. A war with the Indians above the Hudson Highlands had also given the governor much trouble; but his energy and wisdom had brought it to a close. The anthems of a Thanksgiving day had died away, and the governor, assured of peace, had gone to Fort Orange (Albany), when news reached him of the coming English armament. He hastened back to his capital, and, on Saturday, the 30th day of August, Nicolls sent to the governor a formal summons to surrender the fort and city. He also sent a proclamation to the citizens, promising perfect security of person and property to all who should quietly submit to English rule.

The Dutch governor hastily assembled his magistrates at the fort to consider public affairs; but, to his disgust, they favored submission without resistance. Stuyvesant, true to his superiors and his

"PETER THE HEADSTRONG," UNABLE TO CONTROL HIS PASSION, TORE THE LETTER INTO PIECES.

own convictions of duty, would not listen to such a proposition, nor allow the inhabitants to see the proclamation. The Sabbath passed without any answer to the summons. It was a day of great excitement and anxiety in Amsterdam, and the people became impatient. On Monday the magistrates explained to them the situation of affairs, and they demanded a sight of the proclamation. It was refused, and they were on the verge of open insurrection, when a new turn in events took place.

Governor Winthrop of Connecticut, who was quite friendly with Stuyvesant, had joined the English squadron. Nicolls sent him as an embassador to Stuyvesant, with a letter in which was repeated the demand for a surrender. The two governors met at the gate of the fort. Stuyvesant read the letter and promptly refused to comply.

"Inform the Englishman if he wants my fort, he must come amid cannon and balls to take it," he said. Closing the gate, he retired to the council chamber and laid the letter before his cabinet and magistrates. After examining it they said:

"Read the letter to the people, and so get their minds."

The governor stoutly refused. The council and magistrates as stoutly insisted that he should do so, when the enraged governor, who had fairly earned the title of "Peter the Headstrong," unable to control his passion, tore the letter into pieces. The people at work on the palisades, hearing of this, hastened to the Statehouse, where a large number of citizens were soon gathered. They sent a deputation to the fort to demand the letter. Stuyvesant, storming with rage, cried:

"Back to the ramparts! mend the palisades, and we will answer the letter with cannon."

The deputies were inflexible, and a fair copy of the letter was made from the pieces, taken to the Statehouse and read to the inhabitants. At that time the population of New Amsterdam did not exceed fifteen hundred souls. Outside of the little garrison, there were not over two hundred men capable of bearing arms, and it was the utmost folly to resist. Nicolls, growing impatient, sent a message to the silent governor saying:

TOMB OF STUYVESANT.

"I shall come for your answer to-morrow with ships and soldiers," and anchored two war-vessels between the fort and Governor's Island. Stuyvesant's proud will would not bend to circumstances, and, from the ramparts of the fort, he saw their preparations for attack, without in the least relenting, and when men, women and children, and even his beloved son Balthazzar, entreated him to surrender, that the lives and property of the citizens might be spared, he replied:

"I had much rather be carried out dead."

At last, however, when the magistrates, the clergy and many of the principal citizens entreated him, the proud old governor, who had "a heart as big as an ox, and a head that would have set adamant to scorn," consented to capitulate. He had held out for a week. On Monday morning, the 8th of September, 1664, he led his troops from the fort to a ship on which they were to embark for Holland, and an hour after, the red cross of St. George was floating over Fort Amsterdam, the name of which was changed to Fort James as a compliment to the Duke.

The remainder of New Netherlands soon passed into the possession of the English, and the city and province were named New York, another compliment to Prince James, afterward James II. Colonel Nicolls, whom the duke had appointed as his deputy governor, was so proclaimed by the magistrates of the city, and all officers within the domain of New Netherland were required to take an oath of allegiance to the British crown.

The new governor took up his abode in the Dutch fort, if the strange structure within the palisades could be called a fort. It contained, besides the governor's house and barracks, a steep gambrel-roofed church with a high tower, a windmill, gallows, pillory, whipping-post, prison and a tall flagstaff. There was generally a cheerful submission to the conquerors on the part of the inhabitants, and after the turmoil of surrender a profound quiet reigned in New York.

So passed into the domain of perfected history the Dutch dominion in America after an existence of fifty years, by that unrighteous seizure of the territory which had been discovered and settled by the Dutch. England became the mistress of all the domain stretching along the coast of the Atlantic Ocean from Florida to Acadie, and westward across the entire continent; but in New Netherland, in that brief space of half a century, the Dutch had stamped the impress of their institutions, their social and religious habits, their modes of thought and peculiarities of character, so that they remained unconquered in the loftier aspect of the case. The characteristics of the Dutch of New Netherland were so indelibly stamped, that, after a lapse of more than two centuries, they are still marked features of New York society.

Saucy New England underwent fewer changes by

reason of the restoration than all the other colonies. The New Englanders were men and women of iron who dared everything. They were always cool, cautious, yet bold, and when they made an effort to gain a right, they always won. They clung to all their rights and demanded more. The bigotry of the Puritans of Massachusetts was vehemently condemned at the time of their iron rule and has been ever since; but their theology and their ideas of church government were founded upon the deepest heart-convictions of a people not broadly educated. Having encountered and subdued a savage wilderness for the purpose of planting therein a church and a commonwealth, fashioned in all their parts after a narrow but cherished pattern, they felt that the domain thus conquered was all their own, and that they had the right to regulate the internal affairs according to their own notion of things. They boldly proclaimed the right to the exercise of private judgment in matters of conscience, and so tacitly invited the persecuted of all lands to immigrate and settle among them. This invitation brought "unsettled persons," libertines in unrestrained opinions, from abroad to disseminate their peculiar views. The Puritans, fearing the disorganization of their church, early took alarm and, with a mistaken policy, resisted such encroachments upon the domain and into their society with fiery penal laws implacably executed.

Among the sects of the time dangerous to Puritanism, were the Quakers or Friends. The first of the sect who appeared conspicuously in New England were Mary Fisher and Anna Austin, who arrived at Boston in the summer of 1656, when John Endicott was governor. There was no special law against them; but under a general act against heretics, they were arrested; their persons were searched to find marks of witchcraft, with which they were suspected; their trunks were searched, and their books were burned publicly by the hangman. After several weeks of confinement in prison, they were sent back to England. Mary Fisher, a violent religious enthusiast, afterward visited the Sultan of Turkey and, being mistaken for a crazy woman, was permitted to go everywhere unmolested.

The harsh treatments of the first comers fired the zeal of the more enthusiastic of the sect in England, who sought martyrdom as an honor and a passport to the home of the righteous. They flocked to New England and fearfully vexed the souls of the Puritan magistrates and ministers. One woman came from London to warn the authorities against persecutions. Others came to revile, denounce and defy the powers of the church. From the windows of their houses they would rail at the magistrates, and mock the institutions of the country, while some fanatical young women appeared nude on the streets and in the churches, as emblems of "unclothed souls of the people." Others with loud voices proclaimed that the wrath of the Almighty was about to fall like destructive lightning on Boston and Salem. The Quakers of 1659 were quite different from that honorable body of people of the present age.

Horrified by their blasphemies and indecencies, the authorities of Massachusetts passed some cruel laws. At first they forbade all persons "harboring Quakers," imposing severe penalties for each offence, then followed mild punishment on the Friends themselves. These proving ineffectual, the Puritans passed laws which authorized the cropping of the ears, boring the tongues with hot irons, and hanging on the gibbet offending Quakers.

Even these terrible laws could not keep them away. On a bright October day in 1659, two young men named William Robinson and Marmaduke Stevenson, with Mary Dyer, wife of the Secretary of State of Rhode Island, were led from the Boston jail, with ropes around their necks and guarded by soldiers, to be hanged on Boston Common. Mary walked between her companions hand in hand to the gallows, where, in the presence of Governor Endicott, the two young men were hung. Mary was unmoved by the spectacle. She was given into the care of her son, who came from Rhode Island to plead for her life, and went away with him; but the next spring this foolish woman returned and began preaching and was herself hung on Boston Common.

The severity of these laws caused a revulsion of public sentiment. The Quakers stoutly maintained their course, and were regarded by the more thoughtful as real martyrs for conscience' sake, and, in 1661, the severe laws against them were repealed. Puritanism, which had flourished under republicanism in England, with the restoration of the Stuarts was threatened, and doubtless fear of the vengeance of the church party caused the New Englanders to temper their laws.

A restless spirit on the part of the New Englanders with an uneasy feeling in regard to the result of the restoration caused many to emigrate to Carolinia, which was a mysterious, far-away land where everybody lived at peace. Removed from the grasp of kings and tyrants, many went to the infant town planted on Old-town Creek, near the south side of Cape Fear River. However, the Carolinias were growing from fugitive settlements into commonwealths, and, in 1666, William Drummond, the friend of John Stevens, was appointed governor of North Carolinia.

Claybourne, who, after a struggle of twenty years, had succeeded in conquering Maryland, saw, with the decline of the commonwealth of England, his own hopes go down. In 1658, the Catholics of St. Mary's and the Puritans of St. Leonard's consulted, and the province was surrendered to Lord Baltimore. Claybourne had no sooner gained that for which he had battled, than his power began to crumble beneath his feet, and he was even ejected from the Virginia council.

The restoration of 1660 produced a most wonderful effect on Virginia. All was changed in the twinkling of an eye, so to speak. The cavaliers, who had been sulking for years under the mild rule of the commonwealth, threw up their hats and cheered from Flower de Hundred to the capes on the ocean, as only a victorious political party can cheer.

The sentiment of the Virginians in favor of royalty was strong and abiding; with the restoration of monarchy they had achieved the main point. The representatives in the colony of the psalm-singing fanatics of England would have to go now. Silk and lace and curling wigs would be once more in fashion, the hated close-cropped wretches in black coats and round hats would fade into the background, and the good old cavaliers, like the king, would have their own once more.

The king's men became prominent, and their plantations resounded with revelry. It was thought that Charles II. would grant special favors to Virginia, as Berkeley had invited him to be their king even before he was restored to the throne of England. The country is said to have derived the name of the "Old Dominion" from the fact that the Charles might have been king of Virginia before he was king of England.

In March, 1660, the planters assembled at Jamestown and enacted: "Whereas, by reason of the late distractions (which God, in his mercy, put a suddaine period to), there being in England noe resident absolute and ge'll confessed power, be it enacted and confirmed: that the supreme power of the government of this country shall be resident in the assembly, and that all writts issue in the name of the grand assembly of Virginia until such command or commission come out of England as shall by the assembly be adjudged lawful." The same session declared Sir William Berkeley governor and captain-general of Virginia. In October of the same year of the restoration, Sir William Berkeley was commissioned governor of Virginia by Charles II.

No one in all the colony rejoiced more at the

restoration of monarchy than did Dorothe Stevens. Her fortunes had mended. Her husband's brother was appointed governor of Carolinia, and, while he was acting in the capacity of governor, he managed to secure the fortune his grandfather had left in St. Augustine. It was large, and fully twenty thousand pounds fell to the heirs of John Stevens, which was a godsend to the widow, who purchased a fine house in Jamestown and once more entered the society of the cavaliers and church people.

For twelve years she had been a widow, and now that she was wealthy and the charm of cavalier society, she began to entertain some serious thoughts of doffing her widow's weeds.

"It's all because of that cavalier Hugh Price," said Ann Linkon spitefully. "The hateful thing will wed him, because he is rich and the king is restored."

The widow left off her weeds and, in silk and lace, with ruffles and frills, became the gayest of the gay. The flush came to her pale cheek, and people said she smiled on Hugh Price. It is quite certain that Hugh Price, after the restoration, was known to be frequently in the society of his lost friend's wife.

CHAPTER VIII.

THE STEPFATHER.

> Mother, for the love of grace
> Lay not that flattering unction to your soul,
> That not your trespass but my madness speaks.
> It will skin and film the ulcerous place;
> While rank corruption, winning all within,
> Infects unseen—
> —SHAKESPEARE.

WITH the return of prosperity Mrs. Stevens deserted and forgot her husband's relatives notwithstanding their kindness to her in adversity. Mrs. Stevens possessed a ruinous pride and vanity combined with a haughty spirit and small gratitude. She was wealthy, again the cavaliers were in power, and she was the gayest of the gay. She was still youthful and beautiful and out of widow's weeds.

"Hugh Price will surely wed her," said Sarah Drummond.

No sooner was Governor Berkeley inaugurated, after receiving his commission from Charles II., than he gave a grand reception at which there was music and dancing. The young widow was there in silk, lace and ruffles, her black eyes sparkling with pleasure. Hugh Price, a great favorite of the governor, was one of the most dashing gentlemen in Virginia at the time. He was a handsome fellow with hair bordering on redness and eyes a dark brown. His mustache was between golden and red, and he possessed an excellent form.

He was seen much in the society of the widow Stevens, and some of his friends began to chaff him on his attentions, which made the cavalier blush.

"Verily, Hugh is a good cavalier, Dorothe is a royalist and was never happy with John Stevens; it is better that she wed him."

Robert Stevens was twelve or fourteen, when his mother, laying aside her widow's weeds, became young again. Robert remembered his father and their days of privation, and he did not forget that all they had, they owed to that father. He witnessed his mother's smiles and blushes with some anxiety. One day, as he was going an errand to Neck of Land, he was accosted by a meddlesome fellow named William Stump, with:

"Master Robert, do you know you are soon to have a father-in-law?" (Stepfather was in those days known as father-in-law.)

"No!" cried the boy, indignantly.

"By the mass! you are. Don't you observe how Hugh Price is continually with your mother?"

Robert's eyes filled with tears, and he cried:

"I will kill him!"

William Stump, laughing at the misery he had occasioned, answered:

"Marry! lad, you can do naught. Better win the favor of Hugh, for he can be a cruel master."

Robert went on his errand, hating both Hugh Price and William Stump, and he determined to appeal to his mother to have no more to do with Hugh Price.

Robert had been sent on the errand by the mother, that he might be away when Hugh Price came. She had an intuition, as women sometimes do, that the supreme moment had arrived in which Hugh would "speak his mind." The widow looked very pretty in her lace and silk and frilled cap, from which the raven tresses peeped. She had also managed to dispose of little Rebecca, so the coast was clear when Mr. Price, on his gayly caparisoned steed, arrived. To one not acquainted with the state of Hugh Price's mind, his appearance and behavior on the occasion of his ride from Greensprings to Jamestown would have been mysterious and unaccountable.

Dismounting at the stiles he gave the rein to a gayly dressed negro, who led the animal into the barn while the negro girl showed him to the parlor, which was furnished gorgeously. The harp which the widow played was in the corner with her Spanish guitar. The room was unoccupied when Hugh entered. He paced to and fro with nervous tread, popped his head out of the window at intervals of three or four minutes and glanced at the hourglass on the mantel, manifesting an impatience unusual in him.

It was quite evident that some subject of great importance occupied his mind. At last Mrs. Stevens entered, quite flustered, almost out of breath and her cheeks crimson with youth and beauty. Wheeling about from the window through which he had been nervously gazing, he accosted her with:

"Mrs. Stevens, I have chosen this opportune moment——"

Here he choked. Something seemed to rise in his throat and cut off his speech. Dorothe glanced at him, her great dark eyes wide open in real or affected wonder and asked:

"Well, Mr. Price, for what have you chosen this moment?"

"It is, madame, to tell you—ahem, this day is very hot."

"So it is," Dorothe answered, her dark eyes beaming tenderly on him. "Won't you sit? Your long ride has fatigued you."

"Indeed it has," answered Hugh, accepting the proffered seat. The fine speech which Hugh had been studying all the way to Jamestown had quite vanished from his mind; but the widow was inclined to help him on with his wooing. After three or four more efforts to clear his throat, he began:

"Mrs. Stevens, I came—ahem—all the way here to ask you—to get your opinion—that is to say——"

Here he stopped again. The words in his throat had become clogged, and Hugh's face was purple, while great drops of sweat stood out in beads on his forehead.

Dorothe, free from the embarrassment which tortured him, waited a respectable length of time for him to clear away that annoying obstruction in his throat, and then to help him along, began:

"Why, Mr. Price, you have always been one of my best friends, and I assure you that any suggestion or information I can give you, will be freely given," and here the widow blushed to the border of her cap, and touched her mouth with the corner of her apron.

Price, fixing his eyes on the ceiling, gathered courage enough to begin again:

"I have come to remark, Mrs. Stevens, that —ahem—that—do you think the restoration of monarchy is permanent?"

"Oh, I hope so," replied the widow very earnestly and softly, with a glance at the cavalier.

"Under the restoration, do you—ahem—think it is a much greater expense to keep two people than to keep one?" He was getting at it at last.

"Oh, dear me, Mr. Price!" said Mrs. Stevens, coloring again, for she fancied she saw in the near future a proposal coming. "Oh, what a question!"

The cavalier, having gotten fairly started, now came boldly to the charge. He had asked a question and demanded an answer. She thought it did not make the expense very much greater if the people were economical and careful, and then the pleasure of being in the society of some one was certainly very great.

That was just what Mr. Price had all along been thinking, and then, with his great manly heart all bursting with human kindness, he said:

"You must be very lonely, Mrs. Stevens."

"Lonely, oh, so lonely!" and the white apron was changed from the corner of the mouth to the corner of the eyes.

"I have thought so often of you living here alone with those children, who need a father's care."

By this time the widow was whimpering. He grew bolder and, falling on his knees, began an impassioned avowal of love. The widow, startled by the earnestness of her lover, rose to her feet in dismay.

At this juncture the door was thrown open, and the boy Robert entered to take a part in the scene. He carried a stout staff and, raising it with both hands, brought it down with a resounding whack on the shoulders of his mother's suitor.

Then a scene followed. Robert was ejected from the room and the mother made it all right with the injured party. A few days later it was currently reported that the widow Stevens was to wed Hugh Price the handsome cavalier. Mr. Stevens, the brother of her former husband, was shocked at the announcement and, in conversation with his wife, said:

"She who has always been an enemy to second marriages is now to bring a father-in-law over her children to the house."

"Poor children when Hugh Price becomes their master, as he will."

"I believe it is my duty to expostulate with her."

"Nay, nay, husband, it will be of no avail. You will have your trouble for your pains."

On a second thought, he was convinced that it would be folly to interpose.

"It will be better to let her have her way," he concluded. "Marry! she hath never sought advice or shelter save when her trouble overwhelmed her. In prosperity we are strangers, in adversity friends. Alas, poor children!"

THE STEPFATHER. 133

The cavalier Price was seen frequently on the streets of Jamestown, and his friends noticed that he spent much of his time with the widow. He was smiling. His fat face and dark brown eyes

THE DOOR WAS THROWN OPEN AND THE BOY ROBERT ENTERED
TO TAKE A PART IN THE SCENE.

seemed to glow with happiness. He never looked ugly, save when he encountered Robert's scowling face, and then he felt unpleasant sensations about the shoulders.

Grinding his teeth in rage, he said:

"I will have my revenge on him when he is under my control."

Hugh Price was not in a great hurry. He bided his time, and not even a frown ruffled his brow. He greeted the children with sunny smiles calculated to win their hearts, and under ordinary circumstances they might have done so. But from the first he was regarded with aversion, as an intruder upon their sanctuary and love. The dislike was mutual, for, though Price concealed his feelings, there rankled in his breast an enmity which he could not smother.

Robert was open in his resentment. It was the first time he had ever opposed his mother. Even when younger, in their trouble and sore distress, he was her counsellor. He had not complained when the heaviest burdens were laid on his young shoulders. He had done the work of a man long before he was even a stout lad. Privation and hardship were borne without complaint. He rejoiced on his mother's account when their fortunes so suddenly and unexpectedly changed. Toil was over. Rest came and with it the improvement he desired.

It was hoped by her best friends that the bitter lesson which Dorothe had learned would prove effective, but it did not. Women of her disposition never learn by experience, and she plunged once more into extravagance and folly. The boy was old enough to realize his mother's weakness, yet his great love for her placed her above censure. He was silent and would have borne a second misfortune like the first uncomplaining; but when he learned that she was to bring one to take the place of that father who slept beneath the sea, he rebelled.

Dorothe knew the disposition of her children, and she decided to get them out of the way until after the wedding. At last she hit upon a plan. Once more in her need she had recourse to the relatives of her husband. Her husband's sister had married Richard Griffin, a planter, and lived at Flower de Hundred. The children had always loved their paternal relatives, and, though they had not been permitted to visit them since the restoration, they had by no means forgotten them. They hailed with joy the announcement that they were to go to Flower de Hundred.

One morning in early June three horses were saddled, and Robert and Rebecca, accompanied by a trusty negro named Sam, started on their journey. Most of the travel, especially to a country as far away as Flower de Hundred, was on horseback.

"I am so glad we are going," said Rebecca, as they galloped along the road through the woods. "Mother was good to let us go."

"I am s'prised at the missus," the negro said, shaking his head. "Sumfin am gwine to happen now fur sure, sumfin am gwine to happen."

"Why?" asked Robert.

"Misse neber gwine to dem people less dar be sumfin for a-gwine ter happen."

Little Rebecca cast furtive glances about in the dark old wood through which they were riding and with a shudder asked:

"Is there any danger of Indians?"

So often had the savages drenched the earth with blood, that the child had a dread of them.

"Dun know, Misse Rebecca. Sam gwine ter fight if Indians come."

"But they must not come."

"No Injun hurt Misse. Sam not let um."

Robert, young as he was, had little faith in the negro's boasts as a protector, for he knew that Sam was a coward and would fly at the first intimation of danger. The journey was made without incident. It was a journey through a country romantic and picturesque to the youthful Robert. The grand old forest, with its untrodden paths, the tall trees, the dead monarchs of the forest, with branches white and bare spread like ghost's fingers in the air, filled his imagination with picturesque visions. Next they journeyed through a strip of low lands covered with tall, coarse grass, which came almost to the backs of the horses. Then they swam streams in which the negro held the girl on her horse. At night Flower de Hundred was reached, and the children were with their aunt.

Sam left them to return to Jamestown with the horses. As he went away, he took Robert aside and, with a strange look on his ebony face, said:

"Spect sumfin bad am gwine ter happen, Masse Robert. She neber sent ye heah but for bad luck ter come. Look out for it now, lem me told ye; look out foh it now."

Robert knew that all negroes were superstitious, and Sam's strange warning made very little impression on him. He and his sister were happy with their relatives who were kind to them.

Occasionally the uncle and the aunt were found talking in subdued tones with eyes fixed on Robert and Rebecca; but he did not think it could have any relation to them.

The days were spent in frolicsome glee among the old Virginia woods, and the nights in healthful repose. Robert felt at times a vague, strange uneasiness. It seemed so odd that his mother should send them away, and that so many days should elapse without hearing from her. It was not at all like her; but he was so free and so happy in his new existence, that he did not allow it to trouble him.

One day a wandering hunter from Jamestown came by the house where Robert was playing with his cousins and called to him:

"Ho! master Robert, I have news for you," he called to the lad.

"William Stump, when did you come?" he asked.

"But this day," was the answer.

"Where are you from?"

"Jamestown, and, by the mass! my young gay cavalier, I have news for you. Marry! have you not heard it already?"

"I have heard nothing."

"Your mother hath married," cried Stump with a fiendish chuckle.

"It is false!" cried Robert.

"By the mass! it is true, my young cavalier," and Stump laughed at the expression of misery which came over the young face. "It was a gay notion to send you brats away until the ceremony was over. You might make trouble, you know. Ha, ha, ha! You laid your stick about the shoulders of Mr. Hugh Price, now he will return blow for blow," and, with another chuckle, Stump sauntered away, his gun on his shoulder.

On going to the house Robert had the report confirmed. Some one from Jamestown had brought news of the wedding, and his little sister, with her great dark eyes filled with tears, took him aside and said:

"Brother, mother is married; what does it mean?"

She clung to him, placed her curly head on his bosom and wept. Robert restrained his own tears and sought to soothe his sister.

"Will that man Hugh Price come to live at our house?" she asked.

"Yes."

"But I can never love him. I don't know what it is to love any but you and mother. I don't remember my own father; but you do, Robert?"

"Yes."

"Was he like Mr. Price?"

"No. He was a grand, noble man, with a kind heart."

"Will he let us live at home, now that he has come?" she asked.

Robert, though his own heart was heavy, and he felt gloomy and sad, strove to look on the bright side.

"Yes, he cannot drive us from home," he said.

"But mother will love us no longer."

"She will, sister. No man can rob us of mother's love."

Then they went apart to discuss their sorrow

dat fellah wat go a loped wid de stock. Ef,! but
I wish ye kib um."

The long journey to Jamestown was made. They
left at sunrise one morning and rode until noon,
when they halted in the wilderness to allow the
horses an hour to rest and graze, while they sat on
a blanket spread on the grass under a tree. Robert
and his sister fell asleep, and the negro was nod-
ding, when a snake came gliding through the grass
toward the sleeping children. San, rose in a
moment and, seizing a stout stick, struck the snake
and killed it before it could reach the children.
They were awakened by the blow and, trembling
at their narrow escape, once more set out for Jamestown.

Though they put their horses to their best and
the afternoon, the sun was sinking behind the western hills and forests as they came in sight of the
settlement. Twilight's sombre mantle was falling
over the earth, when they arrived at the door of
their home and were assisted by the servants to
alight.

Robert and his sister were so sore and tired they
scarcely could stand. A candle had been
lighted in the house, and the soft rays came through
the open casement; but the house was strangely
silent. No mother came to welcome them home
with a kiss, and a sense of death fell upon those

young hearts. Robert dared not ask where she was and why she was not at the stiles; but Rebecca was younger, more inexperienced and impulsive.

"Where is mother, Dinah?" she asked her mother's housekeeper.

"In de house, chile, waitin' for you," she answered.

Poor, tired, heart-broken little Rebecca forgot all save that she was her mother, and she ran upon the piazza and burst into the room where Mr. Hugh Price and her mother were.

"Come here, my darling," said Mrs. Price, kissing her daughter. "This man is your father now, and he will be very good to you."

It was like a dash of cold water on the warm little heart, and, starting back, she glanced at him from the corners of her pretty black eyes and answered:

"I cannot call him father."

"You will learn to, my dear," Price answered with a smile.

"Come, Robert, come and greet your new father," said the mother.

Robert remained stubbornly at the door and, with a dangerous fire flashing in his eyes, answered:

"Call him not my father; he is no father of mine!"

"You will learn to like me, children," answered Mr. Price, with an effort to be pleasant; but it needed no prophet to see that there was trouble in the near future.

CHAPTER IX.

THE MOVING WORLD.

If we could look down the long vista of ages,
  And witness the changes of time,
Or draw from Isaiah's mysterious pages
  A key to this vision sublime;
We'd gaze on the picture with pride and delight,
  And all its magnificence trace,
Give honor to man for his genius and might,
  And glory to God for his grace.
                          —PAXTON.

AFTER the surrender of New York to the English, in the year 1665 Peter Stuyvesant went to Holland to report to his superiors. In order to shift the responsibility from their own shoulders, they declared that the governor had not done his duty, and they asked the States-General to disapprove of the scandalous surrender of New Netherland. Stuyvesant made a similar counter-charge and begged the States-General to speedily decide his case, that he might return to America for his family. The authorities required him to answer the charges of the West India Company. He sent to New York for sworn testimony, and at the end of six months he made an able report, its allegations sustained by unimpeachable witnesses. The company made a petulant rejoinder, when circumstances put an end to the dispute. War between Holland and England then raging was ended by the peace concluded at Breda in 1667, when the former relinquished to the latter its claims to New Netherland. This brought to an end the controversy between Stuyvesant and the West India Company.

Stuyvesant went to England and obtained from King Charles permission for three Dutch vessels to have free commerce with New York for the space of seven years. Then he sailed for America, with the determination of spending the remainder of his life in New York. He was cordially welcomed by his old friends and kindly received by his political enemies, who had learned by experience that he was not a worse governor than the Duke had sent them. Stuyvesant retired to his *bowerie* or farm on East River, from which the famous Bowery of New York City derived its name, and in tranquillity passed the remainder of his life.

The people of New York soon discovered that a change of masters did not increase their prosperity or happiness. Brodhead says: "Fresh names and laws they found did not secure fresh liberties. Amsterdam was changed to New York and Orange to Albany; but these changes only commemorated the titles of a conqueror. It was nearly twenty years before the conqueror allowed for a brief period to the people of New York even that partial degree of representative government which they had enjoyed when the tri-colored ensign of Holland was hauled down from the flagstaff of Fort Amsterdam. New Netherland exchanged Stuyvesant and the West India Company and a republican sovereignty for Nicolls, a royal proprietor and a hereditary king. The province was not represented in Parliament, nor could the voice of its people reach the chapel of St. Stephen at Westminster as readily as it had reached the chambers of the Binnenhof at the Hague."

Nicolls was succeeded by Francis Lovelace in 1667. Lovelace was a quiet man, unfitted to encounter great storms, yet he showed considerable energy in dealing with hostile Indians and French on the northern frontier of New York. He held friendly intercourse with the people of New England, and in the summer of 1672, when a hostile squadron of Dutch vessels of war appeared before his capital, he was on a friendly visit to Governor Winthrop of Connecticut. War had again broken out between England and Holland, and the Dutch inhabitants of New York had shown signs of discontent at the abridgment of their political privileges and a heavy increase in their taxes without their consent. Personally, they liked Lovelace; but they were bound to consider him as the representative of a petty tyrant. When, in menacing attitude, they demanded more liberty and less taxation, the governor in a passion unwisely declared that they should "have liberty for no thought but how to pay their taxes." This was resented, and when the Dutch squadron came, nearly all the Hollanders regarded their countrymen in the ships as liberators. When Colonel Manning, who commanded the fort, called for volunteers, few came, and these not as friends but as enemies, for they spiked the cannon in front of the statehouse.

The fleet came up broadside to the fort, and Manning, sending a messenger for Lovelace, opened fire on the enemy. One cannon ball passed through the Dutch flagship from side to side; but the balls from the fleet began pounding against the walls of the fort. Six hundred Holland soldiers landed on the banks of the Hudson above the town and were quickly joined by four hundred Dutch citizens in arms urging them to storm the fort.

With shouts and yells of triumph the body of one thousand men were marching down Broadway for that purpose. They were met by a messenger from Manning proposing to surrender the fort, if the troops might be allowed to march out with the honors of war. The proposition was accepted. Manning's troops marched out with colors flying and drums beating and laid down their arms. The Dutch soldiers marched in followed by the English troops, who were made prisoners of war and confined in the church. It was the 9th of August, 1672, and the air was quivering with heat, when the flag of the Dutch Republic once more waved over Fort Amsterdam, and the name of the city of New York was changed to New Orange, in compliment to William Prince of Orange.

The Dutch had taken New York.

The New Netherland and all the settlements on the Delaware speedily followed the capture of New York. The other English colonies near the province were amazed and prepared to defend their own domains against the encroachments of the Dutch, and Connecticut foolishly talked of an offensive war. Anthony Clove, the governor of re-conquered New Amsterdam, was wide-awake. He kept his eye on the movements of the savages and Frenchmen on the north, watched every hostile indication in the east, and sent proclamations and commissions to towns on Long Island and in Westchester to compel hesitating boroughs to take the oath of allegiance to Prince William of Orange. His forts about New Orange were strengthened and mounted with one hundred and ninety cannon. A treaty of peace between the Dutch and English, however, made at London in 1674, restored New Netherland to the British crown. Some doubts arising as to the title of the Duke of York after the change, the king gave him a new grant of territory in June, 1674, within the boundary of which was included all the domain west of the Connecticut River, to the eastern shores of the Delaware, also Long Island and a territory in Maine. King Charles had commissioned Major Edmond Andros to receive the surrender of this province of New Netherland (New York) to which he was appointed governor. The final surrender was made in October, 1674, by the Dutch governor, who delivered up the keys of the fort to Major Andros, and the English never lost possession of the colony and city, until the united colonies gained their independence.

The political changes in New York had its effect on the settlements to the west and south. Eastward of the Delaware Bay and River (so called in honor of Lord De la Warr) lies New Jersey. Its domain was included in the New Netherland charter. So early as 1622, transient trading settlements were made on its soil, at Bergen and on the banks of the Delaware. The following year, Director May, moved by the attempt of a French sea-captain to set up the arms of France in Delaware, built the fort called Fort Nassau at the mouth of Timmer

Kill or Timber Creek, a few miles below Camden, and settled some young walloons near it. The walloons (young couples), who had been married on shipboard, settled on the site of Gloucester. This was the first settlement of white people in New Jersey that lived long; but it, too, withered away in time. It was seven years later when Michael Pauw made his purchase from the Indians of the territory extending from Hoboken to the Raritan River and, latinizing his name, called it Pavonia.

In this purchase was included the settlement of some Dutch at Bergen. Though other settlements were attempted, it was forty years before any of them became permanent. Cape May, a territory sixteen miles square, which Captain Heyes bought of the Indians, all the time remained an uncultivated wilderness, yielding the products of its salt meadows to the browsing deer.

After the trouble with Dutch and Swedes the English came under the agent of the Duke of York and captured the New Netherland. While Nicolls was on his way to capture the Dutch possessions in America, the Duke of York conveyed to two favorites all the territory between the Hudson and Delaware rivers from Cape May north to the latitude of forty degrees and forty minutes. Those favorites were Lord Berkeley, brother of the governor of Virginia and the duke's own governor in his youth, and Sir George Carteret, then the treasurer of the admiralty, who had been governor of the island of Jersey, which he had gallantly defended against the forces of Cromwell. In the charter this province was named "Nova Cæsarea or New Jersey," in commemoration of Carteret's loyalty and gallant deeds while governor of the island of Jersey. Colonel Richard Nicolls, the conqueror of New Netherland, in changing the name of the province to New York, ignorant of the charter given to Berkeley and Carteret, called the territory west of the Hudson Albania, in honor of his employer, who had the title of Duke of York and Albany.

Berkeley and Carteret hastened to make use of their patent. The title of their constitution was: "The concessions and agreement of the Lords Proprietors of the Province of Nova Cæsarea or New Jersey, to and with all and every new adventurers and all such as shall settle and plant there." It was a fair and liberal constitution, providing for governor and council appointed by the proprietors, and deputies or representatives chosen by the people, who should meet annually and, with the governor and his council, form a general assembly for the government of the colony. It provided for a choice of a president by the representatives when in session, in case of the absence of the governor and deputy governor. All legislative power was vested in the assembly of deputies, who were to make all laws for the province. These were to be consistent with the laws and customs of Great Britain and not repugnant to the interests of the proprietors. Emigration to New Jersey was encouraged. To every free man who would go to the province with the first governor, furnished with a good musket and plenty of ammunition and with provisions for six months, was offered a free gift of one hundred and fifty acres of land, and for every able man-servant that such emigrant should take with him so armed and provisioned, a like quantity of land. Even the sending of such servants provided with arms, ammunitions and food was likewise rewarded. And for every weaker servant or female servant over fourteen years, seventy-five acres of land was given. "Christian servants" were entitled, at the expiration of the term of service, to the land so granted for their own use and benefit. To all who should settle in the province before the beginning of 1665, other than those who should go with the governor, was offered one hundred and twenty acres of land on like conditions.

It was expected that these tempting offers would rapidly people the country with industrious settlers. Philip Carteret, a cousin of Sir George, was appointed governor, and with about thirty emigrants, several of whom were Frenchmen skilled in the art of salt-making, he sailed for New York, where he arrived about the middle of July, 1665. The vessel having been driven into the Chesapeake Bay the month before, anchored at the mouth of the James River, from whence the governor sent dispatches to New York. Among them was a copy of the duke's grant of New Jersey. Governor Nicolls was astounded at the folly of the duke's grant, and mortified by this dismemberment of a state over which he had been ruling for many months with pride and satisfaction. But he bottled his wrath until the arrival of Carteret, whom he received at Fort James with all the honors due to his rank and station. That meeting in the governor's apartments was a notable one. Mr. Lossing graphically described it as follows:

"Nicolls was tall, athletic and about forty-five years of age, a soldier, haughty and sometimes very irritable and brusque in speech when excited. Carteret was shorter and fat, good-natured and affable, with polished manners which he had learned by being much at court. He entered the governor's room with Bollen, the commissary of the fort, when the former arose, beckoned his secretary to withdraw, and received his distinguished visitor cordially. But when Carteret presented the outspread parchment, bearing the original of the duke's grant with his grace's seal and signature, Nicolls could not restrain his feelings. His temper flamed out in words of fierce anger. He stormed, and uttered denunciations in language as respectful as possible. He paced the floor backward and forward rapidly, his hands clasped behind his back, and finally calmed down and begged his visitor's pardon for his uncontrollable outburst of passion.

"Nicolls yielded gracefully yet sorrowfully to circumstances, and contented himself with addressing a manly remonstrance to the duke, in which he urged an arrangement for the grantees to give up their domain in exchange for 'a few hundred thousand acres all along the seacoast.'"

The remonstrance came too late. New Jersey was already down on the maps as a separate province. Governor Carteret at the head of a few followers crossed over to his domain with a hoe on his shoulder in significance of his desire to become a planter. For his seat of government he chose a beautifully shaded spot, not far from the strait between Staten Island and the main, called the Kills, where he found four English families living in as many neatly built log cabins with gardens around them. The heads of these four families were John Bailey, Daniel Denton, and Luke Watson and one other not known, from Jamaica, Long Island, who had bought the land of some Indians on Long Island.

HIS TEMPER FLAMED OUT IN WORDS.

In compliment to the wife of Sir George Carteret, the governor named the place Elizabethtown, which name it yet retains. There he built a house for himself near the bank of the little creek, and there he organized a civil government. So was laid the foundation of the colony and commonwealth of New Jersey.

The restoration did not so materially change the New England colonies as might have been supposed, considering that they were hotbeds of Puritanism. In the younger Winthrop the qualities of human excellence were mingled in such happy proportions that, while he always wore an air of contentment, no enterprise in which he engaged seemed too lofty for his powers. He was a man whose power was felt alike in the commonwealth and the restoration. The new king had not been two years on the throne when, through his influence, an ample patent was obtained for Connecticut, by which the colony was independent except in name.

After his successful negotiations and efficient concert in founding the Royal Society, Winthrop returned to America. The amalgamation of New Haven and Connecticut could not be effected without collision. New Haven had been unwilling to merge itself in the larger colonies; but Winthrop's wise moderation was able to reconcile the jarrings and blend the interests of the united colonies. The universal approbation of Connecticut was reasonable, for the charter which Winthrop obtained secured to her an existence of unsurpassed tranquillity.

Civil freedom was safe under the shelter of masculine morality, and beggary and crime could not thrive in the midst of severest manners. From the first, the minds of the yeomanry were kept active by the constant exercise of the elective franchise, and, except under James II., there was no such thing in the land as a home officer appointed by the English king. Under the happy conditions of affairs, education was cherished, religious knowledge was carried to the highest degree of refinement, alike in its application to moral duties and to the mysterious questions on the nature of God, of liberty and of the soul. A hardy race multiplied along the *alluvion* of the streams and subdued the more rocky and less inviting fields. Its population for a century doubled once in twenty years, though there was considerable emigration from the valley. Religion united with the pursuits of agriculture gave to the people the aspects of steady habits. The domestic wars were discussions of knotty points in theology. The concerns of the parish and the merits of the minister were the weightiest affairs, and a church reproof the heaviest calamity. The strifes of the parent country, though they sometimes occasioned a levy among the sons of the husbandmen, never brought an enemy over their border. No fears of midnight ruffians disturbed the sweetest slumber, and the best house required no fastening but a latch, lifted by a string.

Happiness was enjoyed unconsciously. Beneath a rugged exterior, humanity wore its sweetest smile. For a long time there was hardly a lawyer in the land. The husbandman who held his own plough and fed his own cattle was the greatest man of the age. No one was superior to the matron, who, with her busy daughters, kept the hum of the wheel incessantly alive, spinning and weaving every article of their dress. Fashion was confined within narrow limits, and pride, which aimed at no grander equipage than a pillion, could exult only in the common splendor of the blue and white linen gown, with short sleeves, coming down to the waist, and in the snow-white flaxen apron, which, primly starched and ironed, was worn on public days. There was no revolution except from the time of sowing to the time of reaping, from the plain dress of the week to the more trim attire of Sunday. Every family was taught to look to the fountain of all good.

Life was not all sombre. Frolic mingled with innocence. Sometimes religion itself wore the garb of gayety, and the annual thanksgiving to God was, from primitive times, as joyous as it was sincere. Nature always asserts her rights, and Christianity means gladness.

The English colonies of the south after the restoration began to show evidence of improvement. Mr. William Drummond, the sturdy Scotch emigrant to Virginia, having been appointed governor of North Carolinia brought that country into the favorable notice of the world. Clarendon gained for Carolinia a charter which opened the way for religious freedom. One clause held out to the proprietaries a hope of revenue from colonial customs, to be imposed in colonial ports by Carolinia legislatures. Another gave them authority to erect cities and manors, counties and baronies, and to establish orders of nobility with other than English titles. The power to levy troops, to erect fortifications, to make war by sea and land on their enemies, and, in cases of necessity, to exercise martial law was granted them. Every favor was extended to the proprietaries, nothing being neglected but the interests of the English sovereign and rights of the colonists. Imagination encouraged every extravagant hope, and Ashley Cooper, Earl of Shaftesbury, the most active and the most able of the corporators, was deputed by them to frame for the dawning states a perfect constitution, worthy to endure throughout all ages.

The constitutions for Carolinia merit attention as the only continued attempt within the United States to connect political power with hereditary wealth. America was singularly rich in every form of representative government. Its political life was so varied that, in modern constitutions, hardly a method of constituting an upper or popular house has thus far been suggested, of which the character and operation had not already been tested in the experience of our fathers. In Carolinia the disputes of a thousand years were crowded into a generation.

"Europe suffered from absolute but inoperative laws. No statute of Carolinia was to bind beyond a century. Europe suffered from the multiplication of law-books and the perplexities of the law. In Carolinia not a commentary might be written on the constitutions, the statutes, or the common law. Europe suffered from the furies of bigotry. Carolinia promised not equal rights, but toleration to 'Jews, heathens and other dissenters,' to 'men of any religion.' In other respects, 'the interests of the proprietors,' the desires of 'a government most agreeable to monarchy,' and the dread of 'a numerous democracy,' are avowed as the motives for forming the fundamental constitutions of Carolinia.

"The proprietaries, as sovereigns, constituted a

close corporation of eight, a number which was never to be diminished or increased. The dignity was hereditary, but in default of heirs, the survivors elected a successor. Thus was formed an upper house, self-elected and immortal."*

Carolinia was an aristocracy, the instincts of which dreads the moral power of proprietary cultivators of the soil, so enacted their perpetual degradation. The leet-men, or tenants holding ten acres of land at a fixed rent, were not only destitute of political franchises, but were adscripts to the soil: "Under the jurisdiction of their lord, without appeal," and it was added: "all children of leet-men shall be leet-men, and so to all generations."

In 1665, Albemarle had been increased by fresh emigrants from New England and by a colony of ship-builders from the Bermudas, who lived contentedly with Stevens as chief magistrate, under a very wise and simple form of government. A council of twelve, six named by the proprietaries, and six chosen by the assembly. An assembly, composed of the governor, the council, and twelve delegates from the free-holders of the incipient settlements, these formed a government which enjoyed popular confidence. No interference from

---

*Bancroft, vol. i., page 495.

abroad was anticipated, for freedom of religion, and security against taxation, except by the colonial legislature, were conceded. As their lands were confirmed to them on their own terms, the colonists were satisfied.

The authentic record of the legislative history of North Carolinia begins with the autumn of 1666, when the legislators of Albemarle, ignorant of the scheme which Locke and Shafetsbury were maturing, formed a few laws, which, however open to objection, were united to the character and manner of the inhabitants. While freedom struggled in the hearts of the common people to assert its rights and declare that all men were equal and ought to be free, scheming nobles sought to enchain them in one form or another of slavery.

CHAPTER X.

THE FUGITIVE AND HIS CHILD.

"Adieu! adieu! My native shore
Fades o'er the waters blue.
The night winds sigh, the breakers roar,
And shrieks the wild sea-mew."

AT the close of a July day in the year of the restoration, a man, travelling on foot and leading a little girl six years of age, entered the town of Boston. The few inhabitants on the streets and at their doors and windows regarded the travellers with amazement and even suspicion, for both were strangers in this part of the world. It would be difficult to meet wayfarers of more wretched appearance. He was tall, muscular and robust, and in the full vigor of life. His age might be anywhere from thirty-five to forty-five, for while his eye possessed the fire of youth, there were streaks of gray in his long hair and beard. His ruffled shirt of well-worn linen was met at the neck by a modest ruff faded and torn like the shirt, and both sadly in need of washing. On his head he wore a round black cap which, if it ever had a peak, had lost it. The trousers of dark stuff came just below the knee, Puritan fashion, and were met by coarse gray stockings. The feet were encased in coarse shoes with steel buckles, and a sable blouse well worn was held close to the body by a belt. His only visible weapon was a knotted stick. Perspiration, heat, exhaustion from travelling on foot, with dust, added something sordid to his general wretched appearance.

No less interesting than the man was the child he led at his side. Her great, dark brown eyes and golden hair were indications of beauty, despite the careworn look and dust-covered features. She wore a hood and frock, stockings and thick English shoes of the period. Like the man, the child had a haggard look, and her clothing was faded and worn. There were leaves and dust in that golden hair, as if her pillow had been the earth, and her beautiful brown eyes had a terrified look, as if some dread possessed her mind.

The appearance of these two travel-stained strangers occasioned much comment in Boston. No one knew them. Where did they come from? The south, perhaps the seaboard, for they made their entrance from the Plymouth and Rhode Island roads. But why had they come by land when travel by water was so much easier? They must

have been walking all day, for the child seemed
very tired. Some women, who had seen them enter the old suburb at the lower part of the town,
asserted that the stranger was carrying the child in
his arms when he came to the town. They saw
him halt under some trees by the big spring and
both man and child drink of the pure sweet waters.
On reaching the corner of what is now Washington Street he paused a moment and glanced toward
the house of the governor as if he would go there;
but, after a few whispered words with the child,
he shook his head and turned his attention toward
the principal inn of the town.

The child evidently caused this change in his
mind, for Mrs. Alice Stevens, who from her window was watching the pair with no little interest,
thought the little girl looked hungry and tired.
She was on the point of going out to offer her some
refreshments and ask the wanderers to come in and
rest, when they went on. The travellers must have
been very thirsty, for the children who followed
them saw them pause at the town-pump and drink
again.

There was at this time in Boston a very respectable inn, at which Bradford the governor of New
Plymouth had been entertained by the elder governor Winthrop. The man and child proceeded
to this inn, the best in the town, and entered the

broad piazza which was on a level with the street. All the ovens were heated, and the host, who was also chief cook, was preparing supper. The savory smell of cooked meats and vegetables filled the air with an odor which seemed to increase the child's hunger. The man and child without a word sank down upon the wooden benches and listened to the conversation of some men who were drinking in the tap-room. The peals of laughter and loud talk certainly were very unlike the staid Puritans of New England. Anon, one of them struck up a cavalier song very popular among that sect at the period, and ended with:

"God save the King!"

No war-horse ever heard the blast of a trumpet with more fire in his soul than did the stranger sitting on the porch holding his child by one hand, and his knotted stick in the other, hear that cry. His hand involuntarily clutched the stick as if it were a sword, and his breath came hard and quick, as if he were eager to rush into battle. The child seemed instinctively to catch the idea of her father and clutched his arm with both her hands, while her soft brown eyes were fixed on his in mute appeal, and he sat enduring the insult without a murmur.

The kitchen was not so far away but that the partridges, grouse and trout on spits and in the oven gave forth their fumes as they browned to tempting perfection. The little girl had not yet spoken since they had entered the town; but now she fixed her eyes on her parent and whispered:

"I am very hungry."

He turned his great brown eyes on her tenderly, and made no answer. At this moment a towheaded son of the host espied the strangers on the porch and went to his father to report. The landlord, with flushed face and greasy apron, appeared on the porch and asked:

"What do you want?"

"Supper and bed," was the answer, and the little girl raised her eyes to the host, giving him a tired hungry stare.

The proprietor of the inn looked at them suspiciously for a moment, and then, as if doubting their ability to remunerate him for his accommodations, asked:

"Have you money to pay for that which you ask?"

"I have," and the mysterious stranger drew from an inside pocket of his blouse a heavy leathern purse. Unfastening its strings he emptied its contents, golden guineas, into his own hands, as if to prove that he had the wherewithal to pay for himself and child. The sight of so much gold caused the landlord's eyes to sparkle with delight, and he said:

"You can have what you ask!"

The stranger returned his money to his purse and put it in the pocket of his blouse. There was an air of mystery about the stranger which puzzled the landlord, and he stood gazing at him, his brow gathered into a knot of wrinkles as if trying to solve some intricate problem. The man was sparing of his words; but when he did speak there was something terrible in his voice; it was deep and heavy like the roar of a cannon. While the landlord was gazing at him, lost in a sort of revery, he was suddenly startled by the awful voice asking:

"Will supper be ready soon?"

"Directly."

The host, being thus recalled to his duty, wheeled about to return to the kitchen. On his way he was met by his wife, whose face was the very picture of terror and superstitious dread.

"Have nought to do with them! Have nought to do with them!"

"Wherefore, good wife, do you say as much?"

She whispered a few words in his ears which made him turn pale, and with eyes starting from their sockets, he asked:

"How know you this?"

"Mrs. Johnson hath told me."

The whole demeanor of the landlord underwent

an immediate change, his eyes no longer sparkled with delight at thought of the golden guineas, and he would sooner have handled a red-hot toasting-fork than have touched one of them. For a moment he stood hesitating and actually quaking, and then he appealed to his wife with:

"What must be done?"

"Be done with them at once. Marry! send them hence without delay."

The good dame ruled the household, and he hastily returned to the porch where the stranger and his child were sitting, and said:

"I cannot make room for you!"

Half starting from his seat, the traveller fixed his terrible eyes on the host and asked:

"What mean you? Be you afraid of your payment? Verily, I will give you the money before I eat your bread," and once more he put his hand into the pocket of the blouse to pull forth the purse; but the landlord raised his own hand and, with a restraining gesture and averted his head, as if he dreaded a sight of the other's gold, answered:

"Nay, it is not that."

"Pray, what is it?"

"I doubt not that you have the money."

"Then why refuse me what I ask?"

"I have no spare beds. When I said you could remain, I knew not that all my rooms were taken."

The child raised her beautiful but dirt-stained face to the host in mute appeal, while her father quietly continued:

"Put us in the stables; we are used to it."

"I cannot."

"Pray why not? Surely the enemies of the son of God would not refuse him that."

The host started at the awful reply, which to him was sacrilege, and answered in a faltering voice:

"The horses take up all the room."

The stranger seemed not entirely put out by the persistent refusal of the landlord and said:

"We will find some corner in which to lie after supper."

"I will give you no supper."

This declaration, made in a firm tone, brought the mysterious traveller to his feet.

"Can you, a Christian, speak thus?" he cried. "We are dying of hunger. I have been on my legs since sunrise, and have walked ten leagues to-day, for most part carrying my child on my back. I have the money, I am hungry, and I will have food."

"I have none for you," said the landlord.

"What are you cooking in your kitchen, the savory odors of which are maddening to a hungry man?"

"It is all ordered,"

"By whom?"

"Merchants and travellers from Plymouth and New Amsterdam."

"You can surely spare a crust for my child, she is starving."

The stern landlord hesitated, when a loud authoritative "Ahem!" from his invisible wife strengthened him, and he said:

"I have not a morsel to spare."

"I am at an inn. I am hungry, I have money, and I shall remain," answered the stranger, sitting by the side of the little girl, who nervously clutched his arm. The landlord seemed quite put out, if not a little awed by the determined manner of the stranger, and turning about re-entered the house, where he held a whispered consultation with some one. Terror overcame the hunger of the tired child, and, clinging to her father, she whispered:

"Let us go from this house. I am not hungry now, let us go to some other place where we will not be injured."

He laid his hard, rough hand assuringly on the shoulder of the frightened child and sought to soothe her fears. At this moment the landlord, who had had his courage renewed by his wife, came quite up to the stranger and, in a voice that was terribly in earnest, said:

"I know more of you by far than you realize,

HIS TIRED CHILD WAS AT HIS SIDE, UNCOMPLAINING

I am usually polite to everybody, so pray be off."

For a single instant a flash blazed from the eyes of the stranger, then his face grew deathly white, and he rose, taking the hand of his child in his own and went off. They walked along the streets at hap-hazard, keeping close to the houses like a sad and humiliated pair. His tired child was at his side, uncomplaining, though scarcely able to drag one weary little foot after the other. They did not look back once. Had they done so they would have seen that the landlord stood with all his guests and the passers-by, talking eagerly and pointing to them. Judging from the looks of suspicion and terror, they might have guessed that ere long their arrival would be the event of the whole town. They saw nothing of this, for people who are oppressed do not look back, they know too well that evil destiny is following them.

Though sad and humiliated, the man was proud, and had the consciousness of right on his side. Only for his child, he might have defied the landlord and all the people, but the dread of leaving her alone and uncared for almost made a coward of a lion. They walked on for a long time, turning down streets new and strange to them, and in their sorrow forgetting their fatigue. The sun had set and darkness was falling over the landscape, when the father, roused once more to a sense of duty for his child, began to look around for some sort of shelter. The best inn was closed against them, so he sought a very humble ale-house, a wretched den which he would have shuddered to have his child enter under other circumstances. The candles had been lighted and the travellers paused for a moment to look through the windows. Even that miserable place had something cheerful and inviting about it. Some cavaliers who had come from England since the restoration were drinking beer, while over the fire in the broad chimney bubbled a caldron hanging from an iron hook. The traveller went to the front entrance and timidly raised the latch and entered the room, bringing his child after him.

"Who is there?" the landlord asked.

"A traveller and his child who want supper and bed."

"Very good. They are to be had here."

A long wooden bench was in the room, and the traveller sat down on it and stretched out his tired feet, swollen with fatigue. The child fell into the seat at his side and, laying her soft curly head on his lap, despite the fact she had travelled all day without food, fell asleep. As the stranger sat there in the gloom of twilight, for no candle had been brought into the room, all that could be distinguished of his face was his prominent nose, and firm mouth covered with beard. It was a firm, energetic and sad profile. The face was strangely composed, for it began by being proud and ended with humility, it commenced in stern austerity and ended in kindness. One moment the eyes beneath the shaggy eyebrows gleamed with fires of hate, next they were softened in love as the glance fell on the sleeping, supperless child. The hand was hardened by grasping the sword-hilt, and the heart, which had so often defied the bullets of the enemy, was humble and child-like in the presence of the little girl.

The landlord was about to prepare supper for the hungry wanderers, when a man suddenly entered by the kitchen door, quite out of breath with running. His eyes were opened wide with terror, and he was trembling from head to foot. He proceeded to whisper some words in the ears of the landlord, which caused him to start and quake with dread.

"What would I better do?" asked the landlord in amazement.

"Drive them hence. No good ever comes to one harboring such."

This being made the plain Christian duty of the landlord, he was not slow to act. He went into the adjoining room, walked up almost to the stranger, holding his sleeping child on his knee, and said:

"You must be off."

At first the eyes glared at the host fiercely, then became more gentle, as he remarked:

"You know me?"

"Yes."

"We were turned away from the other inn."

"So you will be from this."

"Where would you have us go?"

"Anywhere so you leave my house."

The stranger had made no effort as yet to rise, and the child who sat at his side with her head on his knee still slept. Some one brought in a lighted wax taper, and the strange man, gazing on the face of the sleeping child, asked:

"Can she remain? See, she has had no food all day and has journeyed, oh, so far! Won't you let her remain?"

"No, I will have none of you with me."

"But she hath done no wrong," persisted the father.

The stubborn landlord shook his head and answered:

"It brings ill luck to one having such about. You must away and take her with you."

The large, sad-eyed man bent over the sleeping child and whispered:

"Ester!"

She awoke in a moment and cast a bewildered glance about the room, as a child will on being suddenly aroused.

"We must go," the father said, sadly.

She made no complaint, but, rising, with a feminine instinct common even in a girl of her tender years, adjusted her ruffled hood and dress.

They went out into the night, for the sun had long since set, and the far-off stars one by one opened their little eyes, until the heavens were glittering with diamonds. They entered a small street in which there were numerous gardens, some being merely enclosures with stone fences. Among these gardens and fences he saw a house the window of which was illuminated, and he looked through the open casement as he had done at the inn. It was a cozy, whitewashed room, with a bed, a rude cradle, a few chairs and an old-fashioned matchlock hanging on a rack made of deer's antlers on the wall. A plain table was laid for supper in the middle of the room, a wax taper burned on the mantel lighting up the interior of the Puritan's home. A man forty years of age sat at the table with a baby on his knee. Two children, one four and the other two years old, sat at his side, while the mother was placing supper on the table. What a tempting sight for a hungry man! Could one conceive a more happy family picture? The travellers looked on, and the father was almost maddened when he glanced at his own child.

"Papa, I am so hungry and so tired," she whispered. "Won't you ask them if we can stay here?"

Fugitives from the law must have a care where they go, and to whom they appeal, yet Ester's father was growing more desperate every moment. He went boldly to the door and gave a timid rap with his knuckle. That hand once bold enough to strike a king from his throne was weak and trembling on this night. At sound of the knock, the husband and father seemed to have suddenly changed. The lion may sport and play with his whelps in his lair, but when the intruder enters his domestic abode, all is changed. He rose, took up the light and went to the door. He was a tall man and, judging from his charcoal-begrimed features, a blacksmith, and he wore a large leathern apron which came quite to his shoulder. As he threw back his head the shirt-front opened, displaying his bare neck and hairy chest. His face was sullen, with a bull-dog expression on it. Without a moment's hesitation, the stranger began:

"I am weary, and my child hath had no food to-day. Would you, for money, give us a morsel to eat and a blanket and corner in which to sleep?"

"Who are you?" asked the smith.

"We came from New Plymouth, and have walked all day. I will pay you well for what you give us."

The blacksmith loved money; but those were troublesome times, and people had to be careful whom they admitted into their houses. The king had been restored and was pursuing his enemies with a vengeance, and to harbor a *regicide* might mean death on the scaffold. The smith thought of all this, and asked:

"Why do you not go to one of the inns?"

"There is no room there."

"Nonsense! that is impossible. Have you been to Robinson's?"

"I have been to all."

"Well?"

The traveller continued with some hesitation, "I do not know why; but they all refuse to take us in."

The man knew there was something wrong with the travellers, and turning about, he held a whispered consultation with his wife. She was heard to say in a faint whisper: "It is the same, a man with a child." Then the smith turned on the stranger, and said:

"Be off."

The proud eye of a daring trooper in despair is

the saddest sight one ever gazed upon. Such was the look of the humiliated man, as, with his starving child, he turned from the last door. At times the spirit of revenge rose in his breast, and he was inclined to turn on the men who refused his child food, drink and shelter, and with his stout knotted stick beat out their brains; but, on second thought, he restrained himself and said:

"No—no; I will not make an outlaw of myself. I am not a robber."

He who had been the commander of thousands, the king of the battle-field, at whose name princes grew pale and thrones tottered, was now a wanderer from house to house, rejected at every door.

"I am so hungry," murmured Ester. "If I had but a morsel of food, I could sleep under a tree."

He heard the plaintive appeal, and it wrung his fatherly heart. Through his teeth he hissed:

"If I am made a savage let all the world beware."

They were climbing a hill to enter another part of the town, when they came upon a kind old Puritan woman, who paused to gaze in compassion on the wayfarers. If others kept off from them as though they were creatures to contaminate by a touch, she seemed to entertain no such fears. Coming quite close, she said:

"Prythee, friend, why do you not get this child to bed?"

"I would, good woman, had I a bed for her; but, alas, all doors are shut against us."

"Surely not all!"

"I have tried the inns and the home of the smith; but they seem to fear us, as if we were polution."

"Have you called at that house?" she asked, pointing to a steep-roofed building, the top of which was just visible over the hill in the light of the rising moon.

"No, who lives there?"

"Mathew Stevens, a very good old man."

"Has he a heart? Is he brave?"

"He has a heart tender enough, and he is brave enough to shelter the oppressed, in spite of other people's opinions."

The woman went her way, and the traveller and his weary child went slowly over the hill to the house. It seemed a great distance. Many a time after that Ester traversed the distance alone and thought it short; but on that night rods were lengthened out into miles. As they were passing the window, Ester saw a man about the age of her father reading a Bible. He sat at a table on which burned a taper, and his wife and children were gathered about listening. Surely a man who would read the Bible would not refuse them food and shelter. She staggered up to the door by her father's side, in a dazed, half-conscious manner, and was cognizant of his knocking, and the door being opened. Their story was told briefly, and then warm arms encircled the little fugitive, a colored slave prepared a supper, and Ester was awakened to eat it, after which she sank into slumber on her father's breast.

CHAPTER XI.

TYRANNY AND FLIGHT.

> "Oh, for a lodge in some vast wilderness,
> Some boundless contiguity of shade,
> Where rumor of oppression and deceit,
> Of successful or unsuccessful war,
> Might never reach me more."
> —COWPER.

WHEN Virginia came back to the royal fold, her people little suspected that she was to be fleeced by the very men for whom they had clamored. No event worthy of note had occurred in the colony until September, 1663, when what was known as the "Oliverian Plot" was concocted. A number of indented servants conspired to "anticipate the period of their freedom," and made an appointment to assemble at Poplar Spring in Gloucester, with what precise designs is not known. They were betrayed by one of their number, and Berkeley, who already seemed to thirst for blood, had the four ringleaders hung.

Jamestown was the gay city of the South; but the halcyon days promised on the restoration of

Virginia to royalty were never realized. The common people were made worse for the change, and only the favorite few were bettered.

At the home of Mrs. Dorothe Price matters went on fairly well. Her children from the first seemed to whisper rebellion; but the stern cavalier husband met them with firmness. Robert Stevens, who had incurred the man's dislike before he had wed his mother, realized that his stepfather had not forgotten and was not likely to forget the assault. His face, which at times could be pleasant, was firm and immovable with Robert. He never smiled on the boy nor gave him one encouraging word.

When the cavaliers and ladies assembled at the house, the children were sent away. Robert was strong and athletic. His early hardships had bred in him a spirit of fearless independence and freedom, which few of his age realized. Mr. Price saw that unless he early mastered him, he would not be able to do so, for Robert was rapidly growing larger. The gloomy taint in Hugh Price's blood was his religion, which was austere and wrathful. He could assume a character of firmness when he chose to do so, and then, despite his silk, lace, and ruffles, he became terrible. One day when Robert had exhibited a strong spirit of insubordination, he took his arm and, sitting on a chair, held him standing before him for a long time, gazing into his face. The little fellow met his glance without quailing, though he could feel his heart within his bosom giving great thumps.

"Robert," he said, pressing his lips firmly together, "do you know what I do if my horse or dog will not obey me?"

"No," was the answer.

"I beat him and make him smart until I have conquered him. I would drain every drop of blood from his veins, but I would conquer him."

Glaring at him with a fury that made the strong man wince, the lad answered:

"If you beat me I will kill you."

For several minutes the stepfather sat glaring at Robert who met his gaze with defiance. Hugh Price read in the face of the child hate, and inwardly realized that there was a struggle in the near future which might end in the death of one or the other; but if those forebodings were in his mind, he did not let the boy see them, and in a voice quite calm and intended to be gentle, he said:

"Go away, Robert, until you are more reasonable."

Robert Stevens might have been improved for his whole life by a single kind word at that moment; but the haughty cavalier would not bow to the will of any one, much less to the boy he already hated. A word of encouragement, explanation, pity for his childish ignorance, of reassurance that his mother's roof was to be his home, might have made him really dutiful.

On his way out he heard a sob, and, going into his mother's room, found her on her knees weeping bitterly. Tenderly he wound his arms around that weak mother, whom he loved with all the fervency of his young soul, and his own tears mingled with hers. They were in this position when Hugh Price, on his way to mount his horse, paused a single instant to gaze on the scene, and then, muttering something about weakness of women, added an oath and hurried from the house.

When he was gone, Dorothe rose from her knees and, clasping Robert in her arms, cried:

"Oh, Robert, I heard it all!"

"Mother, I mean it!" he answered.

"No, no; for my sake, promise me you will not, Robert."

"Mother," said the boy, "my own father never struck me a blow. He who had the right to punish me never found it necessary, and he shall not."

Dearly as Robert loved his mother, he would not yield to Hugh Price. He would have suffered torture rather than caused his mother a single tear; but to yield to the haughty cavalier was impossible.

Public schools were unknown in that day, and

what little learning was to be acquired was by private tutors. Sometimes Price talked of sending the boy to England to school, more to get rid of him than from any real desire to improve his mind. The mother objected to this. Then the stepfather tried to effect a compromise by sending him to Harvard College in Massachusetts, for he had relatives in Boston who might keep an eye on the incorrigible youth; but the fond mother clung to her son, and having a fair education herself, Robert and his sister, a pale little creature, whose great dark eyes were like her mother's, became pupils with the mother for teacher. She was an indulgent preceptress and, for a short season, renounced the pleasures and follies grown so dear to her heart, and devoted herself to the improvement of her children's mind. Mrs. Price was so blind as to believe that it was her husband's real interest in Robert's welfare that made him wish to send the boy away. She soon found her labor as teacher irksome. She employed a private tutor and again mingled with the lords and ladies, and became one of the sparkling lights of Greensprings Manor.

Hugh Price was kind and indulgent to her. Her temperament suited his own ideas of living, and but for the children they might have been happy.

It is possible that Mr. Price entertained some fear that Robert would execute his threat and kill him, for though he often laid his hand on the slender cane as if he would like to use it on the boy, he had thus far refrained; but a crisis was coming. Price not only entertained an aversion to Robert, but disliked Rebecca. She shrank from him in a way that increased the dislike, although he made some efforts to reconcile her to him.

One day, a year and a half after his marriage, he accosted the child, and she, shrinking with dread, failed to do his bidding. He boxed her ears, and she cried out with pain.

That scream roused Robert, and he flew tooth and nail at the stepfather. Hugh Price, unprepared for this violent attack, shook the lad off, held him at arm's length for a moment and said:

"I may as well do it now as ever."

Robert was in a maze, and to him it seemed a dream. His mother was weeping and imploring, his sister screaming, and the faithful slave Dinah howling. As Price took him toward the door, his mother ran toward them; but the husband angrily raised his disengaged hand and growled:

"Dorothe, you are a perfect fool!"

Robert saw her stop her ears, then heard her crying, as he was led slowly and gravely to his room. The supreme moment had arrived when Mr. Hugh Price was to glut his vengeance. Price was delighted with this formal parade to the execution of justice, for he had made up his mind to conquer the lad's spirit or break it, and when Robert's room was reached, he suddenly twisted his head under his arm, saying:

"The moment has arrived, Robert, when I must convince you that I am master of the house."

"Mr. Price, beware! Pray don't beat me, it will only make matters worse. I could not see you strike my sister; but if you will not beat us, we will try to obey you in the future."

"No, no, indeed, Robert!" he answered. "The time has come to convince you that I am master."

He held the boy's arm until it ached with pain, but Robert continued to gaze in his face and implore him for the sake of the future not to strike him. The stepfather was in a rage, and at that moment little cared what he roused in the breast of the boy. Heedless of his pleading, he raised his slender cane and struck at him, but the active lad dodged the blow and caught his arm with his sharp teeth.

It now became a fight to the finish. Hugh Price was enraged and struck fast and furious. Above the din of the combatants in the room, the angry, smarting boy could hear the darkies flying in terror from room to room, and his little sister at the door imploring mercy for her brother. Mingled with this noise were the screams and supplications of his mother until she fainted in the arms of the negress, after which came only the shrill cries of little Rebecca. Then the stepfather was gone, and the door bolted on the outside. The badly bruised lad lay raging and sobbing on the floor, breathing threats of vengeance. By degrees he became quiet and listened. A strange, unnatural silence reigned throughout the whole house. When his smarting began to subside his passion cooled a little, yet he felt wicked; and, rolling on the floor, vowed he would kill his stepfather.

After a while he sat up and listened for a long time; but there was not a sound. He crawled from the floor, and the wounds made by the cane of the cavalier were so fresh and sore that they made him weep anew.

He sat by the window. It had began to grow dark, and he was turning away to lie on the couch, when he heard the clatter of hoofs and saw Hugh Price mounted on his favorite black charger, riding toward Greensprings. Shortly after, Dinah's step was heard on the stairway, and his door was opened.

" Where is Rebecca?" he asked.

" Waiten," was the answer.

" Waiting for what?"

" For you, Massa Robert. You is gwine away."

" Where?"

The negress did not know; but Robert soon

learned that their uncle from Flower De Hundred had come to Jamestown and agreed to take the children and rear them.

"When are we to go, Dinah?"

"To-morrow, Massa."

"Is that why Mr. Price left?"

"Yes um. Him say neber want to see you again."

"Shall I see mother?"

"Yes, in de mornin'. Heah am yer suppah chile; now eat it an den go to sleep, honey, for it am all ober."

Consequently next morning at early daylight the children were mounted on horses, the chief mode of travel in Virginia at that time, and, accompanied by their aunt's husband and two negro slaves, they set off on the long journey. Mrs. Price kissed them a tearful adieu and wept as if her heart would break. This unfortunate woman was more weak than bad. By one who has not made a study of the human heart and is incapable of an analysis of woman, Mrs. Price will not be understood. There are many women like her, and, disagreeable as the type may seem, it exists, and the artist who is true to nature must paint nature as he finds it.

Three years were passed by Robert and his sister at the home of their relative, and in those three years Robert imbibed a spirit of republicanism which at that time was rapidly growing in Virginia. As Robert's uncles were republicans, he learned the doctrine from them. If for no other reason than that his stepfather was a royalist, he would have been a republican.

Nothing is more uncertain than political friendship, a friendship selfish and treacherous. It assumes all things, absorbs all things, expects all things, and disappoints in everything. A merely political friend can never be trusted. Robert was seventeen or eighteen years of age, when he became acquainted with Giles Peram, a young man two or three years his senior. Peram was a caricature on nature. He was short of stature, had a round, fat face, eyes that bulged from his head like those of a toad, a corpulent body, and a walk about as graceful as the waddling of a duck. His short legs and arms gave him a decidedly comical appearance.

He was egotistical, with flexible opinions and liable to be swayed in any course. When he was at Flower De Hundred, living in the atmosphere of liberalists and republicans, he was one of the most outspoken of all. He would strut for hours before any one who would listen to his senseless twaddle and would harangue and discourse on the rights of the people.

"Are you favorable to royalty?" he asked Robert one day. "Don't you believe in the rights of the common people?"

"I certainly do," Robert answered, for he was thoroughly democratic.

"So do I—ahem—so do I;" and then the angry little fellow shook his fist at an imaginary foe. "Would you fight for such principles?"

"I would."

"So would I—ahem, so would I," cried Mr. Peram. Giles had a very disagreeable habit of repeating his words. A wag once said that his ideas were so few and his words so many that he was forced to repeat. "I will fight for the rights of the people. I will lead an army myself and hurl King Charles from his throne."

Robert laughed. The idea of this insipid pigmy leading an army to overthrow the king was as ridiculous as Don Quixote charging the windmills.

"Give o'er such thoughts, Giles, or perchance the king will hang you."

"Hang me! I defy him!" cried Mr. Peram.

His manner was earnest, and Robert, who hated Governor Berkeley, suggested they had better begin their republic by overthrowing the governor.

"Do you mean it?" asked Giles. "Aye, do you mean it? Then why not hurl Berkeley from power."

"Verily, you could not more nearly conform to my wishes," answered Robert.

Then Giles, in his impetuous enthusiasm, embraced Robert. Giles Peram was not a spy, and at that time he believed himself a stanch republican. A few days later he went to Jamestown. Robert little dreamed that his remark would bring trouble upon himself.

At this time Governor Berkeley was growing uneasy. He felt that he stood above a burning volcano, from which an eruption was liable to take place at any moment. He trembled at the slightest whispers of freedom, for royalty dreads independence, and the idle boasts of Giles Peram startled him. He summoned Hugh Price and consulted with him on the boldness of Peram.

"Fear him not, my lord," said Hugh. "He is but an idle, boasting, half-witted fellow, as harmless as he is silly. There is a plot, I am sure; but of it I will learn the particulars and advise you."

Hugh Price was shrewd, and, by a little flattery, he won over the vacillating Giles Peram to the royalists' side.

"Yes, sir, I will draw my sword for the king, ahem—draw my sword for the king at any moment. I am a loyal cavalier of his majesty, Charles II., and woe to the man who says aught against him or his majesty's governor, Berkeley."

Then Hugh told him that there was certainly a deep-laid plot against Governor Berkeley, and he asked the aid of Peram in ferreting out the leaders. There were no leaders and no plot; but Peram, after cudgeling his brain, remembered that Robert Stevens had spoken treasonable words against the governor. Having changed his politics, he was no longer the friend of Robert and was willing to aid in his downfall.

Price received the intelligence with joy. He hated Robert, and this was a good way to get rid of him. Often the cavalier had declared:

"Marry! he is a merry rogue. He will yet ornament the gibbet."

His predictions seemed on the verge of realization. Berkeley, grown petulant and merciless in his old age, would not hesitate to hang Robert on suspicion.

One evening as Robert was going from his mother's house he noticed three or four persons coming down the street. Their manner might have excited the suspicion of a guilty man; but as Robert had committed no crime, he relied wholly on his innocence. No sooner had he stepped on the street, however, than he was arrested.

"Of what offence am I accused?" he asked.

"Treason."

"Treason! it is false; I am guilty of no treason."

The mother and sister, hearing the angry words without, hurried to the street to find him in custody. Wringing their hands in an agony of distress, they demanded to know the cause of the arrest, and were informed that Robert had been accused of treason to the governor and must be committed to jail.

Robert slept behind iron bars that night. He had many friends in the town, who no sooner learned of his arrest, than they began to appeal to the governor for his release. Among them was Drummond, Cheeseman and Lawerence; but all supplications and entreaties were of no avail. Hugh Price made a pretence of defending his wife's son; but the hollow show of his pretended interest was apparent.

One night, as he was lying on his hard prison bunk, Robert heard the sound of footsteps without. Some persons were working at the front door with a key. They seemed to be exercising due caution, and soon the door was open.

They came to the door of his cell. For a long time it seemed to baffle them, but at last it yielded, and the door opened.

"Who are you?" asked the prisoner, as three dark forms appeared before him.

"Friends," a voice which he recognized as Mr.

Edward Cheeseman's whispered. "We have come to liberate you."

He was led from the jail, and then, by the dim light of the stars, he recognized William Drummond, Edward Cheeseman and Mr. Lawerence.

"There is a ship in the harbor ready to sail for Boston," said Mr. Lawerence. "You will go aboard of her and escape."

"Can I see my mother and sister before I go?"

"They are waiting on the beach," Drummond answered.

Thanking his liberators, he followed them from the jail to the beach. It was midnight, and the stars looked coldly down on the youth as he hurried from the prison. His proud spirit rebelled at flying from home. He had done no wrong and consequently had nothing to fly from; but when his mother threw her arms about his neck and implored him to go, he assented.

"I shall appeal to the king, show him my wrong and obtain my right."

"Have you money?" asked Mr. Drummond.

"None."

"Here is some," and Drummond placed in the hand of Robert a well-filled purse.

"My friend, how can one so poor as I repay you?"

"Talk not of repayment," Drummond answered, "but go on, and when you are away, remember us in kindness."

The boat was waiting on the beach, and the sailors sat at their oars ready to take him away to the vessel which lay at anchor. Drummond, Cheeseman and Lawerence withdrew, leaving Robert alone with his mother and sister. A few silent tears, a few silent embraces, and then he bade them adieu, entered the boat, and was rowed away into the darkness.

CHAPTER XII.

THE DAUGHTER OF A REGICIDE.

> When thy beauty appears
> In its graces and airs,
>   All bright as an angel new dropped from the sky
> At a distance I gaze and am awed at my fears,
>   So strangely you dazzle my eyes.
> —PARNELL.

ONE bright morning in autumn a ship from Virginia entered Boston Harbor. The appearance of a vessel was not an uncommon sight, and this one attracted little more than passing comment. Passengers were coming ashore and among them a stalwart youth of eighteen. His eyes wandered about over the town while the breeze played with his long hair hanging about his shoulders. He wore the costume of a cavalier, with a low-crowned, broad-brimmed hat and plume; but his face had all the grave aspect of a Puritan.

He asked no questions on landing, but went up to the Common, where a fencing-master had erected a stage and was walking back and forth upon it with a rapier in his hand, saying:

"Come, any who will, and fight me with swords."

Near him were a dozen or two swords of all kinds. The new-comer paused near the platform on which the boaster stood and gazed at him in wonder.

"I have been on this platform for several days, defying any man to fence with me. Have you no one in Boston brave enough?"

"I will," a voice cried at this moment. All turned at the sound, for the voice was deep and commanding, sounding like the boom of a cannon.

This stranger to all assembled on the Common was most singularly armed and equipped for a fight. On his left arm, wrapped in a linen cloth, was a large cheese for a shield, while he carried, instead of a sword, a mop dipped in muddy water.

"Who is he?"

"Some madman."

"Beware of him, and allow him not to go on the stage," cried another.

But the stranger, with an agility not to be expected in one of his years, sprang upon the platform. The fencing-master evidently thought he had an easy victory, for a smile curled his lip, as he asked:

"Are you ready?"

"Yes," was the answer.

"Guard!"

THE DAUGHTER OF A REGICIDE. 199

He sprang at the fencing-master, who made a thrust at him, burying the point of his sword in the cheese, where the white-haired man held it,

"Are you ready?"

while he smeared the face of his opponent with the mud on his mop.

"Zounds! master what are you about?" cried the fencing-master.

"Marry! I am teaching you new tactics."

Releasing his sword, the fencing-master ran to the other end of the platform and, seizing a broadsword, cried:

"I will have it out with you with these."

At this, the old man cried in a terrible voice:

"Stop, sir! hitherto you see I have only played

with you and done you no hurt; but if you come at me with the broadsword, I will take your life."

The alarmed fencing-master cried out:

"Who can you be? You must be either Goffe, Whalley, or the devil, for there are no others in England who could beat me."

In order to fully explain the meaning of the fencing-master's words, we beg leave to step aside from our story for a moment and recall some historical events which have a bearing upon it. Of the judges who tried and condemned Charles I. three escaped to America. One was Edward Whalley, who had first won laurels in the field at Naseby, had even enjoyed the confidence of Cromwell, and remained a friend of the Independents; one was William Goffe, a firm friend of the family of Cromwell, a good soldier and an ardent partisan, but ignorant of the true principles of freedom. Endicott was governor when these two arrived in Boston. Goffe, with his child, came first, but was known as soon as he entered the town, and lodging was refused him at every house until he came to the home of the kind Puritan, Mathew Stevens, who sheltered the man and his child, though it might endanger his own head.

Charles II. pursued the murderers of his father with unrelenting fury. Whalley and Goffe both had been generals in the army of Cromwell and were men of undoubted courage. When warrants came for them from England, they hurried across the country to New Haven, where it was esteemed a crime against God to betray a wanderer or give up an outcast; yet such diligent search was made for them, that they never knew security. For a time they went in secrecy from house to house, for awhile concealing themselves in a mill, sometimes in clefts of rocks by the seaside, and for weeks together, and even for months, they dwelt in a cave in the forest. Great rewards were offered for their apprehension. Indians as well as English were urged to scour the woods in quest of their hiding-place.

John Dixwell, the third regicide, was more fortunate. He was able to live undiscovered and, changing his name, was absorbed among the inhabitants of New Haven. He married and lived peacefully and happily. Raleigh's history of the world, written during his imprisonment, while he was under sentence of death, was his favorite study. It is said that to the day of his death he retained a firm belief that the spirit of English liberty would demand a new revolution, which was achieved in England while he was on his death-bed.

Another victim of the restoration, selected for his genius and integrity, was Sir Henry Vane, the benefactor of Rhode Island. This ever faithful friend of New England and liberty adhered with undaunted firmness to "the glorious cause" of popular liberty, and, shunned by every one who courted the returning monarch, he became noted for his unpopularity. When the Unitarians were persecuted, not as a sect but as blasphemers, Vane interceded for them. He also pleaded for the liberty of the Quakers, and as a legislator he demanded justice in behalf of the Roman Catholics. When monarchy was overthrown and a Commonwealth attempted, Vane reluctantly filled a seat in the council, and, resuming his place as a legislator, amidst the floating wrecks of the English constitution, he clung to the existing parliament as to the only fragment on which it was possible to rescue English liberty. His ability enabled Blake to cope with Holland on the sea.

SIR HENRY VANE.

After the restoration, parliament had excepted Sir Henry Vane from the indemnity, on the king's promise that he should not suffer death. It was resolved to bring him to trial, and he turned his trial into a triumph. Though he had always been supposed to be a timid man, he appeared before his judges with animated fearlessness. Instead of offering apologies for his career, he denied the imputation of treason with scorn, defended the right of Englishmen to be governed by successive representatives, and took glory to himself for actions which promoted the good of England and were sanctioned by parliament as the virtual sovereign of the realm. "He spoke not for his life and estate, but for the honor of the martyrs to liberty that were in their graves, for the liberties of England, for the interest of all posterity to come." When he asked for counsel, the solicitor said:

"Who will dare speak for you, unless you can call down from the gibbet the heads of your fellow-traitors?"

"I stand single," Vane defiantly answered. "Yet, being thus left alone, I am not afraid, in this great presence, to bear my witness to the glorious cause, nor to seal it with my blood."

Stimulated by the magnanimity of this noble spirit, his enemies clamored for his life. The king wrote:

"Certainly Sir Henry Vane is too dangerous a man to let live, if we can honestly put him out of the way."

Though he could not be honestly put out of the way, it was resolved that he should die. The day before his execution his friends were admitted to his prison, and sought to cheer his drooping spirits. He calmly reviewed his political career, and in conclusion said:

"I have not the least recoil in my heart as to matter or manner of what I have done. Why should we fear death? I find it rather shrinks from me than I from it." His children gathered around him, and he stopped to embrace them, mingling consolation with his kisses. "The Lord will be a better father to you than I could have been. Be not you troubled, for I am going to my father."

His farewell counsel was:

"Suffer anything from men rather than sin against God." When his family had withdrawn, he declared: "I leave my life as a seal to the justness of that quarrel. Ten thousand deaths, rather than defile the chastity of my conscience; nor would I, for ten thousand worlds, resign the peace and satisfaction I have in my heart."

He was beheaded at the block, and Charles II. smiled when news was brought to him of the execution. We must not regard Charles II. as a bloodthirsty man. In fact, he was rather good-natured, thinking more of pleasures and beautiful mistresses than of vengeance; but it was only natural that he should feel anxious to bring the murderers of his father to the scaffold.

He had no love for Puritan Massachusetts and threatened to deprive them of their liberties, demanding the retiring of the charter, which they refused to surrender. Various rumors went to England to the detriment of the people of Massachusetts. The New Englanders were not ignorant of the great dangers they incurred by refusing to comply with the demand of the sovereign. In January, 1663, the council for the colonies complained that the government there had withdrawn all manner of correspondence, as if intending to suspend their obedience to the authority of the king. It was currently reported in England that Whalley and Goffe were at the head of an army. The union of the four New England colonies was believed to have had its origin in the express "purpose of throwing off dependence on England."

Friends of the colonies denied the reports and assured the king that New England was loyal; but despite the fact of their assertions, Whalley and Goffe were still at large.

Even when their pursuers were close on their trail, Goffe, with a daring that was reckless, frequently appeared in Boston, usually in disguise. Long sojourn in rocks and caves had given him a natural disguise, in the long, snowy hair and beard.

It was on one of his daring visits to Boston, that he met and conquered the fencing-master as narrated in the opening of this chapter. Having humbled the boaster, the man with the cheese and mop descended from the platform, threw away his weapons and advanced toward the youth who had been an amazed spectator of the scene.

"Good morrow, friend. Do you belong here?" he asked, taking his hand.

"No, sir, I just came in on the vessel."

"Whom do you wish to see?"

"Some relatives named Stevens."

"Is your name Stevens?"

"It is, sir."

"And you are from Virginia?" the old man asked.

"Verily, you have guessed it, sir. Who may you be?"

Without answering him, the strange swordsman seized his arm, saying:

"Come with me; I am going to the house of Mathew Stevens. What is your father's name?"

"John Stevens was his name; but he is dead. He went on a voyage and was lost at sea when I was quite young."

"And your grandfather was—"

"Philip Stevens, the friend of Captain John Smith."

"I know of him. We will go to the home of your relatives." He led Robert over the hill toward a neat looking house, one of the best in Boston. The old man was nervous and frequently halted to look about, as if expecting pursuit.

"Surely you have no one to fear?" said Robert.

"Whom should I fear—the man whose face I plastered with mud? I carry a sword at my side, and he could not fight me in a single combat."

"But he said something. He called you a name."

"What name?"

"Goffe."

"What know you of Goffe, pray?"

"I have heard of him. My mother's husband frequently spoke of him as a regicide."

The swordsman gazed on him for a moment, and asked:

"Do you know what a regicide is?"

"A king-killer."

"Well, my young cavalier, when a king has been convicted of treason, should he not suffer death as the humblest peasant in the land?"

"He should," cried Robert, on whose republican soul the argument fell with a delightful sensation. "A king is but a man and no better than the poorest in the realm."

"Ha! young cavalier from Virginia, dare you utter those words in your own colony?"

"No; I left my colony because I could not abide there."

"What! a fugitive?"

"I escaped prison by the aid of friends and fled to Boston."

"And wherefore, pray, were you imprisoned?"

"On the charges of my mother's husband and a false friend in whom I trusted."

General Goffe shook his white locks and said:

"So young, and made to feel the grinding heel of the despot! Verily the suffering race of Adam will claim their rights some time."

They reached the home of Mathew Stevens, a large old-fashioned New England house, and were admitted at once.

Robert was conscious of being in the presence of several strange but kindly faces. There was an old man and woman with some young people of his own age. Then he noticed among them a beautiful, fairy-like little creature, some four years younger than himself, who, at sight of the white-haired man, rushed toward him and, placing her arms about his neck, cried:

"Father, father, father!"

"Ester, my child," the swordsman returned, "have you been happy?"

"Happy as one could be with father away."

"Now that I have returned, you need sorrow no more."

All the while Robert Stevens was standing on

THE DAUGHTER OF A REGICIDE.

the threshold waiting an invitation to enter. The aged patriarch at last seized the arm of General Goffe and asked:

"Whom have we here?"

The general, in the joy of meeting his daughter from whom he had been separated, had forgotten Robert.

"This is Robert Stevens, your relative from Virginia."

"Robert, I knew your father; I heard he was lost at sea."

"He was," Robert answered sadly.

"And your mother?"

"Has married Hugh Price, a cavalier."

Robert told a part of his story, ending with the announcement that he was forced to fly from home to escape prosecution for treason. This he told with much reluctance, for it was a poor recommendation that he was an escaped prisoner.

When all was known, Robert found an abundance of sympathy, and was told that he might make his home with his relatives, until he could be provided for.

Then followed long weeks, months and years of the most delightful period of his life. His relatives were kind. Their home was attractive; but kind relatives and an attractive home were not the chief magnets which attracted him to the spot. It was the joy of a pair of soft brown eyes which held him. Ester Goffe was the most interesting person at Boston. She was a creature born to inspire one with love. She was young, hardly yet budded into womanhood, when first he saw her. Day by day and week by week she seemed to him to grow in beauty and goodness.

The third day after his arrival, General Goffe mysteriously disappeared. He had been gone almost a week, when Robert asked Ester where her father was.

"He is gone," she answered. "The king's men learned that he was here, and were coming after him, when he escaped."

"Whither has he gone?"

"Alas, I know not."

"What would be his fate if he should be taken?"

"He would suffer as did Sir Henry Vane. No mercy will be shown to a regicide."

"You must suffer uneasiness."

"I am in constant dread, though my father is brave and shrewd, while the king's officers are but lazy fellows with dull wits, who do not care to exert themselves, yet some unseen accident might place him in their power."

Then he induced her to tell the sad story of their flight from the wrath of an angry king, and how they had walked all the way from Plymouth to Boston.

The year 1675 came, just one century before the shots at Lexington were heard around the world.

There was a restless feeling in all the colonies. The governor of Virginia was a tyrant. The Indians were becoming restless, and a general outbreak was expected.

Robert had been informed by his mother that his friends had procured his pardon from Governor Berkeley, and he was urged to come home. Robert was now twenty-six years of age. Ester was twenty-two, and they were betrothed. Their love was of that kind which grows quickly, but is as eternal as the heavens. The regicide had been home very little for the last five years. He came one night to spend a short time with his daughter. They had scarce time to whisper a few words of affection, when Robert ran to them, saying:

"The king's men are coming."

In a few moments a dozen cavaliers with swords and pistols rushed on General Goffe.

"Do not surrender; I will defend you," cried Robert.

He drew his sword and assailed the foremost of the cavaliers with such implacable fury that they fell back. General Goffe took advantage of the moment to mount a swift horse and fly. A few pistol shots were fired at him; but he escaped, and Robert conducted the half-fainting Ester home.

It was nearly midnight when a friend came to inform Robert that the king's men had procured a warrant against him for resisting his majesty's officers, and he must fly for his life. There was a flutter of hushed excitement. Everybody was awakened. Robert hurriedly gathered up his effects, which were taken to a brigantine ready to sail for Virginia. There was a silent, tearful farewell with Ester; vows were renewed, and he swore when the clouds had rolled away to come and make her his wife.

Then a last embrace, a hasty kiss, and he hurried away to the bay. Ten minutes later the house was surrounded by soldiers.

CHAPTER XIII.

LEFT ALONE.

> Yes, 'twill be over soon,—This sickly dream
> Of life will vanish from my brain;
> And death my wearied spirit will redeem
> From this wild region of unvaried pain.
> —WHITE.

FOR fifteen years John Stevens and Blanche Holmes had lived on the Island of Desolation, and in all that time not a sign of a sail had appeared on the vast ocean. Not a sight of a human being had greeted their eyes, and they had become somewhat reconciled to the idea of passing their lives on this island. The soil in the valley was fertile and yielded abundance to moderate tillage. John studied the seasons and knew when to plant to receive the benefits of the rains. There was no winter in this tropical clime, the rainy season taking the place of winter. The sails and clothing which they had brought from the wreck had been husbanded and made to last as long as possible; and then Blanche, who was industrious, spun and wove cloth for both from the fibre of a coarse weed like hemp. Her wheel and loom were rude affairs constructed by John Stevens, who, thanks to his early experience as a pioneer, knew how to make all useful household implements. When their shoes were worn out he tanned the skins of goats and made them moccasins, and he even wore a jacket of goat's skin.

For a covering for his head, he shot a fox and dressing the skin fashioned himself a cap. In fact, the castaways lived as comfortably as the pioneers of Virginia. John had his days of despondency, however. For fifteen years he had climbed the hill and gazed beyond the reef-girt shore at the broad sea in the vain hope of descrying a sail. He always heaved a sigh of disappointment when he swept the sailless ocean with his glass.

One morning when he had made his fruitless pilgrimage to his point of observation, he sat down upon a stone and, passing his hand over his eyes, brushed away a tear which came unbidden there.

"Alas, I am doomed to pass my life here. Never more can I see my home, friends or kindred; but on this desolate shore I must end my existence. Fifteen years have come and gone— fifteen long years since I left my home. My wife, no doubt, believing me dead, has ceased to mourn for me. Perhaps—but no, Dorothe never believed in it. God knows what they may have suffered. I am powerless to aid them, and to His hands I entrust them."

Heaving a deep sigh, he resumed his painful ruminations:

"It might be worse; yes, it might be worse. I might have perished with the others, or I might not have been spared a single companion. God has given me one, and with her I could almost be happy."

Returning to his humble cabin he was met by Blanche, who greeted him with a sweet smile. Blanche seemed to grow in goodness and beauty. She was his consoler in his hour of grief. When he was ill with a fever, she held his burning head in her tender arms and soothed his pain. She administered the simple remedies with which they were provided and nursed him back to health. Once, when he was only half conscious, he thought he felt her tears fall on his face and her soft warm lips press his; but it might have been a dream.

"You saw no sail this morning, I know; but, there, don't despair, you may yet go home," she said.

"No, Blanche, no; I have given up all hope of ever going home. We must end our days here."

She looked at him with her great blue eyes so soft and tender, and sighed:

"I am sorry for you."

"Are you not sorry for yourself?"

"No, no; I am not thinking of myself. I am all alone in the world, and it makes little difference where I am." Her voice faltered, and he saw that she was almost choking with grief, and John Stevens, feeling that he had been too selfish all along, said:

"Blanche, forgive me. I have had no thought for any one save myself. I have been cruel to neglect you as I have."

"Do not blame yourself," she sighed. "Your anxiety for your wife and children outweighs every other consideration."

"But when I think how kind and how gentle you have been throughout all these years, how, when the fever burned my brow, it was your soft hand which cooled it and nursed me back to life and reason, and how I have neglected and forgotten you, I feel I have been selfish. Surely you are an angel whom God hath sent me in these hours of loneliness."

His natural impulse was to embrace the heroic woman; but he restrained such unholy emotions, and she, with her heart overflowing, sat weeping for joy.

In order to change the subject, he said:

"Blanche, I have thought that the time has come

to explore the peak of Snow-Top." (Snow-Top was the name they had given the tallest mountain in the valley.) "It is the loftiest peak on the island, and from it we might see other islands and continents, and with this glass, perchance, we might get a view of a distant sail."

The exploration of this mountain had been the pet scheme for years. The sides were steep and the ascension difficult. He had spoken of it before, and she had approved of it.

"When do you think of going?" she asked.

"The day after to-morrow, if I can get ready."

"I will go with you."

"No, no, Blanche; the journey will be too great for you. You cannot go that distance."

With a smile, she answered:

"Surely, as I have gone with you on so many perilous journeys, you will not deny me this."

"Deny you, Blanche? I can deny you nothing; but I fear the journey will overtax your strength."

"I can go wherever you do," she answered.

He made no further objection, and next day they prepared to scale those heights which human feet had never trod. John had made for each a pair of stout shoes, the soles of which were of a kind of wood almost as elastic as leather and the tops of tanned goat-skins. Their shoes were well suited for travel through the wilderness and in stony countries.

Knowing what a fatiguing journey lay before them, John travelled slowly and at the end of the first day halted at the foot of the mountain, where he built a fire, and they slept in perfect security.

The island was free from poisonous reptiles and insects, and since the foxes had been nearly exterminated, there was not a dangerous animal on the island. When morning came, they breakfasted and prepared to ascend the mountain. At the base was a dense tangled growth of tropical trees through which they pushed their way, sometimes being compelled to cut their way through. The tall grass, the palms, the matted mangroves and vines made travel difficult.

On and on, up the thorny steep they pressed. The palms and mangroves gave place to scrub oaks, and they in turn to pine and cedar. As they ascended, there was a change in soil, vegetation and climate.

At the base of the mountain grew only the trees and plants of the tropics. Three hours' upward travel brought them into the regions of the temperate zone, and they plucked wild strawberries such as grew in New England. Pressing on up the steep side, scaling cliffs and rocks, which at times almost defied their skill and strength, the air grew cooler. The vegetation was less rank. The grass grew short and in places there was none at all.

"Are you tired?" John asked.

"Not much."

"Let us sit and rest."

"The sun has almost reached the meridian, and we are not half-way up the mountain."

"Yet you must have a few moments' rest, Blanche."

They rested but a moment and again pressed on. They had now reached a great altitude, and the valley below looked like a fairy-land. They found up here a species of mountain goats which they had not seen before. They were very shy of the intruders and went bounding away from cliff to cliff and rock to rock at a speed which defied pursuit.

John shot one. The report of his musket in this lofty region was so slight as to be heard but a short distance, but the birds, soaring aloft, screamed with fear and went still higher up the mountain sides.

Here they found squirrels more abundant than in the valley. The oaks and hickory trees bore an abundance of nuts for them. Further on the nut-bearing trees gave place to grass, and they found themselves on a sloping plain.

Every hour seemed bringing them to new and

unexplored regions. Old Snow-Top, as they called the mountain, contained wonders. The trees had dwindled to dwarfs, and the animals degenerated in proportion. Some fur-bearing animals were found in these lofty regions, and the eyrie of the eagle was in the cold, dark cliffs.

There was a perceptible change in the climate. The clothing suitable for the valley was uncomfortably light in this region.

"Blanche, are you cold?" he asked.

She, smiling, answered:

"Never mind me, I can stand it."

"The air is chill."

"It always is so in ascending a lofty mountain."

"The ascent is more difficult than I supposed; behold the cliff before us!"

"I see it."

"It seems almost perpendicular."

"So it does."

"I see no way to scale it from here."

"Yet, like all other ills in this world, the difficulties may disappear at our approach."

When they advanced toward the cliff, fully two hundred feet in height, a narrow rocky slope was seen ascending on the left, like a flight of winding stairs, to the plateau above. Even with this aid the ascent was difficult.

The rocks were rough, hard and sharp at the

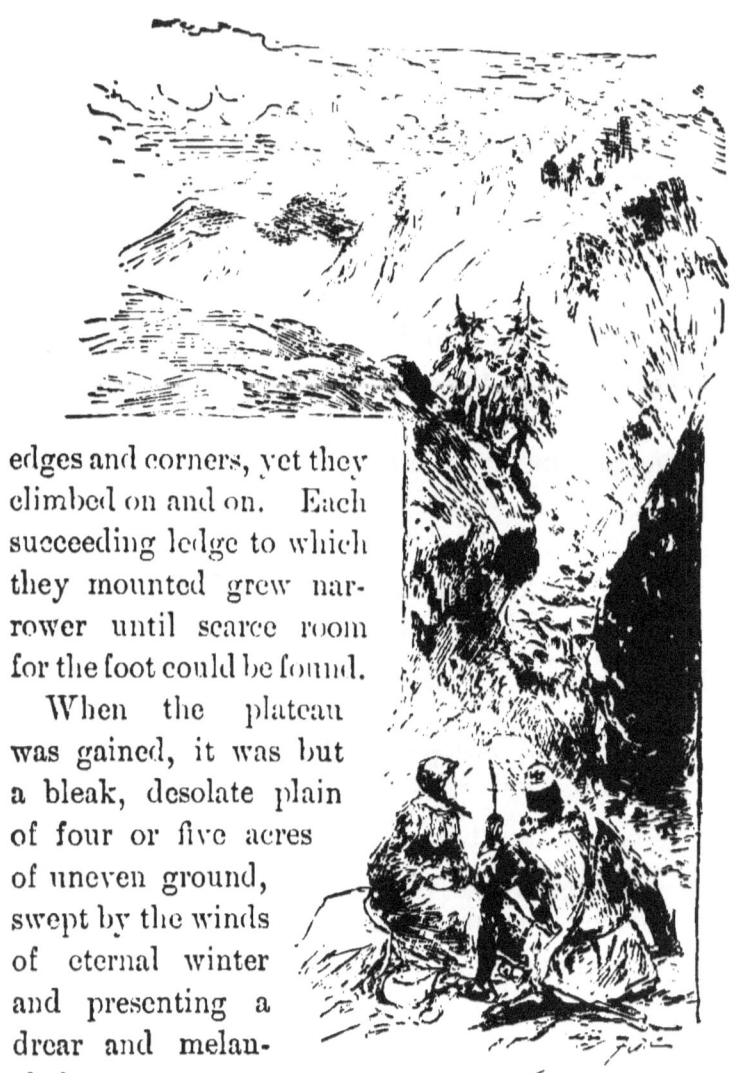

edges and corners, yet they climbed on and on. Each succeeding ledge to which they mounted grew narrower until scarce room for the foot could be found.

When the plateau was gained, it was but a bleak, desolate plain of four or five acres of uneven ground, swept by the winds of eternal winter and presenting a drear and melancholy aspect.

"OUR JOURNEY IS NOT ONE-HALF OVER."

Close under a stone they sat down to partake of the noonday

meal, listening to the shrill winds sweeping over the dreary waste and gazed at the cloud-capped peak above. The only cheerful object was a noisy cataract thundering down the mountain, fed by the melting snows.

"Do you feel equal to the task?" he asked.

"Yes."

"Our journey is not one-half over."

"I know it."

"And the last half will be more trying than the first."

"I will go with you," she answered cheerfully.

To one living in a mountainless country the difficulties and fatigues of mountain scaling is unknown. An ascent, which, to the unpractised cliff climber, might seem the work of an hour, will consume an entire day.

Having finished their meal, they resumed the upward march. Reaching a small cluster of stunted and gnarled pines, they pressed through it and emerged on a great, bleak hillside, almost bare of vegetation. Only here and there grew a tuft of stunted grass or a dwarfed shrub. The temperate zone had given way to the regions of eternal winter. Again and again they were compelled to pause for breath.

"Here it is," John cried, almost gleefully, as a snow-flake fell on his arm.

A little further up, they found snow drifted under a ledge of the rock, while little rivulets, running from the melting snow, joined mountain torrents and cataracts that thundered down below. At last the great summit was gained, and they paused to gaze afar on the land and sea below. John drew his glass and swept the horizon. The slight clouds, from which an occasional flake had fallen, cleared away at sunset, and they had an excellent view as far as the eye could reach.

"Do you see any sail?" she asked.

"None."

"Then we must be in an ocean as unexplored and unknown as the great south sea which Balboa discovered."

"I know not where we are."

The sun set, dipping into the sea and leaving a great, broad phosphorescent light where it disappeared, which broadened and radiated toward the east until it was lost in gloom.

"We cannot return home to-night," said Blanche.

"No; we will seek some suitable spot for passing the night further down the mountain."

The mountain top was covered with snow, and they went down a mile or more before they found the ground free from snow, slush, ice or water. Here, on a mantle made of goat-skins, John induced the shivering Blanche to lie down, while he gathered some stunted brush, small pines and dead grass and built a fire to keep her warm. During the night the sky became obscured, and a cold rain fell. Their condition was miserable enough, for they were soaked to the skin and shivering. There was no shelter near enough for them to reach it, and it was too dark to travel.

"I am freezing," said Blanche, through her chattering teeth. John tried to muffle her in the robe of goat-skin; but it was wet and worse than no covering. His soaked garments were placed about her; but she still shook with cold, until he became alarmed and held her in his arms, endeavoring to instill some warmth in her from his own body.

All things must have an end, and so did that dreary night. Day dawned at last, and the rising sun chased away the clouds, and they saw, far, far below them, the low, green valley which they called home. The morning air was chill and piercing, and John began to fear for Blanche; but she assured him that soon they would reach lower land and warmer temperature. They did not wait for breakfast, but hurried down the mountain just as soon as it was light enough to see. She was weak, and he offered to carry her in his strong arms.

"No, no; I can walk," she said.

"But you are so chilled and so weak."

"Exercise will warm me and give me strength," she answered. It did, and when they reached the valley she was quite herself again. It was the middle of the afternoon when they entered the valley, and gazing back at old Snow-Top, with his towering summit piercing the skies, they thanked God for their deliverance. About the snowy peak there clung a rift of vapor, as if some passing cloud had caught upon it and torn off a fragment.

"I don't care to venture up there again," said John.

"Nor do I," sighed his companion. "So peaceful, so sweet and so dear is our little home, that I am almost content with it."

"I am, likewise."

For two or three days no evil effects were perceivable from their journey save a weariness on the part of Blanche, which John flattered himself would pass away. He sat with her and talked more than had been his custom. She seemed to grow better in his eyes, for he had seen how uncomplaining she was, and how she nobly struggled to make his burden lighter. She spoke encouraging words of Virginia, told him of his wife and children, who had been described so often to her that she had a faithful picture of them in her mind. She would say:

"Your little Rebecca is now sixteen years of

age, quite a young lady. She is beautiful, too. I know she is beautiful, for she has the dark eyes and hair of her mother."

"Blanche, beauty is not confined to black eyes and hair alone," said John.

She went on:

"And your little boy is a man now, twenty years of age, and he is no doubt strong, brave, gallant and noble. Surely you must be proud of such a son. Your wife has grown more wise with her distress, and she still looks to the ocean for the return of one for whom she will wait until the angel of death summons her to meet him in Heaven."

"Blanche, Blanche, how strangely you talk!"

"I fancy I can see them, and they are happy in their little home. The son supports his mother. Oh, they are happy!"

"Blanche, Blanche, your cheeks are flushed, your eyes are unnaturally bright; you have a fever."

She laughingly answered:

"It is only a slight cold, the result of our visit to the peak of old Snow-Top."

He administered such simple remedies as they had at hand, tucked her up warmly in bed and sat by her side until she was asleep. Then he made a bed on the floor in the adjoining room, where he might be within call, and lay down to sleep. Being wearied with the toils of the day, he was soon asleep, and it was after midnight when he was awakened by a cough from Blanche's bed. It was followed by an exclamation of pain.

In a moment he was at her side.

"What is the matter, Blanche?" he asked, uneasily.

"I have a pain in my side."

He stooped over her, put his hand on her face and was startled to find it so dry and hot. Groping about he found a rude lamp, which he had fashioned from an old pewter pot brought from the wreck. Within the lamp was a wick made from the lint of wild hemp, fed with goat's fat. Seizing his flint and steel he kindled a light and found Blanche in a raging fever.

"Blanche, Blanche, you are ill!" said John.

"I am so hot, I burn with thirst," she answered.

"You shall have water." There was a spring of clear, cold water flowing down from the mountain, and John took an earthen jar, and ran to fill it.

"It is so good of you," the sick woman sighed, as he moistened her fevered lips.

John Stevens was now very anxious about her, for she was growing rapidly worse. He knew a little about medicine and had brought some remedies from the ship; but the disease which had fastened itself on Blanche defied his skill. She was at times seized with a fit of coughing which almost took away her breath. When he had exhausted all his efforts, she said sweetly:

"You can do no more."

"Blanche, Blanche," he almost sobbed, "Heaven knows I would give my life to spare you one pang."

"I know it," she answered.

"What will you have me do?"

"Sit by my side."

He brought a stool and sat by her bedside.

"Hold my hand, I have such frightful dreams, and I want you near."

He took the little fevered hand in his own and for hours sat by her side.

Morning came and went, came and went again, and she grew worse.

John never left her save to bring cold water to slake her burning thirst, or prepare some remedy to check the ravages of the fever.

"Oh, God! to be left alone—to be left all alone! Can I endure it?" he sighed. When he was at her side, he said:

"It was the journey to Snow-Top. It was too much for you, Blanche, I am to blame for this."

"No, no, blame not yourself. I it was who insisted on going."

She rapidly grew worse, and John Stevens saw

that she must die. Occasionally she fell asleep, and then he thought how beautiful she was. Once she murmured his name and sweetly smiled. She awoke and was very weak. Raising her eyes, she saw him at her side, and with that same happy smile on her face, she said:

"Oh, I had such a delightful dream. It may be wicked; but it was delightful. I dreamed that I was she."

"Who?"

"Your wife——"

"Blanche!"

"Kiss me, brother—I am going—rapidly going."

He entwined his arms about the being who, for fifteen years, had been his only companion, and pressed his lips to hers.

"Blanche, Blanche, you must not die; for my sake live."

"No, no; I will soon be gone; then you will be all alone. Don't leave me until all is over."

"I shall not, Blanche; I shall not," cried Stevens, holding her tightly clasped in his strong arms.

"It may be wrong—but we have been here so long—meet me in heaven, brother."

"God grant that I may, poor girl."

"Pray with me."

He knelt at her side, and the lips of both moved

in prayer. When he rose, she laid her little hand, all purple with fever, in his and said:

"Brother—when I am gone, bury me in that beautiful valley near the spring, where the wild flowers grow close by the white stone. On the stone write: 'Here lies my beloved sister, Blanche Holmes.'"

An hour later John Stevens knelt beside a corpse. The gentle spirit had flown.

Midnight—and the castaway, despairing, half-crazed with grief, still knelt by the dead body, tearing his hair, and groaning:

"Alone—left alone!"

CHAPTER XIV.

THE TREASURE SHIP.

"O gentle wind ('tis thus she sings)
 That blowest to the west,
Oh, couldst thou waft me on thy wings
 To the land that I love best,
How swiftly o'er the ocean's foam,
 Like a sea-bird I would sail."
—Pringle.

WHEN the heart is full, there seems some relief in pouring out the story of woe into a sympathetic ear; but when one is alone, with no human being to listen or sympathize, grief is a hundred-fold greater.

Day dawned and found John Stevens still kneeling by the side of the cold form of the only being who had shared his unhappy lot. How seldom we realize the worth of companions or friends until they are forever gone, and then, as if to mock our grief, each kind act, each little delicate attention seems to start out as if emblazoned on stone before us. At last the broken-hearted castaway rose and with folded arms gazed on the dead face, still beautiful and holy even in death.

"Blanche, Blanche, must I give you up, you who have so long cheered my lonely life? Must I never listen to the sweet music of your voice again?"

John roused himself at last from the feeling of despair and, taking the best boards left from the wreck, constructed a neat coffin. He dug the grave at the white stone as she had directed and laid her to rest. No one but God listened to him as he read the solemn and impressive burial service, according to the established church. No one but God saw those tears flow in silence as he gazed for the last time on her face. Then, fastening down the lid, he covered the coffin over with boards and began slowly and mournfully shovelling the earth upon it. He heaped up the earth and placed the soft green sod over the mound. Then he cut the inscription on the stone as she had requested at the head of the grave, adding:

"Sweet sister, rest in peace, until Christ comes to claim his own, when there will be a crown given you which outshines the sun." To go about his daily routine of life, to feel that heavy aching load on his heart crushing and consuming him, made his existence almost unbearable.

He lost all interest in the little field, the tame goats and birds, and for two or three days even neglected to take food himself. An appalling silence had fallen upon the island. He seemed to still hear her voice in the house and about it, and when he closed his eyes in sleep, after being utterly exhausted, he saw her sweet face bending over him and felt the sunshine of her smile on him. It was so hard to realize that she was gone, and he could scarcely believe that he would not find her down on the beach gathering shells, as he had so often seen her.

Frequently when alone in the cabin he would start, half expecting to see her enter with her cheering smile; but she was gone forever; her sweet smiles and cheering voice would no more be heard on earth.

It required long months before he could settle down to that life of loneliness. Hitherto he had not lived the life of a Crusoe or Selkirk; but now he was destined to know what real solitude was. John Stevens at last began to take some interest in his domestic affairs. He sadly missed the thousand little attentions which feminine instincts suggested for his comfort; but anon he became accustomed to being alone. He grew morose and melancholy, even wicked, for at times he blamed Providence, first for casting him away on this lonely island, and lastly for taking from him the companion he had failed to appreciate, until he felt her loss; but soon he turned to God and prayed for light.

He read the Bible and from this living fountain of consolation drank deep draughts of that which, to his starving soul, was the elixir of life. Strange as it may seem, in the first ebullition of his grief, John Stevens seemed to forget his wife and children. So long had he been from them, that they had lost their place in his thoughts. Time, the great healer of all wounds, the great reconciler to all fates, the great arbitrator of all disputes, had almost lost to him those tenderest ties which had lacerated his poor heart.

To the fatalist, John Stevens would seem to be one of those unfortunate beings doomed to be made the sport of a capricious fortune. His domestic relations in Virginia were a strange intermixture of good and bad. His business had been decidedly prosperous, he had married into a respectable family, and his wife was popular. His children were beautiful and healthy; but his wife was extravagant and foolish and had swept away his fortune faster than he could accumulate it. Then his voyage and shipwreck seemed the hand of fate. His father had been a sailor by profession and had never been shipwrecked, while he, on his first voyage, was cast away upon an unknown island. Fate gave him at first a companion and, just as he began to appreciate her, snatched her away.

At last he became reconciled even to live and

die alone on that island—to die without a friend to close his eyes, or to soothe his pillow. Horrible as the fate might seem, he was reconciled. No human hand would give him Christian burial, and the vultures which soared about the island might pluck out his eyes even before life was extinct. With this dread on his mind, he shot the vultures whenever he saw them, and almost drove them from the island.

Three years had lapsed since poor Blanche had been laid in her grave, and John was morose, silent and moody, but reconciled. It was eighteen years since he had been cast away, and he had about abandoned all thought of again seeing any other land save this.

Among other things saved from the wreck was a quantity of tobacco seed, and, as tobacco was then thought to be an indispensable article, he planted some and grew his own. He fashioned pipes from the roots of trees, as the Indians did, and his pipe became his greatest solace in solitude.

One night, a little more than three years after he had been left alone, he was lying on his well-worn mattress, smoking his evening pipe, when there came on the air far out to sea a heavy "Boom!"

The trumpet of doom would not have astonished him more. At first he could scarcely believe his ears. Starting up, he sat on the side of his bed listening.

"Boom!"

A second report, more heavy than the first, shook the air.

"God in heaven! can it be cannon?" cried Stevens. He leaped to his feet, pulled on his rude shoes and seized his musket.

"Boom! Boom! Boom!"

Three more shots from the sea rang on the air, and there could now be no doubt that a ship was near the island. The hope which suddenly started up in his heart almost overcame him, and he clung to the door for support.

Only for an instant did he linger thus, then he rushed to the headland from whence his tattered flag had floated all these years. The moon was shining brightly from a cloudless sky, and his vision swept the ocean far beyond the dangerous reefs which formed a natural guard about the island. There he saw a sight calculated to startle him. A large Spanish galleon was coming directly toward the island, pursued by a vessel which from the first he surmised to be a pirate. Even as he looked, he saw the flash of a gun and imagined he coud hear the crash of the iron ball striking into the side of the fugitive ship. He heard the cry of dread from the poor wretches on board, as the pirate drew nearer. On the still evening air came wild shouts of the buccaneers as they fired shot after shot at the prize.

John Stevens was greatly excited. Here was an opportunity to escape or be slain, either preferable to living on this terrible island alone.

The Spanish galleon was being driven directly through the only gap in the reefs to the island. Like a bird chased by a vulture she sought any shelter. She returned the fire as well as she could; but was no match for the well-equipped and daring pirate.

John's whole sympathies were with the unfortunate Spaniards. Their vessel evidently drew considerable water, for entering the gap in the reef, the tide being low, it stranded. The pirate, being much lighter draft, came nearer and poured in her volleys thick and fast. They were so near to the headland that John Stevens, a spellbound spectator, heard the iron balls and shot tearing into her timbers. With his glass he could even see her deck strewn with dead and dying.

The foremast of the galleon was cut through and fell, and the ship's rudder was shot away. The Spaniards, evidently bewildered, lowered boats, abandoned the galleon and pulled toward a rocky promontory two miles to the south.

Their enemies saw them and, manning boats,

headed them off, killing or capturing every one. The captured men were taken aboard the victorious ship.

While these startling scenes were being enacted, a great change had come over the sky. The tide began to rise and floated the galleon clear of the sand, and it drifted into the little bay not a mile from John's house. The sky was obscured with clouds and one of those tropical hurricanes called squalls swept over the island and sea. It struck the pirate broadside, and John Stevens last saw the vessel amid a mountain of waves and spray struggling to right itself. It probably went down, as he never saw or heard of it more.

For hours the amazed castaway stood in the pelting rain and howling wind, with the roaring sea below him. Was it all a dream, or was this only another freak of capricious fate, which doomed him to eternal misery. The storm roared and the hungry sea swallowed up the pirate.

Why could not one have been spared? Even a pirate would have made a companion; but fate had roused his hopes only to dash them to the earth again.

It was pitch dark save when a flash of lightning illuminated the heavens. John Stevens turned slowly about to retrace his steps homeward, half believing it was some terrible dream which had brought him from his bed into the pelting storm, when by the aid of a flash of lightning he saw the Spanish galleon, which had been again stranded within a hundred yards of the beach. The single flash of lightning revealed only her deck and rigging; not a soul was to be seen on board the ship; but the sight of the vessel roused the castaway. In eighteen years this had been the only sign of civilization which had greeted his vision, and he was nearly frantic with delight.

Some one might be on board. Some skulkers from the cannon-balls of the pirates might have sought safety in the hold of the galleon, and he would find them. His heart was full to overflowing. He even began to hope that the ship could be gotten off the bar, and could make a voyage to some land of civilization. Though the ship was between the dangerous reefs and the sea, partially protected by a small land-locked bay, yet the surf was so high that it was madness to think of reaching the vessel that night. He built a fire on shore and all night long heaped on wood in the hope of attracting attention of those on board.

Morning dawned, and he saw the galleon with her head high in the air and her stern low in the sand and water. The tide had gone out, and not more than one hundred yards of water lay between him and the ship. John stripped off his clothes and swam to the wreck.

After no little difficulty he climbed up the mizzen chains.

A silence of death reigned over the ship, and when he had gained the deck a terrible sight met his view. Five men and one boy, the victims of the pirate's guns, lay dead on the deck, which was badly splintered with balls and shot.

The ship was wonderfully well preserved, the chief damage it received being from the cannon of the enemy.

John called again and again but no voice responded. The grim silence of death was about the ship. He found a boat in fair condition, lowered it and, putting the dead Spaniards into it, pulled ashore, where he gave the dead a decent burial on the sands, too high up for the tide to reach them.

Having accomplished this sad rite, he cried from the fulness of his soul:

"Oh, that there had been but one, only one saved, with whom I might converse!"

John Stevens, however, was a practical sort of a fellow, and, instead of repining over his sad fate, he determined to bring away everything valuable on board. Consequently he launched the boat, pulled to the wreck and went aboard. Had he been able to get the ship afloat, a carpenter might have repaired it so that a voyage could have been made; but the strength and skill of a hundred men could not have moved it from the sands in which it was so deeply imbedded. The vessel had been steered through the reefs and almost into the bay when deserted. John loaded his boat with muskets, several chests and casks, which contained food and wine. There was also a powder-horn, some kegs of powder, a fire shovel, tongs, two brass kettles, a copper pot for chocolate, and a gridiron. These and some loose clothes belonging to the sailors formed the first cargo taken ashore.

Next he brought off several barrels of flour, a cask of liquor and some tools, axes, spades, shovels and saws. Every implement that might be useful to him was taken ashore and stowed away. Then he began to search the lower part.

He had been for a week working on the wreck carrying off every conceivable object which might be of any possible use. He found the ship's books; but, owing to his ignorance of Spanish, he was unable to read them.

The name on the stern of the vessel was St. Jago, therefore he reasoned that it must be a West Indian vessel. How the idea entered his mind, Stevens never knew. It came suddenly, as an inspiration, that the galleon must be a Spanish treasure ship. One day, while in the captain's cabin, he found a narrow door opening from it. It was securely locked, and though he searched everywhere for keys and found many, none would fit the lock. At last he seized an iron crowbar, with which he forced the door off its hinges. Before him was a curious sort of compartment like a vault, the inside of which was lined with sheet iron. There lay before him several large, long boxes made of strong wood. He wondered what they contained. He cleared away every obstacle to the nearest box, and saw a lock and padlock and a handle at each end, all carved as things were carved in that age, when art rendered the commonest metals precious. John seized the handles and strove to lift the box; but it was impossible.

"What can it contain, that is so heavy?" he thought. He sought to open it; but lock and padlock were closed, and these faithful guardians seemed unwilling to surrender their trust. Stevens inserted the sharp end of the crowbar between the box and the lid and, bearing down with all his strength, burst open the fastenings. Hinges and lock yielded in their turn, holding in their grasp fragments of the boards, and with a crash he threw off the lid, and all was open.

John Stevens found a tanned fawn-skin spread as a covering over the contents and he tore it off. He started up with a yell and closed his eyes involuntarily. Then he opened them and stood motionless with amazement.

Three compartments divided the coffer. In the first blazed piles of golden coin. In the second bars of unpolished gold were ranged. In the third lay countless fortunes of diamonds, pearls and rubies, into which he dived his hands as eagerly as a starving man would plunge into food.

After having touched, felt and examined these treasures, John Stevens rushed through the ship like a madman. He leaped upon the deck, from whence he could behold the sea. He was alone. Alone with this countless—this unheard-of wealth. Was he awake, or was it but a dream? Before him lay the treasures torn from Mexico, Darien and Peru. They were his—he was alone.

Alas, he was alone! What use would those millions be to him on this island? The reaction came, and, falling on his knees, he cried:

"O God, why is such a fate mine?"

Hours afterward he recovered enough to remove the gold and jewels from the treasure ship to his home on the island. With more jewels than a king, he lived the lonely life of a hermit and a pauper, dreading to die, lest the vultures pluck out his eyes.

CHAPTER XV.

THE ANGEL OF DELIVERANCE.

Strange that when nature loved to trace
As if for God a dwelling place,
And every charm of grace hath mixed
Within the paradise she fixed,
There man, enamoured of distress,
Should mar it into wilderness.
—BYRON.

ON the restoration of monarchy in England, in 1660, the Connecticut colonists entertained serious fears regarding the future. Their sturdy republicanism and independent action in the past might be mortally offensive to the new monarch. The general assembly of Connecticut, therefore, resolved to make a formal acknowledgment of their alliance to the crown and ask the king for a charter. A petition was accordingly framed and signed in May, 1661, and Governor John Winthrop bore it to England. He was a son of Winthrop of Massachusetts, and was a man of rare attainments and courtly manners. He was then about forty-five years of age.

Winthrop was but coolly received at first, for

he and his people were regarded as enemies of the crown. But he persevered, and the good-natured monarch at last chatted freely with him about America, its soil, productions, the Indians and the settlers, yet he hesitated to promise a charter. Winthrop, it is said, finally drew from his pocket a gold ring of great value, which the king's father had given to the governor's grandfather, and presented it to his majesty with a request that he would accept it as a memorial of the unfortunate monarch and a token of Winthrop's esteem for and royalty to King Charles, before whom he stood as a faithful and loving subject. The king's heart was touched. Turning to Lord Clarendon, who was present, the monarch asked:

"Do you advise me to grant a charter to this good gentleman and his people?"

"I do, sire," Clarendon answered.

"It shall be done," said Charles, and he dismissed Winthrop with a royal blessing.

The charter was issued on the first of May, 1662. It confirmed the popular constitution of the colony, and contained more liberal provisions than any yet issued by royal hands. It defined the boundaries so as to include New Haven colony and a part of Rhode Island on the east, and westward to the Pacific Ocean. In 1665, the New Haven colony reluctantly gave its consent to the union; but the boundary between Connecticut and Rhode Island remained a subject of dispute for more than sixty years. That old charter, written on parchment, is still among the archives in the Connecticut State Department.

While King Philip's war raged all about them, the colonists of Connecticut did not suffer much from hostile Indians, save in some remote settlements high up the river. They furnished their full measure of men and supplies, and the soldiers bore a conspicuous part in that contest between the races for supremacy; but while they were freed from dangers and annoyances of war with the Indians, they were disturbed by the petty tyranny of Governor Andros, who, as governor of New York, claimed jurisdiction as far east as the Connecticut River. In 1675, he went to the mouth of that stream with a small naval force to assert his authority.

Captain Bull, the commander of a small fort at Saybrook, permitted him to land; but when he began to read his commission, he ordered him to be silent. The cowardly Andros was forced to yield to the commander's bold spirit and, in a towering passion, returned to New York, hurling the most bitter anathemas against Connecticut and Captain Bull.

It was more than a dozen years after this event

before anything happened to disturb the public repose of Connecticut; but as that event belongs to another period, we will omit it for the present.

Rhode Island was favored with a charter from Parliament, granted in 1644 to Roger Williams. The charter was very liberal, and in religion and politics the people were absolutely free. The general assembly, in a code of laws adopted in 1647, declared that "all men might walk as their conscience permitted them—every one in the name of his God." Almost every religious belief might have been encountered there; "so if a man lost his religious opinions, he might have been sure to find them in some village in Rhode Island." Society was kept in a continual healthful agitation, and though the disputes were sometimes stormy, they never were brutal. There was a remarkable propriety of conduct on all occasions, and the political agitations brought to the surface the best men in the colony to administer public affairs.

Two years after the overthrow and execution of Charles I., 1651, the executive council of state in England granted to William Coddington a commission for governing the islands within the limits of the Rhode Island charter. This threatened a dismemberment of the little empire and its absorption by neighboring colonies. The people were greatly alarmed. Roger Williams and John Clarke hastened to England, and with the assistance of Sir Henry Vane, the "sheet anchor of Rhode Island, the noble and true friend to an outcast and despised people," the commission was recalled, and the charter given by parliament was confirmed in October, 1652.

On the restoration of monarchy, 1660, the inhabitants sent to Charles II. an address, in which they declared their loyalty and begged his protection. This was followed by a petition for a new charter. The prayer was granted, and in July, 1663, the king issued a patent highly democratic in its general features and similar in every respect to the one granted to Connecticut. Benedict Arnold was chosen the first governor under the royal charter, and it continued to be the supreme law of the land for one hundred and eighty years.

Slowly advancing with the other colonies, if she did not even keep abreast of them, was the colony of New Jersey, from the time it first became a permanent political organization as a British colony, with a governor and council. Elizabethtown, which consisted only of a cluster of half a dozen houses, was made the capital. Agents went to New England to invite settlers, and a company from New Haven were soon settled on the banks of the Passaic. Others followed, and when, in 1668, the first legislative assembly met at Eliza-

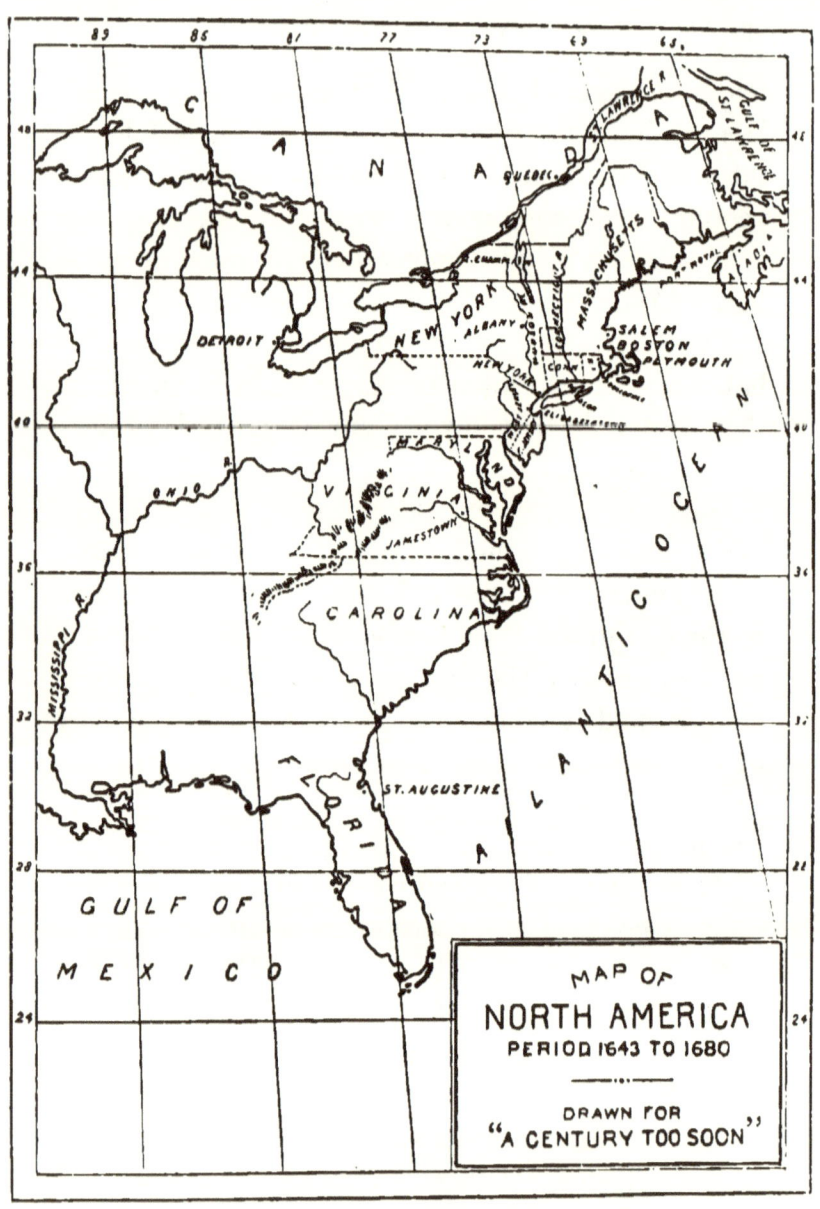

bethtown, it was largely made up of emigrants from New England. Thus we see how early in the history of our country, the restless tide moved westward. The fertility of the soil of New Jersey, the salubrity of the climate, the exemption from fear of hostile Indians, and other manifest advantages caused a rapid increase in the population and prosperity of the province, and nothing disturbed the general serenity of society there until in 1670, when specified quitrents of a half-penny per acre were demanded. The people murmured. Some of them had bought their lands of the Indians before the proprietary government was established, and they refused to pay the rent, not on account of its amount, but because it was an unjust tax, levied without their consent.

For almost two years they disputed over the rents, and kept the entire province in a state of confusion. The whole people combined in resistance to the payment of the tax, and in May, 1672, the disaffected colonists sent deputies to the popular assembly which met at Elizabethtown. That body compelled Philip Carteret, the lawful governor, to vacate his chair and leave the province, and chose a weak and inefficient man in his place. Carteret went to England for more authority, and while the proprietors were making preparations to recover the province by force of arms, in August,

1673, New Jersey and all the rest of the territory in America claimed by the Duke of York suddenly fell into the hands of the Dutch, who were then at war with England.

When, fifteen months later, New York was restored to the English, Carteret had a part of his authority restored to him; but sufficient was reserved to give Andros a pretext for asserting his authority and making himself a nuisance with the people.

Massachusetts never enjoyed the full favor of the Stuart dynasty. The almost complete independence which had been enjoyed for nearly twenty years was too dear to be hastily relinquished. When it became certain that the hereditary family of kings had been settled on the throne, and that swarms of enemies to the colony had gathered round the new government, a general court was convened, and an address was prepared for the parliament and the monarch. This address prayed for "the continuance of civil and religious liberties," and requested an opportunity of defence against complaints.

"Let not the king's men hear your words. Your servants are true men, fearing God and the king. We could not live without the public worship of God. That we might therefore enjoy divine worship without human mixtures, we, not without tears, departed from our country, kindred, and fathers' houses. Our garments are become old by reason of the very long journey. Ourselves, who came away in our strength, are, many of us, become gray-headed, and some of us are stooping for age."

So great was their dread of the new king after the restoration, that, as we have seen, Whalley and Goffe were denied shelter at all the public houses in Boston. Their charter was threatened and commissioners sent to demand it; but, by one device and another, the shrewd rulers of Massachusetts managed to avert the calamity. The government at home was kept busy at this time. There was a threatened war with the Dutch, and then the whole government of England had to be thoroughly renovated. Charles II. was not much of a business monarch. His thoughts were mainly of pleasure, and, despite his merciless pursuit of the men who put his father to death, he was good-natured.

Though the colonists of Massachusetts had levied two hundred men for the expected war with the Dutch, they wished to maintain their spirit of independence, and the two hundred were only a free offering. They regarded the commission sent by the king as a flagrant violation of chartered rights. In the matter of obedience due to a government, the people of Massachusetts made the nice distinction between natural obedience and voluntary subjection. They argued that the child born on the soil of England is necessarily an English subject; but they held to the original right of expatriation, that every man may withdraw from the land of his birth, and renounce all duty of allegiance with all claim to protection. This they themselves had done. Remaining in England, they acknowledged the obligatory force of established laws. Because those laws were intolerable, they had emigrated to a new world, where they could organize their government, as many of them originally did, on the basis of natural rights and of perfect independence.

As the establishment of a commission with discretionary powers was not specially sanctioned by their charter, they resolved to resist the orders of the king and nullify his commission. While the fleet sent from England was engaged in reducing New York, Massachusetts, on September 10th, 1664, published an order prohibiting complaints to the commissioners, and at the same time issued a remonstrance, not against deeds of tyranny, but the menace of tyranny, not against actual wrong, but against the principle of wrong. On the twenty-fifth of October it thus addressed a letter to King Charles II.:

"DREAD SOVEREIGN :—The first undertakers of this plantation did obtain a patent, wherein is granted full and absolute power of governing all the people of this place, by men chosen from among themselves, and according to such laws as they should see meet to establish. A royal donation, under the great seal, is the greatest security that may be had in human affairs. Under the encouragement and security of the royal charter, this people did, at their own charges, transport themselves, their wives and families, over the ocean, purchase the land of the natives, and plant this colony, with great labor, hazards, cost, and difficulties; for a long time wrestling with the wants of a wilderness and the burdens of a new plantation; having also now above thirty years enjoyed the privilege of GOVERNMENT WITH THEMSELVES, as their undoubted right in the sight of God and man. To be governed by rulers of our own choosing and laws of our own, is the fundamental privilege of our patent.

"A commission under the great seal, within four persons (one of them our professed enemy) are impowered to receive and determine all complaints and appeals according to their discretion, subjects us to the arbitrary power of strangers, and will end in the subversion of our all.

"If these things go on, your subjects here will either be forced to seek new dwellings or sink under intolerable burdens. The vigor of all new endeavors will be enfeebled; the king himself will be a loser of the wonted benefit by customs, exported and imported from hence into England, and this hopeful plantation will in the issue be ruined.

"If the aim should be to gratify some particular gentlemen by livings and revenues here, that will also fail, for the poverty of the people. If all the charges of the whole government by the year were put together, and then doubled or trebled, it would not be counted for one of those gentlemen a considerable accommodation. To a coalition in this course the people will never come; and it will be hard to find another people that will stand under any considerable burden in this country, seeing it is not a country where men can subsist without hard labor and great frugality.

"God knows, our great ambition is to live a quiet life, in a corner of the world. We came not into this wilderness to seek great things to ourselves; and, if any come after us to seek them here, they will be disappointed. We keep ourselves within our line; a just dependence upon, and subjection to, your majesty, according to our charter, it is far from our hearts to disacknowledge. We would gladly do anything within our power to purchase the continuance of your favorable aspect; but it is a great unhappiness to have no testimony of our loyalty offered but this, to yield up our liberties, which are far dearer to us than our lives, and which we have willing ventured our lives, and passed through many deaths to obtain.

"It was Job's excellency, when he sat as king among his people, that he was a father to the poor. A poor people, destitute of outward favor, wealth, and power, now cry unto their lord the king. May your magesty regard their cause, and maintain their right; it will stand among the marks of lasting honor to after generations."

The royalists in the days prior to the American Revolution, occupied a similar position that the monopolists, and wealthy do in politics to-day. They were the aristocrats, and for the common people to clamor for political freedom was absurd. The idea of republicanism was as loathsome to them and watched with as much jealousy as an important labor movement is to-day. The royalists called the men who clamored for civil and religious liberty fanatics, just as the monopolists of to-day, who control the dominant parties, call men who cry out against their oppression fanatics. It is sometimes difficult to distinguish the instinct of fanaticism from the soundest judgment, for fanaticism is sometimes the keenest sagacity. Those men wanted liberty and struggled and fought for it until it was obtained, just as the toiling millions of the world will some day sting the heel of grinding monopolies.

From 1660 to 1671, all New England was kept in a perpetual state of alarm and excitement. Plymouth made a firm stand for independence, although the weakest of the colonies. The commissioners threatened to assume control. It was the dawning strife of the new system against the old, of American politics against European politics, and yet those men struggling for liberty were called fanatics.

Secure in the support of a resolute minority, the Puritan commonwealth, in 1668, entered the province of Maine, and again established its authority by force of arms. Great tumults ensued; many persons, opposed to what seemed a usurpation, were punished for "irreverent speeches." Some even reproached the authorities of Massachusetts "as traitors and rebels against the king"; but the usurpers made good their ascendency till Gorges recovered his claims by adjudication in England. From the southern limit of Massachusetts to the

Quebec, the colonial government maintained its independent jurisdiction.

The defiance of Massachusetts was not punished as might have been expected. Clarendon's power was gone, and he was an exile. A board of trade, projected in 1668, never assumed the administration of colonial affairs, and had not vitality enough to last more than three or four years. Profligate libertines gained the confidence of the king's mistresses, and secured places in the royal cabinet. While Charles II. was dallying with women and robbing the theatres of actresses; while the licentious Buckingham, who had succeeded in displacing Clarendon, wasted the vigor of his mind and body by indulging in every sensual pleasure "which nature could desire or wit invent"; while Louis XIV. was increasing his influence by bribing the mistress of the chief of the king's cabal, England remained without a good government, and the colonies, despite bluster and threats, flourished in purity and peace. The English ministry dared not interfere with Massachusetts; it was right that the stern virtues of the ascetic republicans should intimidate the members of the profligate cabinet. The affairs of New England were often discussed; but the privy council was overawed by the moral dignity, which they could not comprehend.

Amid all the discord and threats, the New England colonies continued to advance in population, and their villages assumed the dignity of towns. It is difficult to form exact opinions as to the population of the several colonies in this early period of their history. The colonial accounts are incomplete, and those furnished by emissaries from England are grossly false. The best estimate that can be obtained gives to New England, in 1675, fifty-five thousand souls. Of these it is supposed that Plymouth contained not less than seven thousand, Connecticut, nearly fourteen thousand, Massachusetts proper, more than twenty-two thousand, and Maine, New Hampshire and Rhode Island, each perhaps four thousand. The settlements were chiefly by agricultural communities, planted near the seaside, from New Haven to Pemaquid. The beaver trade, more than traffic in lumber and fish, had produced the village beyond the Piscataqua; yet in Maine, as in New Hampshire, there was "a great trade in deal boards."

A sincere attempt had been made to convert the natives and win them to the regular industry of civilized life. The ministers of the early emigration, fired with a zeal as pure as it was fervent, longed to redeem those "wrecks of humanity," by planting in their hearts the seeds of conscious virtue, and gathering them into permanent villages. No pains were spared to teach them to read and

17

write, and in a short time a larger proportion of the Massachusetts Indians could do so, than the inhabitants of Russia fifty years ago. Some of them wrote and spoke English tolerably well. Foremost among these early missionaries, the morning star of missionary enterprise, was John Elliot, whose benevolence amounted to the inspiration of genius. He wrote an Indian grammar, and translated the whole of the Bible into the Massachusetts dialect. His actions, his thoughts, his desires, all wore the hue of disinterested love.

The frown was on the Indian's brow, however. Clouds were rising in the horizon. Since the Pequod war, there had been no great Indian uprising; but there was a general feeling of uneasiness which seemed to portend a general outbreak. The New Englanders were to feel the effects of it in all its fury. Neither Whalley nor Goffe had been seen since the day that Robert Stevens assisted the latter to make his escape.

The Indians, whose cupidity had been aroused by English gold, had searched the forest far and near for the regicides. Their knowledge of the forest and cunning in following a trail had two or three times brought them face to face with Cromwell's stern old battle-trained warriors. Then they had learned to their cost that they had roused a pair of lions in their lairs; but the regicides finally disappeared. They had last been seen near Hadley, and it was currently reported they were dead.

Rumors of an Indian outbreak were rife; still the good people of Hadley were living in comparative security. It was a quiet sabbath morn, and the drowsy hum of the bees made music on the air. The great meeting-house stood with its doors thrown wide open inviting worshippers. The sun, beaming from the cloudless sky upon the scene, seemed a benediction of peace. The whispering breeze on this delightful twelfth of June swept about the eaves of the church without a hint of danger.

The worshippers at the proper hour were seen thronging to the meeting-house, carrying their guns, swords or pistols with them. It seemed useless to go armed, when there was not a whisper of danger; but scarcely had the worship begun, when a terrible warwhoop broke the stillness. Immediately all was confusion. Children shrieked, some women trembled, and men, pale and stern, began to fire upon the savages, who, seven hundred strong, rushed on the place.

They fought stubbornly, driving away the enemy; but their great lack of discipline promised in the end to defeat them.

"We are lost! We are lost!" some of the weak-hearted were beginning to cry, when suddenly there appeared among them, from they knew not where, a tall, venerable personage, with white flowing beard, clad in a white robe, and carrying a glittering sword in his hand.

"You are not lost, if you follow me!" he cried.

"Who is he?" was the general query, which no one could answer save: "He is an angel sent by God to deliver us."

It soon became quite apparent that this celestial being was well posted in military tactics. He formed the young men in line of battle and taught them in a few moments to deploy and rally.

When the Indians again rushed to the conflict, they were met with a volley that stunned them and strewed the ground with dead. The angel leader of the whites then gave the command to charge, and, with their pistols and keen swords, they flew at the enemy before they had time to recover, and they were thrown into confusion and fled in dismay. After the departure of the Indians, nothing was heard or seen of the white angel deliverer. It has since been ascertained that Goffe and Whalley were at that time concealed at the house of Mr. Russel in Hadley, and it is inferred that Goffe left his concealment when the danger threatened, and, forming the men, led them to victory.

"YOU ARE NOT LOST IF YOU FOLLOW ME!"

CHAPTER XVI.

KING PHILIP'S WAR.

Oh, there be some
Whose writhed features, fixed in all their strength
Of grappling agony, do stare at you,
With their dead eyes half opened.
And there be some struck through with bristling darts
Whose clenched hands have torn the pebbles up;
Whose gnashing teeth have ground the very sand.
—BAILLIE.

MASSASOIT kept his treaty with the English inviolate so long as he lived. He died in 1661, at the advanced age of eighty or ninety years, leaving two sons whom the English named respectively Alexander and Philip. Alexander, the eldest son and hereditary sachem, died soon after his father, when Philip became chief sachem and warrior of the Wampanoags, with his royal residence on Mount Hope, not far from Bristol, Rhode Island. He was called King Philip. He resumed the covenants with the English made by his father, and observed them faithfully for a period of twelve years.

But it had become painfully apparent to Massasoit before his death, that the spreading colonies would soon deprive his people of their land and nationality, and that the Indians must become vassals of the pale race. Long did the warlike King Philip ponder on these possibilities with deep bitterness of feeling, until he had lashed himself into a fury by the continued nursing of his wrath, and resolved to strike the exterminating blow against the English.

There were many private wrongs of his people unavenged. The whites already had assumed a domineering manner, and his final resolution was both natural and patriotic. King Philip was a man of reason, and it is said he had no hope of success when he began the war. It was a war against such odds that it must have but one termination, and he had little if any faith in a successful issue.

The Pokanokets had always rejected the Christian manners, and Massasoit had desired to insert in a treaty, what the Puritans never permitted, that the English should never attempt to convert the warriors of his tribe from their religion.

Repeated sales of land narrowed their domains, and the English had artfully crowded them into the tongues of land, as "most suitable and convenient for them," where they would be more easily watched. The two chief seats of the Pokanokets were the peninsulas now called Bristol and Tiverton. As the English villages now grew nearer and nearer to them, their hunting-grounds were put under culture, their natural parks turned into pastures, their best fields for planting corn were gradually alienated, their fisheries impaired by more skilful methods, till they found themselves deprived of their broad acres, and by their own legal contracts driven, as it were, into the sea.

Mutual distrusts and collisions were the inevitable consequence. There is no authentic evidence of a deliberate conspiracy on the part of all the tribes. Bancroft, who is, perhaps, the best authority on all colonial matters, says the commencement of the war was accidental, and that "many of the Indians were in a maze, not knowing what to do, and ready to stand for the English."

There were many grievances among the Indians. The haughty chieftain, who had once before been compelled to surrender his "English arms," and pay an onerous tribute, was summoned to submit to an examination, and could not escape suspicion.

The wrath of his tribe was roused, and the informer was murdered. In turn the murderers were identified, seized, tried by a jury of which one-half were Indians, and on conviction were hanged. The younger men of the tribe were eager for vengeance, and without delay eight or nine of the English were slain about Swansey, and the alarm of war spread through the colonies.

King Philip was thus unwillingly hurried into war, and he wept when he heard that a white man's blood had been shed. It is a rare thing for an Indian to weep, least of all a mighty chief like Philip; but in the cloud of war hovering over his people, he read the doom of his tribe. He had kept his men about him in arms, and had welcomed every stranger, and yet, against his judgment and his will, he was involved in war almost before he knew it. The English had guns enough, while but few of the Indians were well armed and were without resources when their present supply was exhausted. The rifle, though not in general use, had been invented many years before, and for hunters and backwoodsmen was an effective weapon, though it was regarded as "a slow firing gun" compared with the smooth-bore. Many of the Indians had firearms and were excellent marksmen, and had overcome their superstitious dread of the white man's weapons.

The minds of the English are said to have been appalled by the horrors of the impending conflict, and superstition indulged in wild inventions. There was an eclipse of the moon at which they declared they saw the figure of an Indian scalp imprinted on the centre of the disk. The perfect form of an Indian bow appeared in the sky. The sighing of the wind was like the whistling of bullets. Some heard invisible troops of horses gallop through the air, while others found the prophecy of calamities in the howling of the wolves.

Despite all his aversion to war, Philip found it forced upon him, and when he took up the hatchet he threw his soul into the issue, and fought until death ended the struggle. There were many Christian converts among the Indians, who were firmly attached to the English. One of these, John Sassaman, who had been educated at Cambridge, where John Harvard had established a college, was a royal secretary to Philip. Becoming acquainted with the plans of the sachem, he revealed them to the authorities at Plymouth. For this he was murdered, and his murderers hanged.

Soon after the attack on Swansey, Philip left his place of residence and his territory to the English. The following is the reason of his precipitate retreat. Additional assistance being needed, the authorities of Boston sent out Major-General Savage from that place, with sixty horse and as many foot-soldiers, who scoured the country all the way to Mount Hope, where King Philip, his wife and child were supposed to be at that time.

Philip was at dinner when the news reached him

of the near proximity of his enemies, and he rose with his family, officers and warriors and fled further up the country. The English pursued them as far as they could go for the swamps, and overtook the rear of the detachment, killing sixteen of them.

At the solicitation of Benjamin Church, a company of thirty-six men were placed under him and Captain Fuller, who on the 8th of July marched down into Pocasset Neck. This force, small as it was, afterward divided, Church taking nineteen of the men and Fuller the remaining seventeen. The party under Church proceeded into a point of land called Punkateeset, now the southerly extremity of Tiverton, where they were attacked by a body of three hundred Indians. After a fight of a few moments, the English fell back to the seashore, and thus saved themselves from destruction, for Church perceived that it was the intention of the Indians to surround them. Every one expected death, but resolved to sell their lives as dearly as possible. Thus hemmed in, Church had a double duty to perform—that of preserving the spirit of his followers, several of whom viewed their situation as desperate, and erecting piles of stone to defend them.

Boats had been appointed to attend the English on this expedition, and the heroic party looked for relief from this quarter; but, though the boats appeared, the bullets of the Indians made them preserve a respectable distance, until Church, in a moment of vexation, cried:

"Be off with you, cowards, and leave us to our fate!" The boats took him at his word.

The Indians, now encouraged, fought more desperately than before. The situation of the Englishmen was most forlorn, although as yet not one had been wounded. Night was coming on, their ammunition was nearly spent, and the Indians, having taken possession of a stone house on the hill, fired into the temporary barricade of the English; but at this moment a sloop hove in sight, and bore down toward the shore. It had two or three small cannon on board with which it proceeded to knock down the stone house. The sloop was commanded by a resolute man, Captain Golding, who effected the embarkation of the company, taking off only two at a time in a canoe. During the embarkation the Indians who were armed with muskets and rifles kept up a steady fire from behind trees and stones, and Church, who was the last to embark, narrowly escaped the balls of the enemy, one grazing his head, and another lodging in a stake, which happened to stand just above the centre of his breast.

Captain Church soon after joined a body of English and returned to Pocasset, and Philip, after a skirmish, retired to the swamps, where for a time his situation became desperate; but at length he contrived to elude his besiegers, and fled to the Nipmucks, who received him with a warmth of welcome quite gratifying to the ambitious chieftain.

The governor of Massachusetts sought to dissuade the Nipmucks from espousing the cause of Philip; but they could not agree among themselves, and consented to meet the English commissioners at a place three miles from Brookfield on a specified day. Captains Hutchinson and Wheeler were deputized to proceed to the appointed place. With twenty mounted men and three Christian Indians as guides and interpreters they reached the appointed place, but no Indians were to be seen. After a short consultation, they advanced a little further, when they found themselves in an ambuscade. A volley of rifles and muskets was the first intimation of the presence of Indians. Eight men and five horses fell dead, and Captain Hutchinson and two more were mortally wounded. The Christian Indians led the remnant to Brookfield.

They scarcely had time to alarm the inhabitants, who, to the number of seventy-eight, flocked into the garrison house, when the Indians assailed the town. The house was but slightly fortified about the exterior by a few logs hastily thrown up, while inside the house was padded with feather-beds to deaden the force of the bullets. The house was soon surrounded by the enemy, and shots poured in from all directions. The beleaguered English were no mean marksmen, and they soon taught the Indians to keep at a respectful distance. The Indians filled a cart with hemp, flax, and other combustible materials, which they set on fire, and pushed it backward to the building. The beleaguered people began to pray for deliverance, when, as if in answer to their prayer, a heavy shower of rain fell, extinguishing the fire, and before it could be replenished, Major Willard with a party of dragoons arrived and the Indians raised the siege.

A considerable number of Christian Indians near Hatfield were suspected of being friendly to Philip and ordered to give up their arms. They escaped at night and fled up the river toward Deerfield to join Philip. The English pursued them and early next morning came up with them at a swamp, opposite to the present town of Sunderland, where a warm contest ensued. The Indians fought gallantly, but were finally routed, with a loss of twenty-six of their number, while the whites lost only ten. The escaped Indians joined Philip's forces, and Lathrop and Beers returned to their station at Hadley.

About the 10th of September, while Captain Lathrop was bringing away some provisions and corn from Deerfield, he was attacked at a place called "Muddy Brook." Knowing the English would pass here with their teams and horses, the Indians lay in ambush and, pouring in a destructive fire, rushed furiously to a close engagement. The English ranks were broken, and the scattered troops were everywhere attacked. Seeking the cover of trees, the English fought with desperation. The combat now became a trial of skill in sharpshooting, on the issue of which life or death was suspended. The overwhelming superiority of the Indians, as to numbers, left little room for hope on the part of the English. Every instant they were shot down behind their retreats, until nearly their whole number perished. The dead, the dying, the wounded strewed the ground in every direction. Out of nearly one hundred, including the teamsters, not more than seven or eight escaped from the bloody spot. The wounded were indiscriminately massacred. This company consisted of choice young men, "the very flower of Essex County, none of whom were ashamed to speak with the enemy in the gate." Eighteen were citizens of Deerfield.

Captain Moseley arrived at the conclusion of the fight, just as the Indians began stripping and mutilating the dead. He charged the Indians, cutting his way through with his company again and again, until he drove them from the field.

The Indians near Springfield, supposed to be friendly, on the 4th of October became allies of King Philip, whose cause seemed likely to prevail. They planned to get possession of the fort, but were betrayed by an Indian at Windsor, and when the savages came they found the garrison ready to resist them. The savages burned thirty-two houses and barns, and the beleaguered people were in great distress.

King Philip next aimed a blow at the three towns Hadley, Hatfield and Northampton at once. At this time, Captain Appleton with one company lay at Hadley, Captain Moseley and Poole with two companies were at Hatfield, while Major Treat had just returned to Northampton for the security of the settlement. Philip with seven or eight hundred warriors made a bold assault on Hatfield, on the 19th of October, attacking from every side at the same moment; but after a severe struggle the Indians were repulsed at every point.

After leaving the western frontier of Massachusetts, Philip was next known to be in the countries of his allies, the Narragansetts. The latter had not heartily engaged in the war; but their inclination to do so was not doubted, and it was the design of Philip to arouse them to activity. Conanchet, their sachem, in violation of his treaty with the English, not only received Philip's warriors, but aided their operations against the English, and Massachusetts, Connecticut and Plymouth raised an army of fifteen hundred men and, in the winter of 1675, set out to attack the Indians.

Philip had strongly fortified himself at South Kingston, Rhode Island, on an elevated portion of an immense swamp. Here his men erected about five hundred wigwams, of a superior construction, in which was deposited an abundant store of provisions. Baskets and tubs of corn (hollow trees cut off about the length of a barrel) were piled one upon another around the inside of the dwellings, which rendered them bullet-proof. Here about three thousand Indians had taken up their winter quarters, and among them were Philip's best warriors.

Governor Winslow of Plymouth commanded the English. A heavy snow had fallen and the weather was intensely cold; but on December 19, the English reached the fort and, by reason of their scarcity of provisions, resolved to attack at once. The New Englanders were unacquainted with the situation of the Indians, and, but for an Indian who betrayed his countrymen, there is little probability that the English would have effected anything against the fort. The stronghold was reached about one o'clock in the afternoon, and the English assailed the most vulnerable part of it, where it was fortified by a kind of a block-house, directly in front of the entrance, and had also flankers to cover a cross-fire. The place was protected by high palisades and an immense hedge of fallen trees surrounding it on all sides. Between the fort and the main land was a body of water, which could be crossed only on a large tree lying over it. Such was the formidable aspect of the place, such the difficulty of gaining access to it.

At first the English tried to cross over on the log; but, being compelled to go in single file, they were shot down by the Indians, until six captains and a number of men had been slain. Captain Moseley and a mere handful of men finally rushed over the log and burst into the fort, where they were assailed by fearful odds. This bold act so attracted the attention of the Indians that others rushed in. Captain Church, that indomitable Indian fighter, burst into the fort, dashed through it, and reached the swamp in the rear, where he poured a destructive fire into the enemy in retreat. The Indian cabins were set on fire, and a scene of horror followed. A Narragansett chief afterward stated their loss at seven hundred killed in the fort and three hundred more who died of their wounds in the woods.

18

After the destruction of the place, Governor Winslow set out with his killed and wounded through a driving snow-storm for Pettyquamscott. The march was one of misery and distress, and a number of the wounded died on their march.

On the 19th of February, the Indians surprised Lancaster with complete success, falling upon it with a force of several hundred warriors. The town contained fifty-two families, of whom forty-two persons were killed or captured. Forty-two persons took shelter in the house of Mary Rowlandson, the wife of the minister of the place. It was set on fire by the Indians. "Quickly," says Mrs. Rowlandson in her narrative, "it was the dolefullest day that ever mine eyes saw. Now the dreadful hour had come. Some in our house were fighting for their lives; others wallowing in blood; the house on fire over our heads, and the bloody heathen ready to knock us on the head if we stirred out. I took my children to go forth; but the Indians shot so thick that the bullets rattled against the house as if one had thrown a handful of stones. We had six stout dogs; but none of them would stir. A bullet went through my side, and another through a child in my arms, and I was made captive, having of my family only one poor wounded babe left. I was led from the town where my captors halted to gaze on the burning houses. Down I must sit in the snow, with my sick child, the picture of death in my lap. Not the least crumb of refreshment came within our mouths from Wednesday night until Sunday night except a little cold water."

Mrs. Rowlandson and her child were afterward recovered from the savages.

Shortly after the Lancaster disaster, Captain Pierce, with fifty men and twenty Cape Cod Indians, having crossed the Pawtuxet River in Rhode Island, unexpectedly met a large body of Indians.

The English fell back and took up a sheltered position under the river bank; but here they were hemmed in and fought until all fell save one white man and four Indians, after killing more than one hundred of the enemy.

The Christian Indians of Cape Cod showed their faithfulness and courage in this melancholy affair. Four of them effected their escape and one of these aided in the escape of the only white man who survived. His name was Amos, and after Captain Pierce was wounded he remained by him loading and firing, until it was evident he could do no more. Then he painted his face black as his enemies had done, and thus escaped. Another of the Christian Indians pretended to be chasing the white man who thus escaped with upraised tomahawk. The ruse saved both.

On the 20th of April, an army of Indians made an assault on Sudbury. The people were reinforced by soldiers from Watertown and Concord. The Indians drew the Concord people into an ambuscade and only one escaped.

The best Indian warrior makes a poor general. He has no ability to preserve an organization, and soon calamities began to befall Philip. They were small at first; but they tended to discourage his followers. First the Deerfield Indians abandoned his cause, and many of the Nipmucks and Narragansetts followed. Still, Philip, though he had not been much seen during the winter, and it is doubtful where he had spent the most of it, had no intention of abating his efforts against the English.

In the month of May, 1676, he appeared at the head of a powerful force in northern Massachusetts. Large bodies of Indians about this time took up positions at the Connecticut River falls, where they were attacked and routed by Captain Turner. One hundred were left dead on the field and a hundred and forty more went over the falls. When Turner retreated from the field, the Indians rallied, fell on his rear, shot down the gallant captain and thirty-seven of his men.

On May 30th, Philip, at the head of six hundred men, attacked Hatfield, but was repulsed after a desperate struggle.

Philip's power was on the wane. He was secure in no place; but his haughty spirit was untamed by adversity. Although meeting with constant losses, and among them some of his most experienced warriors, he, nevertheless, seemed as hostile and determined as ever. In August, the intrepid Church made a descent upon his headquarters at Matapoiset, where he killed and made prisoners one hundred and thirty. Philip barely made his escape, and was obliged to leave his wampum and his wife and child, who were made prisoners.

Church's guide had brought him to a place where a large tree, which the enemy had felled, lay across a stream. Church had gained the top end of the tree, when he espied an Indian on the stump of it, on the other side of the stream. Church brought his gun to his shoulder and would have shot the Indian, had not one of his own Indians told him not to fire, as he believed it was one of his own men. On hearing voices, the Indian looked about, and the friendly Indian got a glance at his face and discovered that it was Philip. The friendly Indian fired, but too late, for Philip, leaping from the stump, ran down the bank among the bushes and in a moment was out of sight. Church gave chase to him; but he could not be found, though they picked up a few of his followers.

King Philip's war had now degenerated into a single man hunt. From this time on, Philip was too closely watched and hotly pursued to escape destruction. His followers deserted him, and he was driven like a wild beast from place to place, until at last he came to his ancient seat near Pokanoket, when one of his men advised making peace. Philip killed him on the spot. The Indian thus slain had a brother named Alderman, who, fearing the same fate, and probably in revenge, deserted Philip, and gave Captain Church an account of his situation and offered to lead him to his camp. Early on Saturday morning, August 12, 1676, Church, with his Indian guide, came to the swamp where Philip was encamped, and, before he was discovered, had placed a guard about it so as to encompass it, except at one place. He then ordered Captain Golding to rush into the swamp and fall upon Philip in his camp, which he immediately did, but was discovered as he approached, and Philip fled. Having been just awakened and being only partially dressed, he ran at full speed, carrying his gun in his hand, and came directly upon the Indian Alderman, who, with a white man, was in ambush at the edge of the swamp.

"There comes the devil Philip now!" cried the Englishman, raising his rifle and aiming at the king; but the powder in the pan had become damp, and

HE FELL UPON HIS FACE IN THE MUD AND WATER WITH HIS GUN UNDER HIM.

he missed fire. Immediately Alderman, whose gun was loaded with two balls, fired, sending one bullet through Philip's heart and another not more than two inches from it. He fell upon his face in the mud and water, with his gun under him.

The death of Philip ended the bloodiest Indian war at that time known in the New World. A few of his confederates were captured; but there was no more fighting. Philip's son was sold into slavery in Bermuda. So perished the dynasty of Massasoit.

CHAPTER XVII.

NEARING THE VERGE.

At times there come, as come there ought,
Grave moments of sedater thought,
When fortune frowns, nor lends our night
One gleam of her inconstant light :
And hope, that decks the peasant's bower,
Shines like the rainbow through the shower.
—CUNNINGHAM.

ROBERT STEVENS was warmly greeted by his mother and sister on his return from Massachusetts. He had grown to a handsome young man, whose daring blue eye and bold, honest face seemed born to defy tyrants. Rebecca, his sister, was a beautiful maiden, just budding into womanhood. She possessed her father's quiet, gentle, modest demeanor with her mother's beauty. Her great dark eyes were softer than her mother's, and her face and contour were perfections of beauty.

"How glad I am to see you! Oh, how you have grown!" were among the exclamations of his mother.

Robert noticed a great change in her. She was

no longer the proud-spirited being of old. Even when assailed by poverty, she was not crushed and humiliated. Nothing was said of Mr. Price, though he was uppermost in the minds of all. The stepfather was not present; but Robert thought:

"I shall meet him, and the meeting will come soon enough."

When the house was reached he had almost forgotten him. His mother's pale face and wasted form were indications of poor health; but she smiled once more, and he hoped to see the bloom return to the still youthful cheek.

It was early when he disembarked, and Mr. Hugh Price, the royalist, had gone with Governor Berkeley on a fox chase. He returned late that night, and Robert did not see him until next morning. The greeting between Robert and the man whom he heartily despised was formal and cool.

The cavalier was, as usual, dressed with scrupulous care, and, in lace ruffles and silk, sought to conceal his coarse, beastly nature. His fat face and pursed lips, with his bottle nose, all bore evidence of high living and indulgence in the wine cup. The family assembled at the breakfast table and sat in silence through the meal. When it was over, Mr. Price said:

"Robert, I want to see you in my study."

His "study" was a room in which were a few books and a great many implements of the chase. There were horns, whips, spurs, boar spears and guns on the wall. Mr. Price lighted his pipe and, throwing himself into his great easy chair, said:

"Sit down, Robert, I have something to say to you."

Robert closed his lips firmly, for he intuitively felt that what was coming would have something unpleasant about it. Mr. Hugh Price partially raised himself from his chair to close the door. Robert caught a momentary glance of two anxious faces at the foot of the stairs, watching them and evidently wondering how it was all going to end. Having closed the door and shut those friendly countenances out from view, Hugh Price raised his slippered feet and placed them on the stool before him, and smoked in silence. Robert had lost the little fear he had entertained in childhood for his stepfather; but he did not calculate on the cunning and treachery which in Hugh Price had taken the place of strength. He realized not the powerful weapons which Price could wield in the governor and officers of State.

"Robert, you have come back," began Mr. Price, slowly and deliberately, as if he wished to impress what he was about to say more fully on his hearer. "I have some words of advice to offer, and I trust you will profit by them. If you fail to, don't blame me."

Robert, by a respectful nod, indicated that he was listening, and Mr. Price went on:

"We have reached a period when a great civil revolution seems to be at hand. Virginia is about to be shaken by an earthquake, to writhe under intestine wars, and it may be necessary for you to take sides. I warn you to have a care which side you choose, for a mistake means death. You had better know something of the condition of the country before you make your choice."

"I assure you that I am willing to learn all I can of Virginia," Robert answered.

"Very well spoken. I hope that you have eradicated from your mind all those fallacious and treasonable ideas of republicanism. The failure of the commonwealth in England ought to convince any one that republicanism can never succeed."

Robert was silent. So deeply had republicanism been engrafted in his soul that he might as well attempt to tear out his heart, as to think of uprooting it. His meeting with General Goffe and his love for Ester had more strongly cemented his love for liberty; but Robert held his peace, and the stepfather went on.

"Virginia is ruled by a governor and sixteen councillors, commissioned by his majesty, and a grand assembly, consisting of two burgesses from each county, meets annually, which levies taxes, hears appeals and passes laws of all descriptions, which are sent to the lord chancellor for his approval, as in accordance with the laws of the realm. We now have forty thousand people in Virginia, of whom six thousand are white servants and two thousand negro slaves. Since 1619, only three ship-loads of negroes have been brought here, yet by natural increase the negroes have grown a hundredfold."

The cavalier, who delighted in long morning talks over his pipe, paused a moment to rest, and Robert sat wondering what all this could have to do with him. After a moment, Hugh Price resumed:

"The freemen of Virginia number more than eight thousand horse, and are bound to muster monthly in every county, to be ready for the Indians; but the Indians are absolutely subjugated, so there need be no fear of them. There are five forts in Virginia, mounted with thirty cannon, two on James River, and one each on the other three rivers of York, Rappahannock, and Potomac; but we have neither skill nor ability to maintain them. We have a large foreign commerce. Nearly eighty ships every year come out from England and Ireland, and a few ketches from New England, in defiance of the navigation laws, which the people of New England seem more willing to break than are the people of Virginia. We build neither small nor great vessels here, for we are most obedient to all laws, whilst the New England men break them with impunity and trade at any place to which their interests lead them."

"The New England people are prosperous and God-fearing," Robert ventured to put in.

"Yea; but do they not harbor outlaws and regicides. Do not Whalley and Goffe find in that country aiders and abettors in their criminal proceeding?"

"The New Englanders are friendly to the education of the masses."

At this, Hugh Price for an instant lost control of his passion. His master, Sir William Berkeley, in a memorial to parliament, had just said:

"I thank God that there are no free schools, nor printing, and I hope we shall not have them these hundred years; for learning has brought disobedience into the world, and printing has divulged them, and libels against the best governments. God keep us from both!"

Virginia was the last province to submit to the commonwealth and first to declare for the returned monarch, and the royalists residing in Virginia despised what the common people insisted in calling freedom. The commonwealth had driven many excellent royalists from England to Virginia, and while Hugh Price seeks to smother his anger in clouds of tobacco smoke, we will make a quotation from John Esten Cooke's "Virginia" in regard to some of them:

"The character of the king's men who came over during the commonwealth period has been a subject of much discussion. They have been called even by Virginia writers as we have seen, 'butterflies of aristocracy,' who had no influence in affairs or in giving its coloring to Virginia society. The facts entirely contradict the view. They and their descendants were the leaders in public affairs, and exercised a controlling influence upon the community. Washington was the greatgrandson of a royalist, who took refuge in Virginia during the commonwealth. George Mason was the descendant of a colonel, who fought for Charles II. Edmond Pendleton was of royalist origin, and lived and died a most uncompromising churchman. Richard Henry Lee, who moved the Declaration, was of the family of Richard Lee, who had gone to invite Charles II. to Virginia. Peyton and Edmund Randolph, president of the First Congress, and attorney-general were of the old royalist family. Archibald Cary, who threatened to stab Patrick Henry if he were made dictator, was a relative of

Lord Falkland and heir apparent at his death to the barony of Hunsdon. Madison and Monroe were descended from the royalist families—the first from a refugee of 1653, the last from a captain in the army of Charles I., and Patrick Henry and Thomas Jefferson, afterward the leaders of democratic opinion, were of church and king blood, since the father of Henry was a loyal officer who 'drank the king's health at the head of his regiment'; and the mothers of both were Church of England women, descended from royalist families."

With this brief digression, we will return to Hugh Price, who, having smoked himself into a calmer state, turned his eyes upon his wife's son with a look designed to be compassionate and said:

"Robert, it is the great love I bear you, which causes my anxiety about your welfare. I trust that your recent sojourn in New England hath not established the seeds of republicanism and Puritanism in your heart. I trust that any fallacious ideas you may have formed during your absence will become, in the light of reason, eradicated."

"He who is not susceptible of reason is unworthy of being called a reasonable being," Robert answered.

"I am glad to hear you say as much. Now permit me to return to the original subject. Virginia is on the verge of a political irruption, and your arrival may be most opportune or unfortunate."

"I hardly comprehend you."

"There is some dissatisfaction with Governor Berkeley's course with the Indians. Some unreasonable people think that he should prosecute the war against them more vigorously."

"Why does he not?"

"He has good reasons."

"What are they?"

"He has dealings with the Indians in which there are many great fortunes involved. To go to war with them would be sure to lose him and his friends these profits. I am one concerned in these speculations, and it would be a grievous wrong to me were the war prosecuted."

Robert knew something of the savage outrages in Virginia. He had learned of them while on shipboard, and he had some difficulty in restraining his rising indignation, so it was with considerable warmth that he answered:

"Do you think your gains of more value than the human lives sacrificed on the frontier?"

"Such talk is treason," cried Price. "It sounds not unlike Bacon, Cheeseman, Lawrence and Drummond. Have you seen them since your return?"

"I have not, nor did I ever hear of the man Bacon before."

"Have a care! You would do well to avoid Drummond, Cheeseman and Lawrence."

"Why?"

"They are suspected of republicanism. Have naught to do with them."

Some people are so constituted that to refuse them a thing increases their desire for it. Robert would no doubt have gone to hunt up his former friends and rescuers even had not his stepfather forbidden his doing so, but now that Price prohibited his having anything to do with them, he was doubly determined to meet them and learn what they had to say about the threatened trouble.

His mother and sister were waiting in the room below with anxiously beating hearts to know the result of the conference. Sighs of relief escaped both, when they were assured that the meeting had been peaceful.

"Hold your peace, my son," plead the mother, "and do naught to bring more distress upon your poor mother."

Robert realized that a great crisis was coming which would try his soul. He had never broken his word with his mother, and for fear that his conscience might conflict with any promise, he resolved to make none, so he evaded her, by saying:

"Mother, there is no need for apprehension. We are in no danger."

"But your stepfather and you?"

"We have had no new quarrel."

He was about to excuse himself and take a stroll about Jamestown, when he saw a short, stout little fellow, resembling an apple dumpling mounted on two legs, entering the door. Though years had passed since he had seen that form, he knew him at sight. Giles Peram, the traitor and informer, had grown plumper, and his round face seemed more silly. His little eyes had sunk deeper into his fat cheeks, and his lips were puckered as if to whistle. He was attired as a cavalier, with a scarlet laced coat, a waistcoat of yellow velvet and knee breeches of the cavalier, with silk stockings.

"Good day, good people," he said, squeezing his fat little hands together. "I hope you will excuse this visit, for I—I—heard that the brother of my—of the pretty maid had come home, and hastened to congratulate him."

Robert gazed for a moment on the contemptible little fellow, the chief cause of his arrest and banishment and, turning to his mother, asked:

"Do you allow him to come here?"

"We must," she whispered.

"Why?"

"Hush, son; you don't understand it all. I will explain it to you soon."

"You may; but I think I shall change matters, if he is to be a visitor."

"He is the governor's secretary."

"I care not if he be governor himself; he has no business here."

The little fellow, whose face had grown alternately white and purple, stood squeezing his palms and ejaculating:

"Oh, dear me!—oh, dear!—this is very extraordinary—what can this mean?"

"Why do you dare enter this house?" demanded Robert, fiercely.

"Oh, dear, I don't know—I am only a small fellow, you know."

At this moment Mrs. Price and her daughter interposed and begged Robert, for the peace of the family, to make no further remonstrance. He was informed that Giles Peram was the favorite of the governor and Hugh Price, and to insult him would be insulting those high functionaries.

"Why is he here? Whom does he come to see?"

"Perhaps it is Mr. Price!" the mother stammered, casting a glance at Peram, who quickly answered:

"Yes—yes, it is Mr. Price. Will you show

me up to him? I have a very important message from the governor."

He was trembling in every limb, for he expected to be hurled from the house.

Robert went into the street in a sort of maze.

He felt a strange foreboding that all was not right, and that Giles Peram had some deep scheme on foot.

"I will kill the knave, if the governor should hang me for it the next moment," he said in a fit of anger.

It was not long before Robert was at the house of Mr. Lawrence, where he met his friends Drummond and Cheeseman. The three were engaged in a close consultation as if discussing a matter of vital importance. They did not at first recognize Robert, who had grown to manhood; but as soon as he made himself known, they welcomed him back among them, and warm-hearted Cheeseman said:

"I know full well you can be relied upon in this great crisis."

"What is the crisis?" Robert asked.

"We seem on the verge of some sort of a revolution. Virginia welcomed Charles II. and Governor Berkeley as the frogs welcomed the stork, and they, stork like, have begun devouring us."

"I have heard something of the grievances of

the people of Virginia; but I do not know all of them. What leads up to this revolution?"

Mr. Drummond answered:

"The two main grievances are the English navigation acts and the grant of authority to the English noblemen to sell land titles and manage other matters in Virginia. Why, the king hath actually given to Lord Culpepper, a cunning and covetous member of the commission for trade and plantations, and the earl of Arlington, a heartless spendthrift, 'all the dominion of land and water called Virginia, for the term of thirty-one years.' We are permitted by the trade laws to trade only with England in English ships, manned by Englishmen."

"Is it such a great grievance to the people?"

"It is foolish and injurious to the government as well as to ourselves. The system cripples the colony, and, by discouraging production, decreases the English revenue. To profit from Virginia they grind down Virginia. Instead of friends, as we expected, on the restoration, we are beset by enemies, who seize us by the throat and cry: 'Pay that thou owest!'"

"To these grievances are added the confinement of suffrage to freeholders, which hath disfranchised a large number of persons," put in Mr. Drummond.

"Also the failure of the governor to protect the

frontier from the Indians," added Mr. Cheeseman. "These heathen have begun to threaten the colony."

"What cause have they for taking up the hatchet?" asked Robert. Mr. Cheeseman answered:

"Their jealousy was aroused by an expedition made by Captain Henry Batte beyond the mountains. Last summer there was a fight with some of the Indians. A party of Doegs attacked the frontier in Staffard and committed outrages, and were pursued into Maryland by a company of Virginians under Major John Washington. They stood at bay in an old palisaded fort. Six Indians were killed while bringing a flag of truce. The governor said that even though they had slain his nearest relatives, had they come to treat with him he would have treated with them. The Indian depredations have been on the increase until the frontier is unsafe, and this spring, when five hundred men were ready to march against the heathen, Governor Berkeley disbanded them, saying the frontier forts were sufficient protection for the people."

"Are they?" asked Robert.

"No."

"Then why does he not send an army against them?"

"He is engaged in trafficking with the heathen and fears that he may lose, financially, by a war."

"Is gain in traffic of more consequence than human life?"

"With him, it is."

Robert was a lover of humanity, and in a moment he had taken sides. He was a republican and his fate was cast with Bacon, even before he had seen this remarkable man.

CHAPTER XVIII.

THE SWORD OF DEFENCE.

He stood—some dread was on his face,
Soon hatred settled in its place:
It rose not with the reddening flush
Of transient anger's hasty blush,
But pale as marble o'er the tomb,
Whose ghastly whiteness aids its gloom.
—BYRON.

ROBERT STEVENS returned home, his mind filled with strange, wild thoughts. It was a lovely evening in early spring. The moon, round and full, rose from out its watery bed and shed a soft, refulgent glow on this most delightful of all climes. Below was the bay, on which floated many barks, and among them the vessel which had so recently brought him from Boston. The little town lay quiet and peaceful on the hill where his grandfather and Captain John Smith sixty years ago had planted it. Beyond were the dark forests, gloomy and forbidding, as if they concealed many foes of the white men; but those woods were not all dark and forbidding. From them issued the sweet perfumes of wild flowers and the songs of night birds, such as are known in Virginia.

Young Stevens was in no mood to be impressed by the surrounding scenery. He was repeating under his breath:

"*Tyranny! tyranny! tyranny!*"

Robert loved freedom as dearly as he loved Ester Goffe, and one was as necessary to his existence as the other. Now, on his return to the land of his nativity, he found the ruler, once so mild and popular, grown to a tyrant.

"His office is for life," sighed Robert. "And too much power hath made him mad."

Reaching the house, he heard voices in the front room and among them that of his sister. She was greatly agitated, and he heard her saying:

"No, no, Mr. Peram. I—don't understand you."

"Not understand me? I love you, sweet maid. Do I not make myself plain?"

"No, no; do not talk that way; pray do not."

"But you must promise, sweet maid, to wed me. I adore you."

At this the scoundrel caught her hand, and Rebecca uttered a scream of terror. Her brother waited to hear no more, but leaped boldly into the room and, seizing Mr. Giles Peram by the collar of his coat and the waistband of his costly knee-breeches, held him at arm's length, and began applying first one and then another pedal extremity to his anatomy.

Mr. Peram squirmed and howled:

"Oh, dear! Oh, let me go! This is very extraordinary!" his small eyes growing dim and his fat cheeks pale.

"You knave! How dare you thus annoy my sister?" cried Robert, still kicking the rascal. At last he led him to the door and flung him down the front steps, where he fell in a heap on the ground with such force, that one might have thought his neck was broken. Robert turned to his sister and asked:

"Where is mother?"

"She hath gone with her husband to Greensprings."

"And left you alone?"

"It was thought you would come."

Robert Stevens felt guilty of neglect in lingering too long in the company of men whom Berkeley would regard as conspirators; but he immediately excused himself on the ground that he had had no knowledge of the intended departure of his mother, or that his sister would be left alone.

"Have you suffered annoyances from him before?"

"Yes."

"Does mother know of it?"
"She does."
"And makes no effort to protect you?"

HE FLUNG HIM DOWN THE FRONT STEPS, WHERE HE FELL IN A HEAP ON THE GROUND.

"She does all she can; but—but Mr. Price sanctions the marriage."

"I think I understand why you were left," said Robert, bitterly; "but I will protect you, never fear. That disgusting pigmy of humanity, that silly idiot and false swearer shall not harm you. I will take you to uncle's."

"Alas, he is dead. He was appointed governor to Carolinia and died."

"But our father's sister will give you a home, if the persecution becomes too hard for you to endure."

With such assurances, he consoled her as only a stout, brave brother can, and to win her mind from the subject that tormented her most, he told her of Ester Goffe and their betrothal, with a few of his wild adventures in New England, where, at this time, King Philip's war was raging with relentless fury.

Then his sister retired, and he sought repose. Next morning his mother was at breakfast; but Hugh Price was absent. He asked no questions about him. Nothing was said of the summary manner in which he had disposed of Mr. Peram, and it was a week before he saw his sister's unwelcome suitor.

The little fellow was standing on a platform making a speech to some sailors and idlers. The harangue was silly, as all his speeches were.

"If the king wants brave soldiers to cope with

these rebels, let him send me to command them. Fain would I lead an army against the vagabonds."

At this, some wag in the crowd made a remark about the diminutive size of the speaker, and the ludicrous figure he would cut as a general, at which he became enraged and cried:

"Begone, knave! Do you think I talk to fools? Nay, I speak sense."

"Which is very extraordinary," put in the wag. This so exasperated the orator, that he fumed and raged about the platform and, not taking heed which way he went, tumbled backward off the stage, which brought his harangue to an inglorious close.

Shouts of laughter went up from the assembled group at his mishap, and the orator retired in disgust.

Robert Stevens was more amused than any other person at the manner in which Giles Peram had terminated his speech. He went home and told his sister, who laughed as much as he did.

That night, near midnight, Robert was awakened from a sound sleep by some one tapping on his window lattice. He rose, at first hardly able to believe his senses; but the moon was shining quite brightly, and he distinctly saw the outline of a man standing outside his window, and there came a tapping unquestionably intended to wake him.

"Who are you?" he asked, going to the window.

"I am Drummond," was the answer, and he now recognized his father's friend standing on the rounds of a ladder which he had placed against the house at the side of his window. On the ground below were two more men, whom he recognized as Mr. Cheeseman and the thoughtful Mr. Lawrence.

"What will you, Mr. Drummond?"

"Come forth; we have something to say to you. Dress for a journey and bring what weapons you have, as you may need them."

Robert hurriedly dressed and buckled on a breastplate and sword with a brace of pistols. He had a very fine rifle, which he brought away with him, as well as a supply of flints, a horn full of powder to the very throat, and plenty of bullets. With these, he crept from the house and joined the three men under the tree. Mr. Drummond said:

"The Indians have again risen in their fury, and attacked the frontier, killing many, and have carried some of your kinspeople away captives."

Robert was roused. He was in a frenzy and vowed that if no one else would go, he would himself pursue the savages and rescue his relatives.

"You will have aid," assured Mr. Drummond. "The people are enraged at the carelessness of the governor, and if they can secure a leader, they will go and punish the Indians."

"Leader or no leader, I shall go to the rescue of my relatives. My father's sister and children are captives; think you I would remain at home for lack of a leader?"

"We will find one in Nathaniel Bacon."

"Who is he?" asked Robert, as if he still feared the willingness or ability of the proposed leader to conduct the crusade against the savages. Mr. Drummond answered:

"Bacon is a young man who has not yet arrived at thirty years. His family belongs to the English gentry, for he is a cousin of Lord Culpepper and married a daughter of Sir John Duke. He run out his patrimony in England and hath, by his liberality, exhausted the most of what he brought to Virginia. He came here four years ago and settled at Curles on the upper James River. His uncle, who lives in Virginia, was a member of the king's council. He is Nathaniel Bacon, senior, a very rich politic man and childless, who designs his nephew, Nathaniel Bacon, junior, for his heir."

"Has he ability for a leader?" asked Robert.

"He hath; his abilities have been so highly recognized, that he was appointed soon after his arrival to a place in the council."

This was a position of great dignity, rarely conferred upon any but men of matured age and large estate, and Bacon was only twenty-eight, and his estate small. His personal character is seen on the face of his public career. He was impulsive and subject to fits of passion, or, as the old writers say, "of a precipitate disposition."

Bacon came near being the Virginia Cromwell. Though he never wholly redeemed his adopted country from tyranny, he put the miscreant Berkeley to flight. On that May night in 1676, Bacon was at his Curles plantation, just below the old city of Henricus, living quietly on his estate with his beautiful young wife Elizabeth. He had another estate in what is now the suburbs of the present city of Richmond, which is to-day known as "Bacon's Quarter Branch." His servants and overseers lived here, and he could easily go thither in a morning's journey on his favorite dapple gray, or by rowing seven miles around the Dutch Gap peninsula, could make the journey in his barge. When not at his upper plantation or in attendance at the council, he was living the quiet and unassuming life of a planter at Curles, where he entertained his neighbors, and being by nature a lover of the divine rights of man, he boldly denounced the trade laws, the Arlington and Culpepper grants, and the governor for his lukewarmness in defending the frontier against the Indians. Though one of the gentry, who had it in his power to become a favorite, the manifest tyranny of Governor Berkeley so shocked his sense of right and justice, that he was ready to condemn the whole system of government.

When the report came to him that the Indians were about to renew their outrages on the upper waters of the James River, Bacon flew into a rage and, tossing his arms about in a wild gesticulation, as was his manner, declared:

"If they kill any of my people, d—n my blood, I will make war on them, with or without authority, commission or no commission."

The hour was not long in coming when his resolution was put to the test.

In May, 1676, two days before Robert was awakened from his midnight slumbers by Drummond, the Indians had attacked his estate at the Falls, killed his overseer and one of his servants, and were going to carry fire and hatchet through the frontier. The wild news flew from house to house. The planters and frontiersmen sprang to arms and began to form a combination against these dangerous enemies.

Governor Berkeley had refused to commission any one as commander of the forces, and the colonists were without a head. The silly old egotist who ruled Virginia declared that there was no danger from the Indians, and even while the frontiersmen were battling with them for their lives, he wrote to the home government that all trouble with the natives was happily over. When the Virginians assembled, they were without a leader.

It was on this occasion that Robert was awakened at night, as we have seen, and asked to arm himself and prepare for a journey. That midnight journey was to Curles where the planters were assembled preparatory to making a descent on the enemy, which they were long to remember. When Robert was informed of the plan, he asked for a moment's time to confer with his sister, that he might notify her of his departure.

He knew the room in which Rebecca slept, and going to her door, tapped lightly until he heard her stirring, and the voice within asked:

"Who are you?"

"It is your brother," he whispered. A moment later the pretty face of the sleepy girl, surrounded by the neat border of a night-cap, appeared, and he hastily informed her that the Indians, in ravaging the frontier, had carried away their relatives, and he was going to set out to recover them. She knew the political situation of the country and the danger of the governor's wrath; but she could not detain her brother from such a mission.

Having explained to her that he was going to recover the captives and knew not when he would return, he went hurriedly away to join his companions. A horse was ready saddled for him, and they rode nearly all the remainder of the night, and at dawn were at Curles where was found a considerable number of riflemen. As they came upon the group, Robert saw a young man with dark eyes and hair, a face that was ruddy, yet denoting nervous temperament. He was tall and graceful, and his bold, vehement spirit seemed at once to take fire, and his enthusiasm kindled a conflagration in the breasts of his hearers. He spoke of their wrongs, of their governor's avarice, who would for the sake of his traffic with the Indians sacrifice their lives. They were not assembled for vengeance, but for defence against a ruthless foe. There was no outward expression of rebellion in his speech, yet he enlarged on the grievances of the time. That speech was an ominous indication of coming events.

"Who is that man?" Robert asked.

"Nathaniel Bacon," was the answer.

This was the first time he had ever seen the man so noted in history as the great Virginia rebel, yet from the very first Robert was strangely impressed with the earnestness of the stranger.

Bacon had been chosen as commander of the Virginians, and had sent to Berkeley for his commission. The governor did not refuse the commission; but he did what practically amounted to the same, failed to send it. It was to this that Bacon was referring when Robert Stevens and his friends joined the group.

"Instead of sending the commission which I desired, he hath politely notified me that the times are troubled," Bacon said, "that the issue of my business might be dangerous, that, unhappily, my character and fortunes might become imperiled if I proceed. The commission is refused; his complimentary expressions amount to nothing; the veil is too thin to impose on us; the Indians are still ravaging the frontier. They have been furnished with firelocks and powder—by whom? By the governor in his traffic with them. If you, good housekeepers, will sustain me, I will assault the savages in their stronghold."

All, with one accord, assented and declared themselves willing to be led to the assault. Bacon was at once chosen as the commander of the army. When he learned that Robert and his friends had come from Jamestown to aid the people on the frontier, he came to welcome them to his ranks and to assure them that he appreciated their courage and humanity.

"I have relatives and friends who are captives of the Indians," Robert explained, "and I shall rescue them or perish in the effort."

"Bravo! spoken like an Englishman. We are kindling a fire which may yet consume royalty in Virginia."

Nathaniel Bacon was politic, however, and before setting out against the Indians dispatched another messenger to Jamestown for a commission as commander. The game between the man of twenty-eight and the man of seventy had begun. Both possessed violent tempers; both were proud and resolute, and the man of seventy was wholly unscrupulous. The prospects were good for a bitter warfare. The old cavalier attempted to end it by striking a sudden blow at his adversary. Bacon and his army were on their march through the forest to the seat of Indian troubles, when an emissary of the governor came in hot haste with a proclamation, denouncing Nathaniel Bacon and his deluded followers as rebels, and ordered them to disperse. If they persisted in their illegal proceedings, it would be at their peril.

Governor Berkeley could not have chosen a more effective way of crippling the expedition. The resolution of the most wealthy of the armed housekeepers were shaken. They feared a confiscation more than hanging or decapitation. One hundred and seventy of the followers of Bacon obeyed the order and abandoned the expedition.

Fifty-seven horsemen remained steadfast.

Among them was Robert Stevens, who was young and reckless as his daring leader.

The Indians had entrenched themselves on a hill east of the present city of Richmond, and when the whites approached them, they as usual sent forth a flag of truce to parley with them. The men who remained with Bacon were nearly all frontiersmen who had suffered more or less from the savages.

John Whitney, a frontiersman, had had his home destroyed, and his wife and child slain by the Indians. While the parley was going on, John discovered the Indian who had slain his wife and child, and, recognizing their scalps hanging at the savage's girdle, he levelled his rifle at the savage and shot him dead.

The Indians gave utterance to yells of rage, and from the hill-top poured down a volley at the white men; but the bullets and arrows passed quite over their heads. Bacon saw that the moment for a charge had arrived, and, raising himself in his stirrups, he shouted:

"There are the devils who slew your friends and kindred. It is their lives or ours. Strike for vengeance! Charge!"

Not a man faltered. Never did husbands, fathers and brothers dash forward into battle more fearlessly. Each man thought only of his own little home exposed to the ravages of the enemy, and the whistling of balls and arrows did not deter him. The enemy were entrenched in a fort of logs. They outnumbered the Virginians ten to one; but the latter charged nobly forward, plunging into the stream which lay between them and the fort, and wading through the water shoulder deep.

"There are the enemy; storm the fort!" cried Bacon. Ever in the van, mounted on his dapple gray, where bullets flew thickest, he was here and there and everywhere, urging and encouraging the men by word and example. They needed little encouragement, for the atrocities of the Indian had fired the blood of the Virginians, until the most timid among them became brave as a lion.

Robert Stevens kept at the side of Bacon, imitating his example. Robert was mounted on an English bay, a famous fox-hunter, and accustomed to leaping barriers. Bacon knew nothing of the science of Indian warfare, even if he knew anything of war at all. Indian tactics are entirely different from civilized warfare and require a different mode to meet them; but though the hero of Virginia four years before was thoroughly ignorant of Indians, he seemed to acquire the necessary knowledge in a moment. He was the man for the occasion.

Side by side Bacon and Robert dashed at the palisade and leaped their horses over it. They emptied their rifles and fired their pistols at such close range, that the effect was murderous. Others followed, leaping down among the savages, and opened fire. When guns and pistols had belched forth their deadly contents, the more deadly sabre was drawn, and the Indians were slain without mercy.

The buildings were fired, and the four thousand pounds of powder, which the Indians had procured of the governor, were blown up. One hundred and fifty Indians were slain, while Bacon lost only three of his own party. This victory is famous in history as the "Battle of Bloody Run," so called from the fact that the blood of the Indians ran down into the stream beneath the hill. Among some of the captives taken by the Indians, Robert Stevens found his relatives and restored them to their homes and friends.

The Indians were routed and sent flying toward the mountains, and Bacon went back toward Curles.

Meanwhile Berkeley was not idle. He raised a troop of horse to pursue and conquer the rebels; but to his alarm he found the people quite outspoken and, in fact, in open rebellion in the lower tiers of counties.

When the burgesses met in June, Bacon embarked in his sloop and went to Jamestown, taking Robert Stevens and about thirty friends with him. No sooner had the sloop landed than the cannon of a ship were trained on it, and Bacon was arrested and taken to Governor Berkeley in the statehouse.

The haughty governor was somewhat awed by the turmoil and confusion which prevailed throughout Jamestown, and feared to appear stern with so popular a man as Bacon.

"Mr. Bacon, have you forgot to be a gentleman?" the governor asked.

"No, may it please your honor," Bacon answered, quite coolly.

"Then I will take your parole," said Berkeley.

Bacon was consequently paroled, though not given privilege to leave Jamestown. There was much murmuring and discontent among the people, who vowed that they had only "appealed to the sword as a defence against the bloody heathen."

CHAPTER XIX.

THE MYSTERIOUS STRANGER.

"Do you know the old man of the sea, of the sea?
Have you met with that dreadful old man?
If you haven't been caught, you will be, you will be;
For catch you he must and he can."
—HOLMES.

ROBERT STEVENS and twenty others captured with Bacon were kept in prison. His mother and sisters visited him, but he saw nothing of his stepfather. One evening he was informed that a gentleman wished to see him, and immediately Mr. Giles Peram was admitted to his cell.

"How are you, Robert—ahem?" began Giles. "This is most extraordinary, I assure you, and you have my sympathy, and you may not believe it, no, you may not believe it, but I am sorry for you."

"You can spare yourself any tears on my account," the prisoner answered, casting a look of scorn and indignation on the proud little fellow who strutted before him with ill-concealed exultation. Without noticing the irony in the words of the prisoner, Giles puffed up with the importance of his mission, went on:

"Robert, I have come to you with a singular proposition. Now you are very anxious to know what it is, are you not?"

"I have some curiosity; yet I have no doubt that I shall treat your proposition with contempt."

"Oh, no, you won't. Your life depends on your acceptance."

"I can best answer you when I know what your proposition is."

"It is this. I am enamoured of your sister. She rejects my suit. Now, if she will consent to become my wife, you shall have your liberty."

It was well for Peram that Robert Stevens was chained to the wall, or it would have fared hard for the little fellow. Giles kept beyond the length of the chain and the prisoner was powerless. His only weapon was his tongue; but with that he poured out the vials of his wrath so copiously on the wretch, that he retired in disgust.

Events soon shaped themselves so as to give Robert his liberty. Through the intercession of Bacon's cousin, Nathaniel Bacon, senior, the governor consented to pardon Bacon the rebel, if he would, on his knees, read a written confession of his error and ask forgiveness. This confession was made June 5, 1676. Between the last days of May and the 5th of June, Bacon had been denounced as a rebel; had marched and defeated the savages; had stood for the burgesses and appeared at Jamestown; had been arrested and quickly paroled, and was now, on the 5th of June, to confess on his knees that he was a great offender. The old cavalier Berkeley was going to make an imposing scene of it. The governor sent the burgesses a message to attend him in the council chamber below, on public business, and when they came, he addressed them on the Indian troubles, specially denouncing the murder of the six chiefs in Maryland, though Colonel Washington, who commanded the forces on that expedition, was present. With pathetic emphasis the governor declared:

"Had they killed my grandfather and grandmother, my father and mother and all my friends, yet if they came to treat of peace, they ought to have gone in peace." Having finished this harangue, designed for the humiliation of John Washington and his followers, he rose and with grim humor said:

"If there be joy in the presence of the angels over one sinner that repenteth, there is joy now, for we have a penitent sinner come before us. Call Mr. Bacon."

Bacon came in, holding the paper in his trembling hand, and, kneeling, read his confession. It evidently grieved his lion heart to do so, for at times he faltered, and his voice, usually clear and distinct, was half smothered. When he had finished, Sir William Berkeley said:

"God forgive you; I forgive you," and three times he repeated the words.

"And all that were with him?" asked Colonel Cole, one of the council.

Hugh Price, who was present, was about to interpose some objection; but before he could say anything, Sir William Berkeley answered:

"Yes, and all that were with him." As Bacon rose from his knees, the governor took his hand and added: "Mr. Bacon, if you will live civilly but till next quarter day, but till next quarter day, I'll promise to restore you to your place there," pointing to the seat which Bacon generally occupied during the sessions of the council.

The order to release the prisoners was at once given, and Robert Stevens was again a free man. He hastened to the home of his mother and sister, where he met his stepfather, whose conduct was so odious to the young man that he took up his abode at "the house of public entertainment kept by the wife of a certain thoughtful Mr. Lawrence." Bacon was also living here under his parole, for it was generally understood that he had not been given permission to leave the city.

One morning, just as the excitement incident to the arrest and confession of Bacon had begun to subside, a large ship entered the river and cast anchor before the town. The ship flew English colors and was a veritable floating palace. There are few crafts afloat even at this day that equal it in elegance. It had been built by the most skilful carpenters in the world at that time, and the long, tapering masts, the deck and bows were more of the modern style than ships of that day.

Her cabins were large, roomy and fitted up with more than Oriental splendor. There were Turkish carpets, and golden candelabra. Wealth, strength, ease and grace were evident in every part of the strange craft. No such vessel had ever before entered James River. The ship was well armed, and the crew thoroughly disciplined. There was a long brass cannon in the forecastle, with carronades above and below, for she was a double-decker with a row of guns above and below, and at that time such a formidable craft was able to destroy half of the English navy. The name of the vessel was not in keeping with her general appearance. In spite of the elegance and magnificence of the vessel, on her stern, in great black letters, was the awful word:

"Despair."

What strange freak had induced the owner of

this wonderful craft to give it such a melancholy name? Jamestown was thrown into a flutter of excitement at first, and whispered rumors went about that the vessel was a pirate. If it should prove a pirate, they knew it would be able to destroy the town and all their fleet. This story was perhaps started by some idlers, who sought to go aboard when the vessel first arrived, but were refused admittance to her deck.

Though not permitted to go aboard, those loafers had seen enough to start the report that the vessel was a gilded palace, ornamented with gold. Two days had elapsed, and no one had come ashore, nor had any visitor been admitted to the ship, and the governor, growing uneasy about the strange craft, resolved to know something of it, so he sent the sheriff to ascertain her mission.

The captain of the ship, who gave his name as George Small, answered:

"This vessel is the property of Sir Albert St. Croix, a wealthy merchant from the East Indies, who will this day visit the governor and make known the object of his visit to Jamestown."

That day, a boat fit for a king was lowered, and eight or ten sailors, richly dressed, took their places at the oars. A man, whose long white hair hung about his shoulders in snowy profusion, and whose beard, white as the swan's down, came to his breast, descended to the boat and was rowed ashore.

When he was landed, the sailors returned with the boat to the ship, leaving him on the beach. The old man was richly dressed. He blazed with jewels such as a king might envy, and the hilt of his sword was of pure gold. He wore a brace of slender pistols, whose silver-mounted butts protruded from his belt.

The dark cloak about his shoulders was Puritanic; but the elegance of his attire and the profusion of jewelry which he wore proved that he was not of that order. His low-crowned hat was three-cornered, trimmed with lace and the brim held in place by three blazing diamonds. It was something like the cocked hat, which, half a century later, was worn by most of the gentry.

After watching the boat until it returned to the vessel, the old man went toward the statehouse. He spoke to no one on the way, though he paused under a large oak about half way between the statehouse and the beach, and gazed long on the town and surrounding country.

The tree beneath which he paused was the same under whose wide spreading branches Captain John Smith had halted to take a last farewell look of Virginia, before embarking for England. The spot had already grown historic.

The people were gathered in groups on the streets gazing at the stranger, and various were the comments about him. He noticed the excitement his advent had created, and walked quickly up the street to the statehouse. Though his hair and beard were white as snow, his frame was vigorous and strong, and his step had about it the elasticity of youth. His brow was furrowed with care rather than time, and his eye seemed still to flash with the fires of young manhood. Nevertheless he was an old man. Every one who saw him on that memorable morning pronounced him a prodigy.

Arriving at the statehouse, he asked for the governor, and was at once shown to Sir William, who, gazing at him in wonder, asked:

"Whence came you, stranger?"

"From Liverpool."

"Who are you?"

"I am Sir Albert St. Croix, the owner of the good ship *Despair*, which lies at anchor in your bay."

"But surely you are not of England?"

"I am an Englishman; but I have spent most of my life abroad, and for many years have been in the East Indies. I amassed a fortune in diamonds and jewels and, being in the decline of life, decided to travel over the world. For that purpose, I builded me a ship to suit and engaged a crew faithful even unto death."

The governor's countenance brightened, and he answered:

"Sir Albert, I am pleased to have you in Jamestown. Your arrival is quite opportune, for I am most grievously annoyed with a threatened rebellion."

Sir Albert fixed his great blue eyes on the governor and answered:

"Sir William Berkeley, it is not my purpose to interfere with any political convulsions. I am simply a transient visitor. My home is my ship."

"But your ship is an English craft, and your crew are Englishmen?"

"That is true."

"And as governor of the province, I will command them should their services be needed."

There was a smile on the sad face of Sir Albert, as he answered:

"It would not avail you, governor, for my captain and crew know no other master save myself, no will save mine."

"But the king?"

"They serve me, and I serve the king. I helped Charles II. out of a financial strait, and, for that, an order from our dread sovereign and lord has been issued, exempting my crew, myself and my vessel from any kind of military duty for the term of fifty years."

The old man drew from his coat pocket a legal document proving his assertion.

"Have you ever been in Virginia before?" the governor asked.

"Yes, many years ago. All things have changed since then."

"How long will you stay?"

"I know not. At any moment I may decide to leave, and should I do so, I will sail at once. I linger no longer at any one place than my fancy detains me."

"What is your wish, Sir Albert?"

"I only ask the privilege of going whithersoever I please in your domain, without let or hindrance," and he produced an order from King Charles II., which commanded Governor Berkeley to grant him such privilege.

"This is strange," said the governor. "An armament such as yours might overthrow the colony at this unsettled time."

"I shall take no part in the disturbance, unless it affects me personally." The governor issued a passport for Sir Albert St. Croix, vessel and crew, and the stranger left the statehouse. He walked up the hill, passing the jail, and gazing about on the houses, as if he wished to make himself acquainted with the town. No end of comment was excited by his appearance, and a thousand conjectures were afloat as to the object of his visit.

For a moment, the white-haired stranger paused before the public house in which Bacon was at that moment reposing. Some thought he was going in; but he passed on and addressed no one, until he came to Robert Stevens, who stood at the side of a well, under a wide spreading chestnut tree.

"Will you draw me some water? for I am athirst," said the stranger.

Robert did so, and handed the stranger a drink from an earthen mug, which was kept by the town pump for the accommodation of the public. After drinking, the old man returned the mug and, fixing his eyes on the young man, asked:

"Have you lived long in Virginia?"

"I was born here, good sir."

"Then you must know all of Jamestown?"

"Not so much, good sir, as I might, if I had not passed a few years in New England."

"Your home is still here?"

With a sigh, Robert answered:

"It is, though I do not live in it now."

Robert evidently was alluding to some domestic difficulties, and the stranger very considerately avoided asking him any further questions about himself. He asked about the proprietors of several houses and gained something of the history of the town and people.

All expected that Sir Albert would return to his vessel; but he did not. Instead, he wandered over the hill into the wood and sat down upon a log. Robert saw him sitting there, with his white head bowed between his hands, looking so sad and broken-hearted, despite all his wealth, that his heart went out to him. He was for hours thus communing with nature, then came back to the town and went on board the *Despair*.

After that, he frequently came ashore and strolled about the town, seldom speaking, even when addressed. But for the letters from the governor and the king, he might have been arrested on suspicion. He came and went at will, occasionally pausing to ask a question which was so guarded, that no one could suspect that he was interested in any particular subject. One day, as he was passing the statehouse, Giles Peram, who, with the powdered wig, lace, and ruffles of a cavalier, was strutting before some of the court officials, turning his eyes with an ill-bred stare on the stranger as he passed, remarked:

"Oh, how extraordinary!"

Sir Albert paused and, fixing his great blue eyes on the diminutive egotist, said:

"Marry! the time of king's fools hath past; yet the king of fools still reigns."

Giles Peram felt the retort most keenly, and, as usual, raged and fumed and swore vengeance after the stranger was out of sight and hearing. Sir Albert strolled down to a pond or lake that was near to the town, on the banks of which was an ancient ducking-stool. Three or four idlers were sitting on the bank, and of one of them he asked:

"For what is that ugly machine used?"

"It is a ducking-stool for scolds," was the answer. The fellow, feeling complimented at being addressed by the celebrated stranger, went on, "Well do I remember, good sir, when and for whom the stool was constructed."

"For whom was it built?" asked Sir Albert.

"It was made for Ann Linkon, who had slandered goodwife Stevens as was, but who has, since her husband was drowned at sea, married Hugh Price, the royalist and friend of the governor. Oh, how Ann did scold and rave, and it was a merry sight to see her plunged beneath the water."

The stranger asked some questions about Ann Linkon and was informed that she had died several years before. "But to the last," the narrator resumed, "she hated Dorothe Stevens. She rejoiced when poverty assailed her, brought on by her own extravagance, after her husband had gone away. Then when goodwife Stevens received the fortune from the grandfather of her dead husband, the old Spaniard at St. Augustine, she again went among the cavaliers and was enabled to marry Hugh Price. It is not a happy life she leads now, though, for there is continual trouble between the husband and the children, so she is grievously harassed in mind continually."

Sir Albert listened as an uninterested person might, then asked some questions about Hugh Price and his good wife Dorothe, and the refractory children, who were causing so much trouble. He found the Virginian voluble and willing to impart all the information he had; but he grew heartily tired of the loafer and at last left him.

No one was more interested in the stranger from across the sea than Rebecca Stevens. She had not seen him; but she had heard so much of him from her brother and others, that her girlish curiosity was aroused. One evening, as she was taking her favorite walk about the village, having wandered farther than she intended, she found herself in the wood above the town, near the old building, which Captain John Smith had called the glass-house. She turned and began at once retracing her steps, for already the sun had set, and the shades of night were gathering over the landscape. She was in sight of the church, when a short, fat little man suddenly met her. He was out of breath, as if he had been running. In the gathering twilight she recognized him as her persecutor.

"Ah! Miss Stevens, this is truly extraordinary. Believe me, this meeting is quite providential, for it enables me to pour into your ear my tale of love."

"Mr. Peram, begone, leave me!"

"Oh, no, my dear, I will never let you go until you have consented to take my name."

In his zeal, the ungentlemanly wooer seized her hand, and his vicious little eyes glared at her with such ferocity, that she gave utterance to a shriek of fear. The tread of hurried feet fell on her ears, and through the deepening shades of twilight, she caught a glimpse of a scarlet coat, long white hair and beard and flashing jewels. Hands of iron seized Giles Peram. He was lifted into the air as if he had been an infant, and flung head first into a cluster of white thorn, where he lay for a few moments, confused and bleeding. Then Sir Albert St. Croix raised the half-fainting Rebecca from the ground and said:

"Come, my child, be not affrighted; he will not harm you."

She gazed up at the kind face and asked:

"Are you the owner of the ship *Despair?*"

"I am."

"Thank you, Sir Albert," she began; but he quickly interrupted her with:

"Thank not me, sweet child; but come, tell me what hath gone amiss, and have no fear, for I am powerful enough to save you from any harm."

While the villanous little coward Giles Peram crawled from the hedge and hurried back to town, the old man led the victim of his insults to the church, where they sat upon the step at the front of the vestibule. She had no fear of this good old man, whom she instinctively loved, and who seemed to wield over her a strange and mysterious influence. He asked her all about her tormentor, and she confided everything to him. She told him of the loss of her father at sea, and how they had lived through adversity until better days dawned, then of her mother's second marriage, and the trouble between her brother and Hugh Price. She did not even omit the recent uprising in which her brother had joined Bacon and the rebels in a mad blow for freedom.

"The worst has not yet come, I greatly fear," sighed the little maid. "The rebellion is not over, and my brother will yet, I fear, be hung by the governor, for Mr. Price, his bitter enemy, is a firm friend of the governor."

"He shall not be harmed, sweet maid. I have a great ship, with larger and more destructive guns than were ever in Virginia. I have a crew loyal even unto death, and I could bombard and destroy their town, ere they harm either your brother, yourself or your mother."

He looked so earnest, so like a good angel of deliverance, that the impulsive Rebecca threw her arms about his neck, and he, pressing a kiss upon her fair young cheek, exclaimed:

"God bless you! There, I must go."

He conducted her home, went aboard his ship, and next morning the mysterious craft had disappeared from the harbor.

There were too many exciting incidents transpiring at Jamestown for the public to dwell long on the stranger. The same day on which the ship disappeared, the rumor ran about town:

"Bacon has fled! Bacon has fled!"

The rumor was a truth. Robert Stevens had gone with him, and although Mr. Lawrence explained that Bacon's wife was ill, and he had gone to visit her, yet Berkeley, ever suspicious, construed his sudden breaking of his parole into open hostility, and prepared to treat it accordingly.

CHAPTER XX.

BACON A REBEL.

"Hark! 'tis the sound that charms
The war-steed's wakening ears.
Oh! many a mother folds her arms
Round her boy-soldier, when that call she hears,
And though her fond heart sink with fears,
Is proud to feel his young pulse bound
With valor's fervor at the sound."
—MOORE.

THE day after the mysterious disappearance of the ship *Despair* and the flight of Bacon, a ship from New England arrived in port. Bacon's flight and the disappearance of Sir Albert and his vessel were so nearly at the same time, that a rumor went around the town that the former had escaped in the vessel of the latter. This rumor however was soon dispelled on learning that Bacon was at Curles rallying the planters about him.

The vessel which had just come into port aroused new speculations, until it was learned that it was only a trading ship from Boston doing a little business in defiance of the navigation laws,

The vessel brought only one passenger. That passenger was a beautiful young maid.

She was landed soon after the vessel cast anchor, and her first inquiry was for Rebecca Stevens:

"Is she a relative of yours, young maid?" asked the man of whom she inquired.

"No; I know of her, and would see her."

"Do you see the large brick house upon the hill —not the one on the left of the church, but to the right with the broad piazza and wires in front?"

"I see it."

"She lives there. It is the home of Hugh Price, who married her mother."

The sailors brought some baggage ashore which was carried to a warehouse to remain until the fair traveller should send for it, and pay the costs of transfer.

"Do you travel alone, young maid?" asked the man whom she had addressed.

"I do."

"Where is your mother?"

"Dead," she answered sadly.

"Then you are an orphan?"

"I am. War is raging with the Indians in New England, and I was not safe there, so I came to Virginia."

She thanked the man who had so kindly directed her, and went to the house of Hugh Price. This house, next to the home of Governor Berkeley, was the most elegant mansion in Virginia. On the front door was a large brass knocker, common at the time, and, seizing it, the young girl struck the door. It was opened by a negro woman whose red turban and rich dress indicated that she was the household servant of an aristocratic family. The stranger asked for Rebecca Stevens, and was shown to her room. Rebecca was astonished to see the pretty stranger; but before she could ask who she was, the maid said:

"I am Ester Goffe from Massachusetts. The war with the Indians rages sorely in that land, and my friends and relatives sent me here."

"Ester — Ester Goffe," stammered Rebecca. "Then you are my brother's affianced."

"I am."

In a moment the girls were clasped in each other's arms, mingling their tears of joy and grief. Then Rebecca held her at arm's length and, gazing on the beautiful face and soft brown eyes, said:

"I don't blame Robert. How could he help loving you?" and once more she clasped her in her arms.

"Where is he—where is Robert?"

Rebecca started at the question, and an expression of pain swept over her face, which alarmed Ester.

"Alas, he is gone. He hath fled with Bacon,

and I fear that you have escaped from one calamity only to fall into another." Then she explained the distracted condition of the country, concluding with:

"You must not be known here as Ester Goffe. Were it known by Sir William Berkeley, or even my mother's husband, that the child of a regicide was here, I know not what the result would be; but, alas, I fear it would be your ruin."

"But can I see him?" asked Ester.

"Who, Sir William Berkeley or Mr. Hugh Price?"

"Robert."

A pallor overspread the sister's face at this request, and she answered that she knew not how they could communicate with him.

"Have you no faithful servant?"

There was old black Sam who had always been faithful. Usually the negroes were cunning as well as treacherous, for, having been but recently brought from Africa, they had much of the heathen still in their natures; but old black Sam had been faithful to the brother through all trying scenes and adversities, and, though he dared not "cross Master Price," he secretly aided Rebecca in many small schemes objectionable to the step-father. Sam was summoned, and Rebecca asked:

"Sam, could you find my brother?"

"I doan know, misse; but I believe old black Sam could."

"Would you take a small bit of writing to him?"

"If misse want um to go, ole black Sam, him try. De bay hoss, him go fast, an' black Sam, him go on um back."

Rebecca hastily wrote on a slip of paper:

DEAR BROTHER;—
Ester is at our house and would like to see you. Do not come unless you can do so safely, for Sir William Berkeley is furious.
Your sister,
REBECCA.

Meanwhile, the fiery General Bacon was not at Curles nursing his sick wife, as was reported (and who was not sick at all); but he, in company with Robert Stevens, was riding to and fro, at the heads of the rivers, sounding the slogan. At the word from Bacon, his friends rose in arms, and among them were a part of the eight thousand horse which Berkeley had reported in the colony. The people had borne enough of Berkeley's tyranny, and the masses sided with Bacon. Even those who did not take up arms in his defence were friendly to his interests. The clans were gathering. They hastened from plantation and hundred, from lowland manor-house and log cabin in the woods of the upland, well-armed housekeepers, booted and spurred, armed with good broadswords and fusils for the wars that were plainly coming. Bacon in a little while had collected a force of nearly six hundred men. In fact, it was not more than three or four days after his escape, before, at the head of this force, he was marching on Jamestown.

Berkeley was alarmed and dispatched messengers to York and Gloucester for the train-bands; but only about one hundred soldiers could be mustered, and before these could reach Jamestown, Bacon entered it at the head of his army, and about two o'clock in the afternoon drew up his troops, horse and foot, upon the green, not an arrow's flight from the end of the statehouse. All the streets and roads leading into the town were guarded, the inhabitants disarmed and the boats in the harbor seized.

Jamestown was thrown into confusion. Sir William Berkeley and his council were holding a council of war, when the roll of drums and blast of trumpets announced that Bacon was in possession of the city.

The house of burgesses was called to order, though little order was preserved on that day, when a collision between law and rebellion seemed inevitable. Between two files of infantry Bacon advanced to the corner of the statehouse, and the governor came out. Bacon, who had perfect control over himself, advanced toward him. Berkeley was in a rage. Walking straight toward Bacon, he tore open the lace at his bosom and cried:

"Here! Shoot me! 'Fore God, a fair mark!"

Bacon curbed his rising anger and replied:

"No, may it please your honor, we will not hurt a hair of your head, nor of any other man's. We are come for a commission to save our lives from the Indians, which you have so often promised, and now we will have it before we go."

Without a word in response, the governor and council wheeled about and returned to their chamber, and Bacon followed them, his left arm akimbo, his hand resting on the hilt of his sword. As they made him no answer, Bacon became furious and tossed his arms about excitedly, while the fusileers covered the window of the assembly chamber with their guns, and continually yelled:

"We will have it! We will have it!" (Meaning the commission.)

One of Bacon's friends among the burgesses shook his handkerchief from the window and answered:

"You shall have it! You shall have it!"

The soldiers at this uncocked their guns and waited further orders from Bacon. Their leader had dashed into the council chamber swearing:

"D—n my blood! I'll kill governor, council, assembly and all, and then I'll sheathe my sword in my own heart's blood!"

The wildest excitement prevailed in the town. Everybody was on the street, and the massacre of the governor and his council was momentarily expected. Two young girls ran toward an officer in the army of the rebel. One of Bacon's young captains met them and clasped an arm about each. It was Ester and Rebecca meeting the brother and lover. The excitement was too great for many to bestow more than a passing glance on the trio. There was a murmured prayer by all three, and they were silent.

A scene so ridiculous as to excite the laughter of many followed the assault on the statehouse. A sleek, plump little fellow, frightened out of his wits, was seen trying to climb out of a window on the opposite side from which danger was threatened. He got out and clung to the window with his hands, his short, fat legs dangling in the air and kicking against the wall.

"Marry! help me! Mother of God, I will be killed if I fall, and shot if I don't!"

It was Giles Peram, whose legs were six feet from the ground. He howled and yelled; but all were too busy to pay any attention to him, and at last his strength gave out, and he fell with a stunning thud upon the ground, where he lay gasping for breath, partially unconscious, but with no bones broken.

After half an hour's interview, Bacon returned. The burgesses hesitated; but the governor held out some promises for next day. Giles Peram, having regained his strength and breath, sprang to his feet and ran as fast as his short legs could carry him to the far end of the street to escape from the town; but half a dozen mounted Virginians with broadswords blocked up his passage. He next ran to the left and was met by men with pikes, one of whom prodded him so that he yelled and ran under some ornamental shrubs, beneath which a pair of frightened dogs had taken shelter. A fight for possession followed, and for a while it was doubtful; but Giles, inspired by fear, fought with the desperation of a madman and drove the dogs forth. With his scarlet coat and his silk stockings soiled, his wig lost and lace and ruffles all torn and ruined, he crouched under the shrubs, groaning:

"Oh, Lordy, Lordy! I will be killed! I know I will be killed!" The governor's valiant secretary presented a deplorable sight, indeed.

Next day Bacon was commissioned by the governor as general and commander-in-chief of the forces against the Indians. It was a great triumph for the young republican. Berkeley even wrote a letter to the king applauding what Bacon had done on the frontier.

Robert Stevens paid his mother, sister and sweetheart a visit. Not having received Rebecca's letter, he was ignorant of Ester's presence in Virginia, until he discovered her, as they were drawn up for battle. Many hoped that trouble was over; but Robert said:

"It is not. I know Berkeley too well. He is a cunning old knave, and as soon as he has recovered from the fright into which the appearance of an armed force precipitated him, he will relent and do something terrible."

"Brother, do not place yourself in his power," said his sister.

"Fear not, sweet sister, I shall have a care for myself. Where is Mr. Price?"

"At the governor's."

"Does he know that Ester is General Goffe's daughter?"

"No."

"He must not. He would report it to the governor, who, in his idiotic love for monarchy, would adjudge her responsible for a deed committed before she was born."

"We will keep the secret, brother."

"When do you go?" asked Ester.

"The army marches against the Indians on the

morrow." He was about to say something more, when they espied Mr. Giles Peram coming toward them. His face was smiling, though there were a few scratches upon it.

"Marry! friend Robert, good morrow! Did you learn of my great speech in the house of burgesses yesterday, when they were about to refuse your general his commission?"

"I knew not that you were a member of the house."

Peram, blushing, answered:

"Nor am I; but I forced myself, at the peril of my life, into their presence, and I swore—yes, God forgive me, but I swore if they did not give the commission, I would annihilate them, and, by the mass, they were afraid of me, and they granted it." With this the diminutive egotist strutted proudly before his auditors.

Black Sam, who had overheard his remark, with his native impetuosity put in:

"'Fore God, massa, what a lie! Why, he war all de time under de thorn bushes fighten wid de dogs fur a hiden-place."

Giles gave utterance to an exclamation of rage and flew at the negro with upraised cane; but black Sam evaded his blow and, with a laugh, ran into the kitchen, yelling back: "It am so. Jist see dem scratches on him face."

Quite crestfallen, Mr. Peram retired, and for several days did not annoy Rebecca with his presence.

Next morning Bacon started on his campaign against the Indians. The burgesses were then dissolved and went back to their homes. The fact that that body sat in June, 1676, and in the same month instructed the Virginia delegates to propose independence of England, has been a theme of much discussion among historians.

Bacon, at the head of his army, duly commissioned, was marching against the Indians. All things in Virginia were virtually under his control as commander of the military. Mr. Lawrence and Mr. Drummond, ex-governor of Carolinia, though they were his friends, remained in Jamestown to look after his interests there. Drummond declared he was "in over-shoes, and he would be over-boots." Had Bacon been uninterrupted, there can be no doubt that his power on the Indians would have been felt; but Berkeley began to relent that he had ever commissioned him, and issued a proclamation declaring him a rebel and revoking his commission. The news was brought to Bacon while on the upper waters, by Lawrence and Drummond. When he heard it, the general declared:

"It vexes my heart for to think that while I am

hunting wolves, tigers and foxes, which daily destroy our harmless sheep and lambs, I and those with me should be pursued with a full cry, as a more savage or no less ravenous beast."

Bacon began his march back to the lower waters. On the way, they captured a spy sent by Berkeley to their camp and hung him. Bacon went to the Middle Plantation, afterward Williamsburg, and camped.

Berkeley, hearing of the return of Bacon's army, which was not disbanded, hastened to Accomac for recruits, and Drummond urged Bacon to depose Berkeley, and appoint Sir Henry Chicheley in his place. When the leader of the rebellion murmured against this, the Scotchman answered:

"Do not make so strange of it, for I can show you ancient records that such things have been done in Virginia."

This, however, was carrying matters too far, even for Bacon. He remembered that Governor Harvey, who had been deposed in a similar manner, was reinstated by the king. He issued a remonstrance against Berkeley's proclamation denouncing him as a rebel, declaring that he and his followers were good and loyal subjects of the king of England, who were only in arms against the savages. Then followed a list of public grievances. He declared that some in authority had come to the country poor, and were now rolling in wealth, likening them to sponges, that have sucked up and devoured the common treasury. He asked, "What arts, sciences, schools of learning, or manufactures have been promoted by any now in authority?"

The governor's beaver trade with Indians, in which he thought more of his profits than the lives of his subjects on the frontier, was not forgotten.

Bacon was declared a rebel, his life was forfeited to Berkeley if captured, and while at the Middle Plantation, he required an oath of his followers to even resist the king's troops if they should come to Virginia. The people of Virginia had not yet learned the true principles of liberty. They still supposed that liberty could be gained while they retained their allegiance to the king of England. It required a hundred years more to convince them that freedom was incompatible with royalty. The paper signed at Middle Plantation on this third day of August, 1676, was a notable document. It began by stating that certain persons had raised forces against General Bacon, which had brought on civil war, and if forces came from England they would oppose them.

The next step of the rebels was to organize a government. Bacon issued writs for the representatives of the people to assemble early in September. The writs were in the king's name, and were signed by four of the council.

This done, Bacon set off on his Indian campaign, leaving behind him a mighty tumult. The new world had defied the old. At midnight by torchlight, the grim-faced pioneers of Virginia had sworn to be free. Everywhere men and women hailed the oath with enthusiasm.

"Now we can build ships and, like New England, trade with any other part of the world," they declared. Sarah Drummond, the wife of the Scottish conspirator, exclaimed:

"The child that is unborn shall have cause to rejoice for the good that will come by the rising of the country." And when a person by her side said, "We must expect a greater power from England, that will certainly be our ruin," Drummond's wife took up a stick, broke it in two and cried disdainfully:

"I fear the power of England no more than a broken straw! We will do well enough."

The women took great interest in public affairs at this time. The wife of Cheeseman urged him to join Bacon and fight for their liberties, which he did, as she afterward declared, at her own request. The whole country was with Bacon, and, after instructing them to resist any force that might come from England, he crossed James River at

Curles with a force of three hundred men, and fell upon the Appomattox Indians at what is now Petersburg, with such fury that he killed or routed the entire tribe. Bacon fought so viciously, that his name was a dread to the savages fifty years after his death. For one without training, he displayed wonderful military ability. Having completely routed all the Indians, early in September Bacon with his army returned to the settlements, and had reached West Point when he received news that Sir William Berkeley, with a thousand men and seventeen ships, was in possession of Jamestown.

Berkeley had not all gloom and disaster on his side. Captain Bland, who had been sent by Bacon with a considerable force to capture Berkeley, was led into a trap and captured by Captain Larramore. Shortly after, the governor returned to Jamestown with a large number of longshoremen and loafers, great enough in quantity, but inferior as soldiers in quality.

While Jamestown was deserted by both belligerent parties, and its frightened inhabitants were waiting in feverish anxiety the next event in the great drama, there suddenly appeared in the harbor the wonderful vessel *Despair*. The ship entered in the night as mysteriously as it had disappeared, and again the white-haired Sir Albert was seen on the streets of Jamestown. He met Rebecca the day of his arrival, and she said:

"I feared you had gone, never to come back."

"Did you want to see me again, child?" he asked, in such a fatherly voice, that she could scarce resist the impulse to embrace him.

"I did, Sir Albert, for I remembered your promise, and I depend on you."

"The war rages again?"

"It does, and I fear for my brother. Sir William is coming with a thousand men."

"If the worst comes, sweet maid, I will take you aboard my ship."

"But my brother—oh, my brother!"

"He, also, will be safe."

"Would you take us all, and Ester, too?"

"Who is Ester?"

She told him all, for she felt that in this mysterious man she had a friend on whom she could rely. When she had finished, Sir Albert shook his snowy locks and remarked:

"You would do well to keep this from the ears of Sir William, sweet maid."

Then he went away into the forest. That evening, as he sat at the roadside, not far from Jamestown, the wife of Hugh Price, who had been to Greenspring, was returning home on her favorite saddle-horse. The animal became frightened at some object by the roadside, and leaped madly forward. The saddle turned and the woman would have fallen had not Sir Albert rushed to her rescue.

He lifted her from the saddle, and, while the horse dashed madly away, seated the rider safely at the roadside.

"Are you injured?" he asked the half-fainting woman.

"No."

"You are fortunate to escape so narrowly, madam. Do you live at Jamestown?"

"I do, sir. You are Sir Albert of the *Despair*, are you not?" asked Dorothe Price.

"I am."

"I have often heard of you. I thank you for your kind service, sir."

"Shall I see you home?"

"If not too much trouble."

As they walked along the road, he asked:

"Are you Mrs. Price?"

"I am."

"Mr. Hugh Price is your second husband?"

"He is."

"When did your first husband die?"

"Many years ago. He was lost at sea."

"Did he leave two children?"

"Yes, sir, two," she sighed, and the white-haired stranger, glancing at her face, asked:

"Was he a good man?"

"Good man! Oh, sir, he was an angel of goodness; but, alas, I never appreciated him, until he was gone. I oft recall that fatal morning when he bade me farewell, when he kissed the baby and left a tear on her cheek. I was happy then!" Tears were now trickling down her cheeks.

"Are you happy now?"

"Alas, no. I am miserable."

"Why?"

"My husband is an enemy to my son. Price is a royalist while Robert is a Puritan and a republican."

"Is your son with Bacon?"

"He is, and Sir William would hang Robert if he could."

"He shall not hang him."

"If he captures him, who will prevent it?"

"I will." They parted at the door, and as the old man went down to his boat, she gazed after him, murmuring:

"Heaven surely hath sent us a protector at last."

CHAPTER XXI.

BURNING OF JAMESTOWN.

"At every turn, Morena's dusky height
Sustains aloft the battery's iron load,
And, far as mortal eye can compass sight,
The mountain-howitzer, the broken road,
The bristling palisade, the foss o'erflowed,
The stationed band, the never-vacant watch,
The magazine in rocky durance stand,
The holster'd steed beneath the shed of thatch,
The ball-piled pyramid, the ever-blazing match."
—BYRON.

SIR WILLIAM BERKELEY, with the motley crowd of sailors, longshoremen, freed slaves, and such as he could collect, sailed for Jamestown and reached it safely September 7th, 1676. The news of his approach reached Jamestown long before he did, and Colonel Hansford, one of Bacon's youngest and bravest officers, with eight hundred men prepared to resist. A terrible conflict was anticipated, and Sir Albert, on the morning of the expected fight, landed and took Mrs. Price, her daughter and Ester Goffe on board his ship, and dropped down the river a mile or two, to be out of harm's way.

These were the first people who had been aboard the wonderful ship *Despair*.

Rebecca was charmed and entranced at the display of wealth and splendor on board the vessel. The elegance was marvellous.

"You must be very rich," she said to Sir Albert.

"This represents but a small part of my possessions."

"I would I were your heiress."

"You may be, sweet maid. I have no nearer relative to inherit the millions which are burdensome to me."

"Have you no wife—no children?"

He shook his head, looked so sad, and turned away with such a deep drawn sigh, that she could not bear to ask him more.

Berkeley appeared that evening before Jamestown and summoned the rebels to surrender, promising amnesty to all but Lawrence and Drummond, who were then in the town. Hansford refused; but, on the advice of his friends, they all left the town that night. At noon next day Berkeley landed on the island and, kneeling, thanked God for his safe arrival. Only a very few people were found in the town, and Lawrence and Drummond were gone. Mr. Lawrence fled so precipitately that he left his house with all its effects to fall into the hands of the enemy.

Drummond and the thoughtful Mr. Lawrence hastened to find Bacon, who was at West Point at the head of the York River.

Bacon acted with an energy and rapidity that would have done Napoleon or Cromwell credit. With his faithful body guard, among whom were Robert Stevens, Drummond, Cheeseman and Lawrence, he set out for Jamestown. Carriers, sent in every direction, summoned the Baconites to join him, so that his small band increased so rapidly, that when he reached Jamestown he had a force of several hundred.

The governor prepared to receive the rebels. He threw up a strong earth-work, and a palisade had been erected across the neck of the island. Bacon, on reaching Jamestown, rode forward to reconnoitre it. He then ordered his trumpeters to sound the battle cry, and a volley was fired into the town; but no response came back.

Bacon made his headquarters at Greenspring, in Governor Berkeley's own house, and while Sir William dined at the board of the thoughtful Mr. Lawrence, the rebel fed at the table of the governor. Resolving on a siege, Bacon threw up earth-works about the town in front of the palisades. Berkeley's riflemen so annoyed the men at work, that Bacon had recourse to a strange device to protect them. He sent a detachment of horse into the surrounding country, captured and brought to camp the wives of all the prominent gentlemen who fought with Berkeley. Perhaps Mrs. Price only escaped by being on board the ship *Despair*. Madame Bray, Madame Page, Madame Ballard and Madame Bacon, the wife of Bacon's cousin, were among the number. These women were placed before the workmen in the trenches to protect them from the bullets of Berkeley.

"Have no apprehensions from us, good-wives," said Bacon. "We shall not harm a hair of your head. If your husbands shoot you we are not to blame."

Bacon has been censured for this ungallant strategy; but it worked well and saved his workmen from further annoyance. He sent one of the good-wives into the town under a flag of truce to inform her own and the others' husbands, that he meant to place them "in the forefront of his workmen," during the construction of the earth-works, and if they fired on them, the good-wives would suffer.

No attack was made on Bacon until the earthworks were completed, and then the women were sent to their homes during the night. Next morning at early dawn, Berkeley sounded his battle-cry, and his men mustered at the roll of the drum. Bacon was on the alert. His eagle eye glanced along his earth-works and the gallant men enrolled under him.

"They are coming! They are coming with their whole force!" he shouted, as he stood on the ramparts, his sword in his hand and his eye flashing with the glorious light of battle. Matches were burning, the cocks of the fusees raised, and the Virginians stood cool and undaunted.

There came a puff of smoke from the palisades at Jamestown, a heavy report of a cannon, and an iron ball struck the earth-work.

"Come down, general!" cried the thoughtful Mr. Lawrence. "You endanger your life up there."

Bacon paid no heed to the warning. He was watching the manœuvres of the enemy, about eight hundred strong, who were about to assault him. Robert Stevens sprang to his side, and both smiled at the lack of courage and discipline which Berkeley's longshoremen displayed. Giles Peram, at the head of the company, marched forth. He wore a tall hat with a feather in it, and strutted about, until his eye caught sight of the enemy, when he wheeled about as quickly as if he were on springs and bounded away toward Jamestown, yelling loud enough to be heard in Bacon's camp:

"Oh, I will be killed! I will be killed!"

A shot was fired from Jamestown, and Giles, believing himself struck, fell on the ground and rolled over and kicked, producing such a ridiculous scene, that Robert and Bacon laughed outright. Berkeley, himself, headed the army, with which he intended to storm the earth-works, and, after some little difficulty, he got his forces formed, and the advance began.

"Don't fire, until I give you the command," said Bacon, coolly. "We will soon disperse this motley crowd, have no fear."

He and Robert were prevailed upon to descend from the ramparts, and all awaited the arrival of the enemy. They came slowly, doing plenty of yelling, and firing their fusees at random. The bullets either buried themselves in the earth-works, or whistled harmlessly through the air. Not one of Bacon's men was touched.

Nearer and nearer they came, until within easy pistol range, when Bacon cried:

"Fire!"

Pistol, musket and cannon belched forth fire and death, while a cloud of smoke rolled up above the fort. One volley had done the work. Alas! the motley crowd from Accomac were no fit adversaries for those stern backwoodsmen. Berkeley's recruits had come over to plunder, and, finding lead and bullets instead of gold and treasure, they fled with light heels to Jamestown, leaving a dozen of their number stretched on the ground as the only proof that they had fought at all.

Bacon now opened a cannonade in earnest on the town. The first ball that came screaming over the town to crash into the house which was the governor's headquarters was answered by a wild yell of fear, and the boastful Mr. Peram might have been seen flying as fast as his short legs would carry him to another part of the fortification. Another boom, and a shot struck the ground ten paces from him, and he wheeled about and ran, until a third shot struck a house before him. Then he ran to the church and crawled under it, where he lay until night.

Berkeley realized that he was in no condition to resist Bacon with such a set of knaves as he had for soldiers.

"We cannot long hold out, Mr. Price," he said as the sun was setting.

"No, Sir William, we must evacuate the city this very night."

"I believe it. Where is that coward Giles Peram?"

"He hath taken refuge under the church."

"Drag him hence. Robert Stevens is among the rebels, and the fool will fare hard if he falls into his hands."

A few moments later the wretched, trembling

Giles was brought before the governor. His scarlet coat, lace and ruffles were torn and disordered. He was reprimanded for his cowardice, and the army at once began to evacuate. When day dawned Berkeley was gone and Bacon entered the town. Mr. Drummond, Mr. Lawrence and Mr. Cheeseman went to their homes.

The ship *Despair*, which had been near enough to witness the scene, now bore down nearer to the town. Boats were lowered and the three women set on shore. Robert greeted his mother, his affianced and his sister with the most ardent affection. He had suffered much uneasiness about them, not knowing where they were, and he was overjoyed to see them.

That evening, while Mr. Lawrence, Mr. Drummond and Mr. Cheeseman were holding a council at the house of the former, the door suddenly opened and a tall white-haired stranger entered. Each started to his feet at the appearance of this apparition and seized pistols and swords.

"Never fear, friends; I came not to harm you," said Sir Albert, in his mild, gentle, but stern voice.

"You intrude—you disturb us!" cried Cheeseman. "We want no spy on our deliberations."

"Verily, my good man, you speak truly. These are deliberations at which there must be no spy.

Let no whispering tongue breathe aught of this meeting."

His words were so strange, that they stood amazed, gazing at him in wonder. Drummond at last gasped:

" 'Fore God, who are you?"

" A man like you," was the answer; "a man no older, yet whom sorrow hath crushed and bowed with premature age; a man with a heart to feel and a brain to think; a man who would willingly exchange places with you, though you stand within the shadow of a scaffold; a man, whose heart—O God!—must speak, or it will break; a friend who loves you, who never wronged any one, but has been made the puppet of outrageous fortune; a man who has more wealth than all Virginia, and yet is poorer than the lowest beggar; a man born to misfortune; a child of sorrow and of tears; one who never loved, but to see the object of his affections blighted or stolen; a man to whom dungeons, chains, slavery, death, hell itself would be heaven compared to what he hath endured; such a poor wretch, my friends, is now before you."

He could say no more, but, sinking upon a chair, buried his face in his hands and burst into tears. The three friends gazed at him for several seconds in astonishment; then they looked at each other for some solution to this mystery.

"What meaneth this?" Drummond asked when he regained his voice. "Surely I have heard that voice before. It takes me back, back into the past, many years ago, when we were all young."

Before any one could say a word, Sir Albert started up, laid aside his cocked hat and, brushing back his long snow-white hair from his massive brow, said:

"Drummond, Lawrence, Cheeseman, friends of my youth, look on this face and, in God's name, tell me you recognize one familiar feature left by the hand of misfortune."

The three looked,—started to their feet, and Drummond cried:

"God in heaven! hath the sea given up its dead? It is John Stevens!"

"It is John Stevens, alive and in the flesh," he quickly answered. At first they could hardly believe him, until he briefly told them the story of his shipwreck and wonderful adventures on the island, of the treasures untold thrown into his hands, and finally of a ship, in search of water, putting into his poor harbor. After no little trouble he got his treasure aboard this vessel without the crew suspecting what it was and sailed to Europe. His vast wealth had procured all else— ship, faithful men, the king's favor and all needful to his plans.

"Then I sailed for Virginia to meet sorrow, good friends, and live a living death," he concluded.

"Did you know of her marriage before your arrival?"

"Yes, I was told in London by a Virginian of whom I made some inquiry. I could not believe it at first, for Dorothe always condemned second marriages, and oft, when ailing, predicted that I would wed when she died, and bring a second mother over her children."

Drummond struck his fist upon the table vehemently, answering:

"'Fore God, it is always thus with the howling wenches! That which they most disclaim will they do. She hath not waited until her husband was dead, but hath married——"

"Drummond, hold your peace; she is the mother of my children and was true to me while my wife. Unless you would lose my friendship, speak not against the woman whom I still love," and John Stevens buried his white head in his hands and trembled as if in an ague fit.

"Forgive me, my friend; forgive me; I was hasty," said Drummond. "I have naught to say against the woman who was and still is your wife. Verily, she hath had her punishment,—and the poor children, how they have suffered."

"I know all," John sobbed.

"What will you do?"

"Alas, I know not."

"Why not declare yourself to the world and claim your wife?"

"What! Illegalize the marriage and make an adulteress of my wife? No, never! I pray you, my friends, pledge me on your oaths as gentlemen never to reveal my identity, while she or I shall live."

Drummond, who was impetuous and hated Hugh Price, cried:

"And will you leave her to him?"

"Yes," was the low, meek answer.

"Will you not seek revenge?"

"'Vengeance is mine, I will repay, saith the Lord.'"

Drummond was choking with fury and amazement. After a moment he regained control over himself, and gasped:

"Heavens! can God permit such injustice? And you will surrender her to him?"

"They believe themselves lawfully married. She hath committed no crime in the sight of heaven."

"But wherefore not tear her from his arms and fly to some foreign land?"

"Nay, my friend, we have two children, a son

and daughter, for whose peace we must have a care. Dare I for their sakes declare who I am?"

Drummond was eager to put a bullet into the brain of Price; but John Stevens was a man of peace and not of blood. His days were few on earth; his race was almost run, and the prime and vigor of his manhood had been wasted on a desert island. His only desire was to hover unknown about those he loved, that they might not want or suffer while he lived, and he had already arranged his fortune so it would descend to Robert and Rebecca when he died.

"Yet I must live unknown, my friends. Swear to keep my secret."

They swore on their honor, and the miserable old man, whose fine apparel was only a disguise, rose and left them. The three friends were sitting looking at each other in speechless amazement, when the door again burst open, and the impetuous Bacon, accompanied by Robert Stevens, entered.

"Why sit you here?" cried the general. "Have you not heard the news?"

"No; what is it?"

"Berkeley hath been reinforced, they say, by troops from England, and is coming upon the town."

Drummond, Cheeseman and Lawrence were on their feet in a moment, their faces evincing alarm.

No one doubted the truth of the story, and they began to hurriedly discuss the situation.

"Are we able to defend Jamestown against them?" asked the thoughtful Mr. Lawrence.

"No," answered Bacon.

"Then we must abandon it."

"They shall not find the town when they come," cried Bacon. "D—n my blood! I will burn Jamestown, and not a stone shall be left standing upon another. Burn it, yes burn it, so that three centuries hence naught but its ashes and ruins will mark where it stands to-day!"

What Bacon ordered in the heat of passion was indorsed by sober reason, and it was resolved to burn the town.

RUINS OF JAMESTOWN.

"But your own house, Mr. Drummond, will have to be burned," cried Robert.

"I will fire it with my own hand. It will be the first that burns," answered Drummond. Immediately the news spread that the town had been doomed. The troops were assembled in the streets, and the people summoned to vacate their houses. There were wailings and shrieks that night. Robert ran to his home and told his mother, what was to be done. She came weeping into the street and asked:

"What will become of us, my son? Whither shall we fly? We are three helpless women without a roof to protect us."

"Until this storm hath blown away, let my ship be your home," said a deep, sad voice at her side, and, turning about, she beheld Sir Albert St. Croix, the man who had so strangely impressed her.

"Mother, go, take Ester and sister and go aboard the *Despair*," cried Robert. Then, turning to the strange old man, he seized his hand and continued, "Kind sir, you look the soul of honor. Will you care for them until this hour has passed?"

Sir Albert's breast heaved a moment like the tumultuous storm; then he answered:

"I will, I swear by the God we all worship!"

Robert hastily gathered up some personal effects and precious family relics, and carried them aboard the ship with his mother, Ester and Rebecca. On his return, he saw a bright flame dart up from the corner of Drummond's house and heard that gentleman say:

"Farewell, dear home! Better perish thus than be a harbor for tyrants."

Drummond had fired his own house. Mr. Lawrence did the same. The street was now filled with weeping and shrieking women and children and piles of household goods. A moment later, and Robert saw the burning flames leaping up about the home of his childhood—the house his father had erected. They leaped and crackled angrily and licked the roof with their hot, thirsty tongues, and he turned away his head. An hour later Jamestown was no more. It has never been rebuilt, and only the ruins of the old church mark the spot where once it stood.

Bacon and his army retreated up the country.

CHAPTER XXII.

VENGEANCE WITH A VENGEANCE.

> The longer life, the more offence ;
> The more offence, the greater pain:
> The greater pain, the less defence ;
> The less defence, the greater gain :
> The loss of gain long ill doth try,
> Wherefore, come death and let me die.
> —WYAT.

BACON still tarried at the Greenspring manor-house after the destruction of Jamestown, till a messenger came with the alarming intelligence that a strong force of royalists was advancing from the Potomac.

With his little army of dauntless patriots, he marched to face this new danger, for there was little more to fear from Sir William Berkeley, who remained at the kingdom of Accomac, and who would only find smoking ruins at Jamestown.

"You do not look well," said Robert to the patriot at whose side he rode. "Your cheek is flushed, and I believe you have a fever."

Bacon, who had contracted a disease in the

trenches about Jamestown, was very irritable. His excitable nature took fire at the slightest provocation; but with Robert he was ever reasonable.

"I shall be better soon," he answered. "When once we have met these devils and had this fight over with, I will be well; but I shall free Virginia, or die in the effort."

"Have a care for your health."

"I shall live to see the tyrant more humbled than when he fled Jamestown."

Bacon was angry and more eager to fight as his illness increased than when well. They crossed the lower York in boats at Ferry Point and marched into Gloucester, where he made his headquarters at Colonel Warner's and issued his "Mandates" to the Gloucester men to meet him at the court house and subscribe to the Middle Plantation oath. They hesitated; but as Colonel Brent was reported to be advancing at the head of a thousand men, Bacon ordered the drums beat, mustered his men, and they set out toward the Rappahanock in high spirits.

On that afternoon Bacon was occasionally irritable; at other times he became hilarious, and at others stupid. Robert, who rode at his side, saw that he was burning with fever, and he was glad that night when they camped.

"Spread a tent for the general, for he is sick,"

said Robert. The men could not realize how sick he was. Camp fires blazed. Brent was but a few miles away, and his forces were deserting him by scores and coming over to Bacon, who was not thought to be dangerously ill. When Robert entered his tent at ten that night, he found him sitting up giving some directions for the quartering of new troops.

"Are you better, general?" he asked.

"I am very tired. I shall lie down and sleep. I will be over this in the morning."

As long as Robert lived, he remembered those words. He knew the general was in a raging fever, yet he little thought it would prove fatal. He went to his own quarters on that October night and sought repose. It was an hour before daylight, when Mr. Drummond and Mr. Lawrence awoke him.

"General Bacon is dead," they said.

"What! dead?" cried Robert.

"Yes, dead and buried. We thought it best to bury him in the forest where his enemies could not find him. Brent is crushed; his men have deserted him, and all are with us. The general died very suddenly in the arms of Major Pate."

It was the purpose of the friends of liberty to keep the death of Bacon a secret, and there is some dispute in history as to where and when he died.

News of this character cannot be suppressed. It came out, and the republicans of Virginia began to lose heart from that hour, while the royalists' hopes increased.

Another general was elected to fill the place made vacant by Bacon. Drummond, Stevens, Cheeseman, or Lawrence might have organized the army and led them to victory; but the foolish frontiersmen chose, instead of either of these wise men, a grotesque personage named Ingram, who had been a rope dancer, and had no more qualifications for so important a position than an organ grinder, as the result soon proved. He was unable to hold them together. Colonel Hansford, the most daring young officer in Bacon's whole army, was captured at the home of his sweetheart, and Berkeley, to whom he was taken, decreed that he should be hung.

"Thomas Hansford," cried Berkeley, "I will quickly repay you for your part in this rebellion!"

Colonel Hansford answered, "I ask no favor but that I may be shot like a soldier and not hanged like a dog."

The governor replied, "You are to die, not as a soldier, but as a rebel."

Hansford was a native American and the first white native (say some historians) that perished on the gibbet. On coming to the gallows he said:

"Take notice, I die a loyal subject and a lover of my country."

Terror-stricken, the followers of Bacon began to desert the new general. In a few skirmishes that followed, they were worsted and broke up into small bands.

Hugh Price was foremost among the royalists searching for the rebels. He hoped to find his wife's son and bring him to the gibbet, for Price hated Robert with a hatred that was demoniacal. Giles Peram took courage, and mounting a horse, joined the troopers in galloping about the country and capturing or shooting the rebels, who, now that their spirits were broken, seldom made any resistance.

One day at sunset Hugh Price and Giles Peram suddenly came upon a wild-eyed, haggard young man, mounted upon a jaded steed. He had slept on the ground, for his uncombed hair had leaves still sticking to it, and his clothes were faded, soiled and torn. The evenings were cold, it being late in October, and the fugitive was looking about for a place to sleep. At a glance, both recognized him as Robert Stevens. They were armed with loaded pistols, while Robert, though he had weapons in his holsters, was out of powder.

"There he is, Giles; now slay him!" cried the step-father.

Robert realized his danger, and, with his whip, lashed his horse to a run. There came the report of a pistol from behind and a bullet whistled above his head.

"Come on, Giles; he is unarmed," cried Mr. Price.

"Oh, are you quite sure?" cried Giles.

"I am sure. He is out of ammunition."

"That is extraordinary, very extraordinary." Mr. Peram, who had been lingering behind, with this assurance urged his horse alongside the stepfather.

"He is heading for the river!" cried Price.

"Can he cross?"

"No; his horse could scarcely swim it. Try a shot at him."

Giles Peram, who was as cruel as he was cowardly, drew one of his pistols, as he galloped along over the grassy plain, and cocked it.

It is no easy matter even for an experienced marksman to hit a running object from the back of a flying horse. Giles, after leaning first to one side, then to the other, and squinting along the barrel of his pistol, shut both eyes and pulled the trigger. When the smoke cleared away Robert was seen sitting bolt upright in his saddle.

"He heads for the river. By the mass, I believe he is going to plunge into it!" cried Price.

The river was in view, and the young fugitive was riding toward it at full speed. His pursuers pressed their tired steeds in his rear, and Robert knew his only chance for life was to swim the stream. He uttered an encouraging shout to his horse as that noble animal sprang far out into the water. Robert's hat fell off and floated near the shore; but his horse swam straight across. Hugh Price, with an oath, drew his remaining pistol, galloped to the water's edge and fired. The ball struck four or five feet to Robert's left and in front of him, splashing up a jet of water where it plunged in. At the instant Hugh fired, Giles Peram's horse, unable to check his speed, would have rushed into the river, had not Price seized the bit and stopped him. Giles, unprepared for so sudden a halt, went over his horse, head first into the water.

Being a poor swimmer and greatly frightened, he would no doubt have drowned, had not Hugh Price gone to his rescue and pulled him out. By the time Giles Peram was rescued and placed safely on shore, Robert Stevens had crossed the river and was ascending the bank.

It was so dark that they could just see the outline of the fugitive, before he disappeared into the wood. Giles Peram was shivering from his sudden plunge and begged to go to camp, so Hugh Price, sympathizing with him, gave up the man hunt, and re-

THE BALL STRUCK FOUR OR FIVE FEET TO ROBERT'S LEFT, AND IN FRONT OF HIM, SPLASHING UP A JET OF WATER.

turned to the nearest camp of royalists. "We will have him yet. He shall hang!" said Mr. Price, by way of consoling his friend for his ducking.

They went to York, where Berkeley had established himself, and the latter commenced a reign of terror and vengeance, which has made him infamous in history as the most bloodthirsty tyrant of America. Major Cheeseman was captured with Captains Wilford and Farlow. The two captains were hung without trial, and Cheeseman was thrown into prison. When Edmund Cheeseman was arraigned before the governor and was asked why he engaged in Bacon's wicked scheme, before he could answer, his young wife stepped forward and said:

"My provocation made my husband join in the cause for which Bacon contended. But for me, he had never done what he has done. Since what is done," she sobbed, falling on her knees in an attitude of supplication, with her head bowed and face covered with her hands, "was done by my means, I am most guilty; let me bear the punishment, let me be hanged, but let my husband be pardoned."

The angry governor gazed on her for a moment with eyes which danced in fury; then he cried:

"Away with you!" adding a brutal remark at which manhood might well blush. Mrs. Cheeseman fainted, and her husband was carried away to the gallows.*

So fearful, at first, was the cruel old baron that some of his intended victims might escape through a verdict of acquittal by a jury, that men were taken from the tribunal of a court-martial directly to the gallows, without the forms of civil law.

For a time after Berkeley was established at York, Ingram still made a show of resistance, but accepted the first terms offered and surrendered. Only two prominent leaders remained uncaptured. These were Lawrence and Drummond. Berkeley swore he could not sleep well until they were hanged. The surrender of Ingram destroyed even the faintest hope of reorganizing the patriot army, and Mr. Drummond, deserted by his followers, was captured in the Chickahominy swamp and hurried to York to the governor, who greeted him with bitter irony.

"Mr. Drummond," he said, "you are very welcome! I am more glad to see you than any man in Virginia. Mr. Drummond, you shall be hanged in half an hour."

"What your honor pleases," Mr. Drummond boldly answered. "I expect no mercy from you. I have followed the lead of my conscience and did

---

*Authorities differ as to the death of Cheeseman. Some say he was hanged, others that he died in prison.

what I might to free my countrymen from oppression."

He was condemned at one o'clock and hanged at four. By a cruel decree of the governor, his brave wife Sarah was denounced as a traitress and banished with her children to the wilderness, where, for a while, they were forced to subsist on the charity of friends almost as poor as they.

Berkeley's rage was not yet fully satisfied. The thoughtful Mr. Lawrence had taken care of himself, for he knew but too well what to expect, should he be captured. Weeks passed and winter was advanced before Berkeley heard of him. Then from one of the upper plantations came the report that he and four other desperadoes with horses and pistols had marched away in snow ankle-deep. Some hoped they had perished in trying to swim the head-waters of some of the rivers; but they really traveled southward into North Carolinia, where they were safely concealed in the wilderness.

Berkeley proved himself a tiger, as he had proved himself a ruffian in insulting Mrs. Cheeseman. The taste of blood maddened him. He tried and executed nearly every one on whom he could lay his hands. Virginia became a vast jail or Tyburn Hill. Four men were hung on the York, several executed on the other side of the James River, and one was hanged in chains at West Point. In February, 1677, a fleet with a regiment of English troops arrived, and a formal commission to try rebels was organized, of which Berkeley was a member. This commission determined to kill Bland, who had been captured in Accomac. The friends of the prisoner in England had procured and sent over his pardon; but the commissioners were privately informed that the Duke of York (afterward James II.) had sworn that "Bacon and Bland must die," and with this intimation of what would be agreeable to his royal highness, Bland was hung. It was a revel of blood. In almost every county, gibbets rose and made the wayfarer shudder and turn away at sight of their ghastly burdens. In all, twenty-three persons were executed, and Charles II., disgusted with the tyranny of Berkeley, declared:

"That old fool has hanged more men in that naked country than I have done for the murder of my father."

Shortly after the execution of Mr. Edmund Cheeseman, and before the arrival of the English regiment, the first British troops ever brought to Virginia, Mr. Hugh Price, who was very active in capturing rebels, one evening brought in a miserable, half-starved, half-frozen young man, whom he had found lying in the snow, too feeble to fly or resist. Mr. Price was especially delighted with the capture, as the captive was Robert Stevens.

Old black Sam recognized the prisoner, and when he had been thrust in jail to await his trial, the old negro mounted a swift horse and rode all night across the country to the James River. Then, stealing a boat at one of the plantations, he rowed down the stream until he came to the *Despair*, on board of which was Mrs. Price, her daughter and Ester.

Sam's story caused instantaneous action, and next morning at daylight Governor Berkeley was amazed to see the strange ship anchored before his quarters, as near to shore as she could be brought. There was something particularly menacing in the vessel, with her double rows of guns pointed at the shore and the marines all on deck under arms. Berkeley was alarmed. A boat was lowered, and Sir Albert St. Croix came ashore. He hurried at once into the governor's presence.

"Sir Albert, I am pleased to see you; yet I do not understand that demonstration," said the governor, who, like all tyrants, was a coward. "Surely, you do not mean any hostilities toward me."

"That depends on circumstances. Have you a young man named Stevens prisoner?"

"Yes."

"Has he been tried?"

"He has and has been condemned."

"To hang?"

"Yes."

"Has the sentence been executed?" asked Sir Albert, trembling with dread.

"Not yet."

"Then your life is saved."

"But he will be hanged at ten o'clock."

"He shall not!"

"Why, who are you, that dare defy me?"

"Governor Berkeley," said Sir Albert, in a voice trembling with earnestness, as he led him to the window. "Look you on yon ship and see the guns pointed at your town. But harm a hair of Robert Stevens' head, and, by the God we both worship, I will blow you into eternity!"

Governor Berkeley sank in his seat, trembling with rage and fear. Must he let one go, and above all Robert Stevens, whom he hated? The old man continued:

"You have already hanged my friends Drummond and Cheeseman, and were I a man who sought revenge, I would destroy you, as I have it in my power to do."

At this moment the door opened, and Hugh Price, accompanied by Giles Peram, entered.

"The scaffold is all ready to hang Robert Stevens," said Mr. Price.

"Ah! marry, it is, governor, and I trow he will

make a merry sight dangling from it," put in Giles, a smile on his face.

Sir William Berkeley's face was deathly white; but he made no response. Mr. Price, who feared his wife's son might yet escape, urged:

"Governor, the scaffold is ready. Come, give the order for the execution."

Sir Albert coolly drew from his coat pocket a legal looking document and, laying it before the governor, said in a commanding tone:

"Sign, sir."

"What is it?"

"A pardon for Robert Stevens."

"No, no, no!" cried Hugh Price, rushing forward to interfere.

"Back, devil, lest I forget humanity!" cried Sir Albert, and, seizing Hugh Price by the throat, he hurled him against the wall. For a moment, the cavalier was stunned, then, rising, he snatched his sword from its sheath.

Sir Albert was not one whit behind in drawing his own blade, and, as steel clashed against steel, Giles Peram shouted:

"Oh, Lordy! I will be killed!" and ran from the room. There was but one clash of swords, then Price's weapon flew from his hand, and he expected to be run through; but Sir Albert coolly said:

"Begone, Hugh Price! Your life is in my hands; but I do not want it. You are not prepared to die. Get thee hence, lest I forget myself."

Price left the room, and Sir Albert, turning to Berkeley, asked:

"Have you signed the pardon, governor?"

"Here it is."

"Now order his release."

Half an hour later, Robert, who expected to suffer death on the scaffold, was liberated.

"I owe this to you, kind sir," he cried, seizing Sir Albert's hand.

"I promised to save you, and I always keep my promise."

"Do you know aught of my mother, sister, and Ester?"

"All are safe aboard my vessel."

"Why do you take such interest in us, Sir Albert? You are like a father to me."

"Do you remember your father?"

"I can just remember him. He was a noble man with a kind heart. Did you know him?"

"Yes; he was my friend. I knew him well."

"Would to heaven he had remained; our misery would not have been so great."

"We are all in the hands of inexorable fate; but let us talk no more. You will have a full pardon from Charles II. soon, and then that old fool will not dare to harm you. Not only will you be pardoned but Ester Goffe as well."

"How know you this?" asked Robert.

"I have sent to the king for the pardons, and he will deny me nothing."

"Then I shall wed Ester and return to my father's plantation to pass my days in peace."

"Do so, Robert, and ever remember that whatever you have, you owe it to your unfortunate father. God grant that your life may be less stormy than his."

When they went on board the *Despair*, there was a general rejoicing.

"Heaven bless you, our deliverer!" cried Rebecca, placing her arms about the neck of Sir Albert and kissing him again and again.

Years seemed to have rolled away, and once more the father felt the soft, warm arms of his baby about his neck. The ancient eyes grew dim, and tears, welling up, overflowed and trickled down the furrowed cheeks.

CHAPTER XXIII.

CONCLUSION.

So live, that when thy summons comes to join
The innumerable caravan, that moves
To that mysterious realm, where each shall take
His chamber in the silent halls of death,
Thou go not, like the quarry-slave at night,
Scourged to his dungeon; but, sustained and soothed
By an unfaltering trust, approach thy grave,
Like one who wraps the drapery of his couch
About him, and lies down to pleasant dreams.
—BRYANT.

THAT strange ship *Despair* still lingered before the headquarters of the governor, much to his annoyance. In February, 1677, when the ships and soldiers came from England, they brought a full and free pardon for Robert Stevens and Ester Goffe.

"What power hath that strange old wizard that he leads kings as it were by the nose?" asked the governor.

"'Fore God, I know not, governor," put in Hugh Price. "I would rather all the rebels in Bacon's army should have escaped than this one."

As Robert was about to depart from the vessel

to repair his father's estates, near Jamestown, Sir Albert took him aside and said:

"Money you will find in abundance for your estate. Henceforth, take no part in the quarrels of your country. Hot-blooded politicians bring on these quarrels, and they leave the common people to fight their battles. The care of your sister, she who is to be your wife, and your unfortunate mother will engage all your time."

"But Mr. Price, what shall I do with him?"

"Harm him not."

"He will harm me, I trow."

"No, not with the king's favor on you; he dare not."

Robert promised to heed all the excellent advice of Sir Albert, and he set forth with his slaves and a full purse to repair the ruined estates on the James River. He met many old friends to whom he was kind. They asked him many questions regarding his mysterious benefactor; but Robert assured them that he was as much a mystery to him as to them.

Hugh Price and his associate, Giles Peram, were nonplussed, puzzled and intimidated by the strong, vigorous, and at the same time mysterious arm which had suddenly been raised to protect him whom they hated.

"It is extraordinary! It is very extraordinary!"

declared Peram, clearing his throat and strutting over the floor.

"Where is your wife?"

"On board the ship *Despair*."

"Bring her home. Why do you not send and bring her home? The trouble is over, and we have put down the rebellion."

"I will."

After the arrival of the commission and soldiers from England, the hanging went on at a brisk pace, and Mrs. Price had lived like one stupefied on board the *Despair*, not daring to go ashore. She seldom spoke, and never save when addressed. She acted so strangely, that her daughter feared she was losing her mind. All day long she would sit with her sad eyes on the floor, and she had not smiled since she came aboard.

When the messenger came from the shore, with the command from Hugh Price for her to come to the home he had provided, she started like a guilty person detected in crime. Turning her great, sad eyes on the man who had been their protector in their hour of peril, she asked:

"Shall I go?"

"The place of a good wife is with her husband," he answered.

Then Rebecca, appealing to him, asked:

"Must I obey Hugh Price?"

"Is he your father?"

"No."

"You are of age?"

"I am."

"Then choose with whom you will live, Hugh Price, or with your brother on the James River."

"I will live with my brother."

Mrs. Price cast her eyes on the river filled with floating ice and, shuddering, said:

"The water is so dark and cold, and the boat is so frail."

"Shall I take you in mine?" asked Sir Albert.

"Will you?"

"If you desire it."

The boat was lowered, and Mrs. Price was tenderly assisted into it. Then he climbed down into the stern, seized the rudder, and gave the command to his four sturdy oarsmen:

"Pull ashore."

It was a bleak, cold, wintry day. The wind swept down the ice-filled river. From the deck, closely muffled in wraps and robes, Rebecca saw her mother and Sir Albert depart for the snow-clad shore. Her eyes were blinded with tears, for she knew how unhappy her mother was. As she watched the boat gliding forward amid the floating blocks of ice, she was occasionally alarmed at the seeming narrow escapes it made.

The current was very swift, for the tide was running out, and tons of ice were all about the boat; but a skilful hand was at the helm, and the little boat darted hither and thither, from point to point, safely through the waters. Once she was quite sure it would be crushed between two small icebergs; but it glided swiftly out of danger.

The nearer they approached the shore, the denser became the ice pack, and the danger accordingly increased. At almost every moment, Rebecca uttered an exclamation of fear lest the boat should be crushed.

Just as she thought all danger was over, and when they were within a short distance of shore, a heavy cake of ice, which had been sucked under by the current, suddenly burst upward with such fury as to crush the boat. The shrieks of the unfortunate occupants filled the air for a single second, then all sank below the cold waves.

Two heads rose to the surface a second later, and those on the ship as well as those on shore recognized them as Sir Albert St. Croix and Mrs. Price. Holding the screaming woman in one arm, Sir Albert nobly struck out for shore, and no doubt would have reached it, for he was a bold swimmer, had not a large cake of ice borne them down to a watery grave.

When they were found, three days later, they

were closely locked in each other's arms. Robert Stevens came from Jamestown, and he and his sister had the body of their mother buried at the old churchyard in the ruins of Jamestown. Sir Albert was also, by order of his captain, buried at the same place.

All winter long, Captain Small of the *Despair* remained in the York River; but at early spring he came to the James River and, summoning both Robert and Rebecca aboard his vessel, informed them that his dead master had, by a will, left them a vast fortune in money, jewels and lands, in both America and England.

"He also gave you the ship *Despair*," concluded the captain.

"This is very strange," said Robert. "I can scarcely believe it."

Captain Small, however, had the will to prove it.

"Now what will you do with the ship?" the captain asked.

"What do you advise? We know nothing of such matters."

"She would make an excellent merchantman, and I would be willing to rent her of you and give you one half the profits."

"No, no, captain; take her, and give us one fourth."

Captain Small was delighted with his new employer's liberality, and the name *Despair* was changed to *Hope*. The vessel soon became famous as a merchantman all over the world. Her honest master, Captain Small, became wealthy, at the same time increasing the wealth of the owners.

Robert and Ester Goffe were married one year after the death of Mrs. Price. Hugh Price never molested Robert, but gave himself up to dissipation and was killed in a drunken brawl two years after his wife's death. Giles Peram continued to make himself a nuisance about the home of Robert Stevens and to annoy his sister, until the indignant brother horsewhipped him and drove him from the premises. Shortly after Giles was seized with fever of which he died.

Rebecca went with her brother and his wife to Massachusetts on a visit and, while there, met a young Englishman of good family, whom she married within a year and took up her abode in New England, while Robert returned to Virginia to pass his days in the land of his nativity, the wealthiest and one of the most respected in the colony.

One evening, five years after the removal of Berkeley, a stranger rode to Robert's plantation. His face was bronzed and his frame hardened by exposure and hardships; but his eye had the flash of an eagle's. It was dusk when he reached Robert's plantation, and he took the planter aside and asked:

"Do you not know me?"

"No."

"Lawrence," the stranger whispered.

"What! Mr. Lawrence?"

"Whist! do not breathe it too loud. I am proscribed, and though Berkeley is gone, Culpepper, his successor, is no friend of mine. All believe me dead, so I am to the world; but I have something to tell you of yourself and your parents that will interest you."

Then Mr. Lawrence told Robert a sad story which brought tears to his eyes before it was finished.

"I have come at the risk of my life from Carolinia to tell you this, my friend. I promised never to reveal it while he lived; but, now that both are gone, it were best that you know."

Robert tried to prevail on him to remain; but he would not, and, mounting his horse, he galloped away into the darkness. Stevens never saw or heard of the "thoughtful Mr. Lawrence" again.

A few days later a man, passing the old graveyard at Jamestown, observed that the body of Sir Albert St. Croix had been removed and placed by the side of the woman whom he died to save. A month later, on a head-stone, appeared the following strange inscription:

"*Father and mother sleep here.*"

Before closing this volume, it will be necessary to revert once more to the tyrant whose misrule of Virginia had brought about Bacon's Rebellion. At last, the assembly had to beg Berkeley to desist, which he did with reluctance. A writer of the period said, "I believe the governor would have hanged half the country if they had let him alone." He was finally induced to consent that all the rebels should be pardoned except about fifty leaders—Bacon at the head of them; but these chief leaders were attainted of treason, and their estates were confiscated. First to suffer was the small property of the unfortunate Drummond; but here Berkeley found the hidden rock on which his bark wrecked, for this roused the voice of the banished Sarah Drummond, and her cry from the wilderness of Virginia went across the broad Atlantic and reached the throne of England. She had friends in high places in the Old World, and she was restored, and Berkeley was censured for what he had done.

All laws made by Bacon were repealed by proclamation, and the royalists triumphed; but Governor Berkeley was ill at ease. The Virginians hated him for his merciless vengeance on their people, and a rumor reached his ears that he was no better liked in England. The very king whom he had served turned against him, and, worn down by

CONCLUSION.

sickness and a troubled spirit, he sailed for England. All Virginia rejoiced at his departure, and salutes were fired and bonfires blazed, and all nature seemed to rejoice in the blessed hope that the reign of tyranny was ended forever.

Ye End.

HISTORICAL INDEX.

	PAGE
Address of the Massachusetts Legislature to King Charles II	252
Albemarle has Stevens appointed governor	160
Alderman, slayer of King Philip	279
Andros, Major Edward, commissioned to receive the surrender of New York	149
Andros and Captain Ball at Saybrook	246
Angel of deliverance	260
Arlington and Culpepper grants denounced by Bacon	304
Arrival of the first English troops in Virginia	376
Assembly begs Berkeley to desist in hanging rebels	390
Attack on the swamp fort	273
Austin, Anna, the fanatical Quaker	120
Bacon, Nathaniel	303
Bacon's "Quarter Branch"	304
Bacon's threat	305
Bacon sends a messenger to Jamestown for his commission	309
Bacon defeats the Indians	312
Bacon arrested	313
Bacon's confession	316
Bacon's flight	330
Bacon rousing his friends	335
Bacon marching on Jamestown	336
Bacon captures Jamestown	336
Bacon and Berkeley meet	337
Bacon commissioned by Berkeley	339
Bacon hangs Berkeley's spy	343
Bacon urged to depose Berkeley	343
Bacon's Indian campaign	346

HISTORICAL INDEX.

	PAGE
Bacon again rallying his hosts	352
Bacon uses the wives of royalists as shields	353
Bacon repulses the attack of Berkeley's longshoremen.	355
Bacon besieges Jamestown	356
Bacon enters Jamestown	357
Bacon burns Jamestown	365
Bacon marches to meet the foe on the Potomac	366
Bacon ill	367
Bacon's death a mystery	368
Bacon rebels attainted of treason	390
Bacon's laws repealed	390
Baconites deserting Ingram	370
Battle between Claybourne and Calvert on the Potomac	22
Battle of the Severn, March 25, 1654	27
Battle of Brookfield	268
Battle of Bloody Run	312
Bennett, Richard, succeeds Berkeley	26
Berkeley, Sir William, Governor of Virginia	22
Berkeley, Sir William, character of	23
Berkeley's proclamation against Puritan pastors	24
Berkeley invites Charles II. to come to Virginia	26
Berkeley, deposed by roundheads in 1650, retires to Greenspring Manor	26
Berkeley restored in 1660 by Charles II	124
Berkeley's opinion of free schools and printing	285
Berkeley informs home government that all trouble with the Indians is happily over	306
Berkeley's excuse for refusing Bacon's commission	308
Berkeley denounces Bacon as a rebel	309
Berkeley pardons Bacon	317
Berkeley preparing to resist Bacon	336
Berkeley and Bacon meet	337
Berkeley revokes Bacon's commission and denounces him a rebel	342
Berkeley in possession of Jamestown	346
Berkeley demands surrender of Jamestown	351

HISTORICAL INDEX.

	PAGE
Berkeley's attack on Bacon's works	354
Berkeley's tyranny at York	373
Berkeley's departure from Virginia	391
Berkeley's territory conveyed to the Duke of York	150
Bland, execution of	376
Brent reported advancing	367
Buckingham succeeds Clarendon	256
Burning of Jamestown	363
Calvert, Sir George, at Jamestown, 1630	20
Calvert, Governor of Maryland	21
Carolinia, William Hawley, governor of	56
Carolinia settled by New Englanders	57
Carolinia constitution	159
Carteret, New Jersey conveyed to	151
Carteret enters New Jersey with a hoe on his shoulder	154
Carteret, Governor of New Jersey, deposed	249
Census of New England in 1675	257
Charles I. beheaded in 1649	25
Charles II. declared king of England in 1660	112
Charles II. pursuing the judges of his father	200
Charles II., character of	204
Charles II. profligate and careless	259
Charles II.'s opinion of Sir William Berkeley	376
Cheeseman, trial of	373
Cheeseman's death	374
Cheeseman, Mrs., before Berkeley	373
Church and his men surrounded at Punkateeset	266
Clarendon in exile	256
Claybourne, William, the great rebel, at Kent Island	21
Clove, Anthony, governor of reconquered New Amsterdam	148
Coddington's, William, commission for governing islands within limits of Rhode Island charter	247
Commissioners sent to demand Massachusetts charter	251
Connecticut obtains a new charter under Winthrop	155
Connecticut after the restoration	244

HISTORICAL INDEX.

PAGE

Connecticut under Winthrop procures another constitution 245
Cromwell, Oliver, rules England as Protector 25
Cromwell, Oliver, dies in 1658 and names his son Richard as his successor 112
Culpepper, Lord, and Arlington receive from Charles II. grant of all Virginia for thirty-one years 293
Curles, Bacon's home 303
Death of Nathaniel Bacon 368
De Vries robbed by the Indians 39
De Vries chosen president of popular assembly 41
Dixwell, John, one of the executioners of Charles I ... 201
Drummond, William, appointed Governor of Carolinia in 1666 123
Drummond brings North Carolinia into notice of the world 158
Drummond before Berkeley 374
Drummond, execution of 375
Drummond, Sarah, banished with her children 375
Drummond's, Sarah, appeal reaches the throne 390
Dutch capture New York 148
Dyer, Mary, execution of 122
Effect of the restoration on Virginia 123
Elizabethtown, New Jersey, founded by Carteret 248
Elliott, John, missionary among Indians 258
Emigrants to Carolinia 122
Emigrants to New Jersey from New England 249
English government in a state of chaos after the death of Cromwell 112
Endicott, John, Governor of Massachusetts 120
Execution of Robinson and Stevenson 121
Farlow, Captain, hung by Berkeley 273
Fisher, Mary, in Massachusetts 120
Forebodings of war 265
Gathering of Virginians at Curles 307
Goffe and the fencing-master 198

HISTORICAL INDEX. 397

	PAGE
Goffe, William, one of the judges who tried and condemned Charles I	200
Goffe and Whalley hiding from the king's men	201
Gorges recovers his claim	253
Greene, Roger, guide into Carolina wilderness	58
Greenspring Manor, Berkeley's country residence	23
Grievances of Virginians	293
Hadley attacked by the Indians	259
Hansford, Colonel, prepares to resist Berkeley	350
Hansford abandons Jamestown	351
Hansford hung	369
Harvey, Sir John, Governor of Virginia in 1629	20
Harvey, Sir John, deposed by West	20
Hawley, Governor of Carolina	56
Heath, Sir Robert, receives patent to lands south of Virginia	56
Hollanders attack Indians at Hoboken	42
Indian war of 1644	24
Indians in New Amsterdam driven to New Jersey	60
Indian advancement in education	258
Indians' lands taken from them	263
Ingram chosen in place of Bacon	369
Ingram's surrender	374
James, Duke of York, has all New Netherland granted to him by his brother Charles II	113
Jamestown besieged by Bacon	356
Jamestown captured by Bacon	357
Jamestown destroyed by Bacon and has never been rebuilt	363
Judges who tried and condemned Charles I	200
Kieft, Governor of New Netherland, demands the murderer of the wheelwright	40
Kieft sends an expedition against the Indians	42
Kieft recalled, perishes on his way to Holland	44
King Philip aims a blow at Hadley, Hatfield and Northampton	271

HISTORICAL INDEX.

	PAGE
King's men, character of	286
Lancaster attacked by Indians	274
Lawrence escapes into the wilds of North Carolinia	375
Law against Quakers repealed in 1661	122
Laws made by Bacon repealed	390
Longtail, Claybourne's trading ship	21
Lovelace appointed Governor of New York	146
Massachusetts controls the New England confederacy	52
Massachusetts' charter threatened	205
Massachusetts after the restoration	250
Massachusetts not punished for her defiance	256
Massasoit, death of, 1661	261
Matapoiset, attack on	277
Meeting between Carteret and Nicolls	153
Middle Plantation oath	344
Money first coined in North America (in Massachusetts), 1652	52
Muddy Brook, fight at	270
Narragansetts, Philip among	271
Navigation act, one of Virginia's grievances	293
New Amsterdam granted a government like the free cities of Holland	47
New Amsterdam conquered by the English and changed to New York	117
New England confederation	51
New England, growth of	52
New England colonies slandered	205
New Haven colony	155
New Jersey, how effected by change	149
New Jersey charter	151
New Jersey's encouragement to emigrants	152
New Jersey falls into the hands of the Dutch	250
New York not represented in Parliament	146
New York attacked by the Dutch	147
New York re-captured by the Dutch and re-christened New Amsterdam	148

HISTORICAL INDEX.

	PAGE
Nicolls, Col. Richard, arrives at New Amsterdam	113
Nicolls succeeded by Lovelace in 1667 as the governor of New York	146
Nipmucks, Philip among	268
North Carolinia's first legislature in 1666	161
Nutten (now Governor's Island), Indians agree to go to	51
Old Dominion, how Virginia derived the name of	124
Oliverian plot	181
Opechancanough captured when almost one hundred years old and assassinated	24
Orange changed to Albany	145
Parliament orders a fleet to Virginia in 1650	26
Pavonia, the territory of Pauw	150
Philip's, King, opposition to war	262
Philip, King, weeps on hearing that white man's blood has been shed	264
Philip, King, among the Nipmucks	268
Philip, King, pursued	278
Philip, King, death of	279
Pokanokets rejected Christianity	262
Popular assembly, the first at New Amsterdam	41
Population of Virginia	284
Printz, governor of Swedes in Delaware	46
Puritans of New England	53
Quakers persecuted in Massachusetts	120
Quitrents demanded of people in New Jersey	249
Raritans of New Jersey persecuted by the Dutch	39
Rhode Island granted a new charter in 1644	247
Rhode Island granted another charter in 1663	248
Rising, John, on the Delaware	47
Roundheads conquer Virginia in 1653	3
Rowlandson, Mrs., narrative of attack on her house	274
Royalists, triumph of	390
Sassaman, John, Christian Indian who betrayed the plans of Philip	265

HISTORICAL INDEX.

	PAGE
Savage sent to Mount Hope	265
South Kingston, Indians at	272
Stuyvesant, Peter, sent as governor to New Amsterdam	44
Stuyvesant forms treaty with New England	45
Stuyvesant and the Swedes on the Delaware	46
Stuyvesant recaptures Fort Cassimer	48
Stuyvesant's answer to the English demand to surrender	115
Stuyvesant consents to surrender New Amsterdam	117
Stuyvesant goes to Holland	114
Stuyvesant returns to New York	145
Sudbury, attack on	276
Suffrage confined to freeholders, under Charles II	293
Swansey, beginning of King Philip's war on	264
Swedes on the Delaware, trouble with	45
Swen, Schute, captures Fort Cassimer and names it Fort Trinity	47
Van Dyck kills an Indian squaw in his peach orchard	49
Van Dyck killed by Indians in retaliation	50
Vane, Sir Henry, a victim of the restoration	201
Vane, Sir Henry, executed	204
Virginia divided into eight shires	21
Virginia restored to monarchy	124
Virginia threatened with civil war	283
Virginia, home ruled	283
Virginia's defence, 1675	284
Washington, Major John, kills Indians while bringing a flag of truce	294
Whalley, one of Cromwell's generals	200
Wheelwright murdered by Indians	40
Wilford, Captain, hung by Berkeley	373
Windsor, Indian attack on	271
Winthrop and Governor Stuyvesant	115
Winthrop, John, and Charles II	245

CHRONOLOGY.

PERIOD VI.—AGE OF TYRANNY.

A.D. 1643 TO A.D. 1680.

1644. SECOND INDIAN MASSACRE in Virginia; 300 whites killed,—April 18.
1645. CLAIBORNE'S REBELLION in Maryland; Gov. Calvert fled to Virginia.
1649. CHARLES I., King of Great Britain, beheaded,— Jan. 30.
1650. FIRST SETTLEMENT in North Carolina, on the Chowan River, near Edenton.
1653. OLIVER CROMWELL appointed Lord Protector of Great Britain,—Dec. 16.
1655. RELIGIOUS WAR in Maryland between Protestants and Catholics; New Sweden conquered by the Dutch.
1656. QUAKERS came to Massachusetts; cruel treatment by Puritans.
1660. MONARCHY restored in Great Britain; Charles II. king,—May 29.
NAVIGATION ACTS passed restricting colonial trade.
1663. CLARENDON GRANT to Lord Clarendon and others,— March 24. (This grant extended from 30° to 36° lat., and from ocean to ocean.)
CHARTER OF RHODE ISLAND, giving religious liberties, granted,—July 8.

1664. NEW NETHERLANDS granted to the Duke of York and Albany,—March 12.
NEW JERSEY granted to Berkeley and Carteret,— June 24.
STUYVESANT surrenders New Amsterdam (New York City).
FORT ORANGE, N. Y., named Albany,—Sept. 24.
ELIZABETH, N. J., settled by emigrants from Long Island.

1665. CONNECTICUT AND NEW HAVEN united under the name of Connecticut,—May
SECOND CHARTER of Carolina; boundary extended to 29 lat.,—June 30.
CLARENDON COLONY, near Wilmington, N. C., permanently settled.

1670. DETROIT, MICH., settled by the French.
CARTERET COLONY settled on Ashley River, near Charleston, S. C.

1671. MARQUETTE established the Mission of St. Ignatius, at Michilimackinac.

1673. VIRGINIA granted to Culpepper and Islington.
MARQUETTE AND JOLIETTE explored the Mississippi River to the Arkansas.

1674. MARQUETTE founded a Missionary Station at Chicago, Ill.

1675. MARQUETTE founded a mission at Kaskaskia, Ill.
KING PHILIP'S WAR in New England began.

1676. BACON'S REBELLION against Berkeley in Virginia, one hundred years before independence.
QUINQUEPARTITE DEED formed in East and West Jersey—west to the Quakers and east to Carteret. Dividing line from Little Egg Harbor to lat. 41° 41' on the northernmost branch of the Delaware River.

www.ingramcontent.com/pod-product-compliance
Lightning Source LLC
Chambersburg PA
CBHW032141010526
44111CB00035B/707